SAT®
Reading & Writing Prep

OVER 300 PRACTICE QUESTIONS + ONLINE

D1292536

Editor-in-Chief

Alexandra Strelka, MA

Contributing Editors

Dr. Brandon Deason, MD; M. Dominic Eggert; Kathryn Sollenberger, MEd; Glen Stohr, JD

Special thanks to our faculty authors and reviewers

Michael Collins; John Evans; Jack Hayes; Jo L'Abbate; Bird Marathe; Melissa McLaughlin; Gail Rivers; Gordon Spector; Bonnie Wang; and Ethan Weber

Additional special thanks to

Matthew Callan; Paula L. Fleming, MA, MBA; Joanna Graham; Adam Grey; Rebecca Knauer; Michael Wolff; and the countless others who made this project possible

Published by Kaplan Publishing, a division of Kaplan, Inc.
750 Third Avenue
New York, NY 10017

ISBN: 978-1-5062-3682-7

Kaplan Publishing print books are available at special quantity discounts to use for sales promotions, employee premiums, or educational purposes. For more information or to purchase books, please call the Simon & Schuster special sales department at 866-506-1949.

TABLE OF CONTENTS

How to Use This Book

This book will help you prepare for the first two sections of the SAT: the Reading Test and the Writing and Language Test. Your scores from each of these two tests will range from 10–40. These scores will be summed and then scaled to a 200–800 score. The result will be your Evidence-Based Reading and Writing score.

Start by becoming familiar with the structure of these sections. Then work your way through the chapters of this book and do as many of the practice sets as you have time for between now and test day. Be sure to review the explanations carefully. (Review them even for questions you got right, to make sure your reasoning is sound.) As your test date approaches, take the Reading Test and Writing and Language Test found at the end of this book. Do this in a quiet environment and use the indicated timing guidelines. Again, be sure to review the explanations to reinforce what you've learned.

If you're still looking for more practice questions once you've finished the question sets in this book, **go online** at kaptest.com/moreonline.

The SAT Reading Test

The SAT Reading Test will focus on your comprehension and reasoning skills when you are presented with challenging extended prose passages taken from a variety of content areas.

SAT Reading Test Overview	
Timing	65 minutes
Questions	52 passage-based multiple-choice questions
Passages	4 single passages; 1 set of paired passages
Passage Length	500–750 words per passage or passage set

Passages will draw from U.S. and World Literature, History/Social Studies, and Science. One set of History/Social Studies or Science passages will be paired. History/Social Studies and Science passages can also be accompanied by graphical representations of data such as charts, graphs, and tables.

Reading Test Passage Types	
U.S. and World Literature	1 passage with 10 questions
History/Social Studies	2 passages or 1 passage and 1 paired-passage set with 10–11 questions each
Science	2 passages or 1 passage and 1 paired-passage set with 10–11 questions each

The SAT Writing and Language Test

The SAT Writing and Language Test will focus on your ability to revise and edit text from a range of content areas.

SAT Writing and Language Test Overview	
Timing	35 minutes
Questions	44 passage-based, multiple-choice questions
Passages	4 single passages with 11 questions each
Passage Length	400–450 words per passage

The SAT Writing and Language Test will contain four single passages, one from each of the following subject areas: Careers, Humanities, History/Social Studies, and Science.

Writing and Language Passage Types	
Careers	Hot topics in "major fields of work," such as information technology and health care
Humanities	Texts about literature, art, history, music, and philosophy pertaining to human culture
History/Social Studies	Discussion of historical or social sciences topics such as anthropology, communication studies, economics, education, human geography, law, linguistics, political science, psychology, and sociology
Science	Exploration of concepts, findings, and discoveries in the natural sciences including Earth science, biology, chemistry, and physics

Elimination and Guessing

Note that there is no penalty for guessing on the SAT, so it is in your best interest to answer every question. Ideally, taking a strategic guess means eliminating one or more choices and guessing from the rest to boost your chances of getting the question correct. However, if you are pressed for time, taking a guess on a potentially time-consuming question—even without eliminating any of the choices—can help you get to more questions and get more points out of a section.

PART ONE

Reading

CHAPTER 1

SAT Reading

Passage Mapping

The SAT Reading section consists of five passages with a total of 52 questions based on them. You'll have 65 minutes to complete the section, which means that in order to answer all the questions, you'll need to complete each passage and its associated question set in about 13 minutes. Some passages will be longer (and thus more time-consuming) than others, but 13 minutes per passage should be your average pace.

Each SAT Reading passage is accompanied by 10 or 11 questions. Two or three of the questions may ask about the passage as a whole. The others will ask about specific paragraphs, details, or other elements within the passage. You'll need to use deliberate reading strategies to answer all of the questions quickly and accurately, with a minimum of rereading.

Because the SAT Reading section often presents questions that can easily trip you up if you try to answer them from memory, and because some of the questions ask about the passage as a whole, the best reading strategy is one called **passage mapping**. Passage mapping means reading the passage fairly quickly, without trying to memorize every detail, while taking brief notes of the main features of each paragraph. Taking notes accomplishes two goals: it helps you focus on the most important points as you read, and it provides you with an outline that you can use to quickly zero in on the right part of the passage to revisit to find the details for a particular question. Once you have finished reading, take a moment to consider the **author's purpose** in writing the passage and its **main idea**. Then you're ready for the question set.

Try mapping the passage that follows, then compare your notes to ours. Take your time and be deliberate. There are Reading question sets in chapter 6 that you can use to practice timing once you've mastered the various features of the Reading section that we'll introduce in the next few chapters.

Practice Passage

This passage about hydrothermal vent ecosystems was adapted from a popular science magazine.

The preservation of the unique ecosystems surrounding deep-sea hydrothermal vents is of increasing importance to scientists as they face mining companies' growing demand to exploit
5 the mineral resources surrounding these vents. Deep-sea hydrothermal vents are undersea cracks in the earth's crust through which magma escapes; the first such vent was discovered in 1977. Seawater comes into contact with the
10 magma and is superheated, forming something like an underwater geyser shooting up from the ocean floor. The superheated water carries dissolved minerals from the magma, which precipitate out upon contact with the cooler
15 ocean water and fall back to the ocean floor surrounding the vent.

Although the geology of these vents is fascinating, what is of even greater interest to scientists are the ecosystems—found nowhere else
20 on the planet—where life thrives without sunlight, under the extreme pressures and temperatures of the deep ocean, surrounded by concentrations of minerals toxic to any other life forms. Hundreds of new species have already
25 been discovered, including bacteria that provide food for other vent organisms through chemosynthesis, a process by which the bacteria use energy from the oxidation of inorganic vent minerals to convert carbon
30 dioxide into organic nutrients. Just as photosynthesis supports a wide variety of life on the surface of the earth, chemosynthesis supports life in hydrothermal vent systems that ranges in size from microbes, to shrimp, crabs,
35 and giant tube worms.

Because of the inaccessibility of these vent sites—most are more than 2,500 meters deep and some are twice that deep—and their relatively recent discovery, deep-sea hydrothermal vent
40 systems and their ecology have been little studied. Commercial mining interests are eager to begin utilizing the potentially rich mineral deposits

surrounding these vents; however, the environmental impact of such activities remains
45 unknown. In an effort to monitor these potential impacts, scientists are attempting to document the food webs and trophic relationships among the vent species in order to determine each species' position in the food chain. Once baseline
50 studies have established these relationships, the studies can be replicated during and after mining activities to assess any disruptions.

In addition to directly observing organisms and their relationships, which the location of the
55 vents makes difficult, researchers use another method to collect this data. Scientists sample and analyze the isotopes present in tissues and waste products of vent organisms. Every type of plant and animal uses different physiological processes
60 and enzymatic reactions, and these leave distinct isotopic signatures behind. By examining the isotopes in a sample, researchers can ascertain not only the food consumed, but also the proportion of the diet each food provided. From
65 this information, they can determine the position of each organism in the ecosystem's food chain.

Without such research, it will be impossible to assess whether utilization of the mineral resources at deep-sea hydrothermal vents will
70 negatively impact these extraordinary, arcane sites and the creatures that inhabit them. Since vent ecosystems have yet to be fully documented and may include unknown species with singular abilities, mining and any other activities that
75 could disrupt or destroy these ecosystems should be postponed until more complete information is available.

Sample Passage Map

The preservation of the unique ecosystems
surrounding deep-sea hydrothermal vents is of
increasing importance to scientists as they face
mining companies' growing demand to exploit
5   the mineral resources surrounding these vents.
Deep-sea hydrothermal vents are undersea cracks
in the earth's crust through which magma
escapes; the first such vent was discovered in
1977. Seawater comes into contact with the
10 magma and is superheated, forming something
like an underwater geyser shooting up from the
ocean floor. The superheated water carries
dissolved minerals from the magma, which
precipitate out upon contact with the cooler
15 ocean water and fall back to the ocean floor
surrounding the vent.
    Although the geology of these vents is
fascinating, what is of even greater interest to
scientists are the ecosystems—found nowhere else
20 on the planet—where life thrives without
sunlight, under the extreme pressures and
temperatures of the deep ocean, surrounded by
concentrations of minerals toxic to any other life
forms. Hundreds of new species have already
25 been discovered, including bacteria that provide
food for other vent organisms through
chemosynthesis, a process by which the
bacteria use energy from the oxidation of
inorganic vent minerals to convert carbon
30 dioxide into organic nutrients. Just as
photosynthesis supports a wide variety of life
on the surface of the earth, chemosynthesis
supports life in hydrothermal vent systems that
ranges in size from microbes, to shrimp, crabs,
35 and giant tube worms.
    Because of the inaccessibility of these vent
sites—most are more than 2,500 meters deep and
some are twice that deep—and their relatively
recent discovery, deep-sea hydrothermal vent
40 systems and their ecology have been little studied.
Commercial mining interests are eager to begin
utilizing the potentially rich mineral deposits
surrounding these vents; however, the

Topic: deep-
sea vents

sci preserve vs
miners exploit

vents described

why imp to sci

hard to study

miners want to
start

environmental impact of such activities remains
45 unknown. In an effort to monitor these potential
impacts, scientists are attempting to document
the food webs and trophic relationships among
the vent species in order to determine each
species' position in the food chain. Once baseline
50 studies have established these relationships, the
studies can be replicated during and after mining
activities to assess any disruptions.

sci want more info to monitor impact

In addition to directly observing organisms
and their relationships, which the location of the
55 vents makes difficult, researchers use another
method to collect this data. Scientists sample and
analyze the isotopes present in tissues and waste
products of vent organisms. Every type of plant
and animal uses different physiological processes
60 and enzymatic reactions, and these leave distinct
isotopic signatures behind. By examining the
isotopes in a sample, researchers can ascertain
not only the food consumed, but also the
proportion of the diet each food provided. From
65 this information, they can determine the position
of each organism in the ecosystem's food chain.

how sci study: isotope analysis

Without such research, it will be impossible to
assess whether utilization of the mineral
resources at deep-sea hydrothermal vents will
70 negatively impact these extraordinary, arcane
sites and the creatures that inhabit them. Since
vent ecosystems have yet to be fully documented
and may include unknown species with singular
abilities, mining and any other activities that
75 could disrupt or destroy these ecosystems should
be postponed until more complete information is
available.

au pov: no mining w/o research

Purpose: To argue that the ecosystems around hydro-thermal vents should not be disrupted until they have been more thoroughly studied

Main Idea: Deep-sea hydrothermal vents are unique ecosystems that should not be exploited without additional research.

CHAPTER 2

The Method for SAT Reading Questions

Once you have read and mapped the passage, you'll want to get through the question set efficiently and accurately. The SAT Reading section essentially tests two things: (1) your ability to get the gist of a passage quickly and (2) your ability to locate information in the passage. Answering questions from memory often results in picking a trap answer. So does comparing the choices to each other instead of to the passage. Therefore, you'll want to get into the habit of always looking up the facts you need to answer a question and predicting the correct answer before you look at the choices. Follow the steps shown in the table below for each Reading question you do now so that those steps will be second nature on test day.

Method for SAT Reading Questions	
Step 1	Unpack the question stem
Step 2	Research the answer
Step 3	Predict the answer
Step 4	Find the answer choice that matches your prediction

Step 1 means getting all the information you can from the question. For example, imagine that a passage about tree frogs comes with a question that asks, "The author indicates that which of the following is true about red-eyed tree frogs?" There are two clues here. The word "indicates" means that you're looking for a fact stated directly in the passage, not merely implied. And the reference to "red-eyed tree frogs" should help you to focus your research on whatever paragraph discusses this particular species of tree frog. Step 2 means actually going back to that paragraph and looking up the facts it provides about red-eyed tree frogs. Step 3 means phrasing the answer in your own words. Finally, step 4 means trusting your predicted answer and finding the choice that matches.

Give it a try in the following practice set. Be deliberate in your markup of the passage and equally deliberate in answering the questions. Don't rush as you practice. Forming habits can't be done under time pressure. There are practice sets in chapter 6 that you can use to practice timing.

The Method for SAT Reading Questions Practice Set

> **DIRECTIONS:** Take as much time as you need on these questions. Work carefully and methodically. There will be an opportunity for timed practice in chapter 6.

Questions 1–10 refer to the following passage.

This passage describes some potential impacts of self-driving cars on urban centers.

Discussions of the self-driving car, or autonomous vehicle, revolve mostly around matters of it in motion. Proponents marvel at the massive amount of information that a self-driving car's
5 software is able to process as the car drives into a multitude of unknown situations. Skeptics raise questions about its safety and reliability as it shares the roads with traditional human-piloted automobiles, which, admittedly, can be erratic and
10 dangerous themselves. One of the nonobvious, yet critical, concerns about the autonomous vehicle, however, is what it will do when it is stationary. Where will it park?

A recent study by Adam Millard-Ball of UC
15 Santa Cruz suggests that parking costs may prohibit autonomous vehicles from parking at all. In a major metropolitan central business district, parking is likely more expensive than the cost of an autonomous vehicle cruising, or driving
20 aimlessly. There is concern that cruising self-driving cars will add to roadway congestion. Based on current trends in autonomous vehicle technology, these so-called "zombie" cars will be electric and will likely be programmed to save
25 battery charge by cruising at very slow speeds. Millard-Ball estimates that the addition of just 2,000 autonomous vehicles would slow the average speed of traffic in downtown San Francisco to under 2 miles per hour. Additionally,
30 more cars on the road means more damage to the environment. Even though driving electric cars produces no carbon emissions, recharging them often creates greenhouse gas pollution because most electric grids are based on power plants that
35 use nonrenewable energy sources. Electric cars that drive all day instead of parking would significantly increase the energy demands on power plants.

In response to these concerns—increased
40 traffic congestion and pollution—some cities are discussing building more parking garages outside the city center that could house the autonomous vehicles after they dropped off their passengers. Many cities, though, already dedicate an
45 unnecessarily high percentage of their land to parking lots, and the problem of parking lots wasting valuable land is something that self-driving cars can fix. Most retail stores' parking lots are significantly underutilized, and large
50 sports arenas and event centers have thousands of spaces that are mostly empty when there is no game or concert. Autonomous vehicles require much less square-footage of parking area than traditional vehicles need. After an autonomous
55 vehicle drops off its passenger, it does not need space to open its doors when it is parked, and an autonomous vehicle parks more accurately and needs less space to enter and exit the parking area than a traditional vehicle.

60 Reducing, or even eliminating, the need for privately owned autonomous vehicles could increase parking efficiency even more. Some city planners have considered adopting fleets of self-driving cars as public transit or partnering
65 with ride-hailing companies to house fleets of their self-driving cars. A fleet of identical self-driving cars means that the cars are interchangeable and that any car can leave and pick up any passenger. In this case, no extra
70 space is needed for driving through the parking lot to get to a specific space or to exit, and cars can park bumper-to-bumper. When self-driving cars park themselves in these extremely efficient arrangements, they can increase parking lot
75 capacity up to 87%, according to a study by Matthew Roorda, a Professor of Civil Engineering at the University of Toronto. With fewer privately owned self-driving cars to house during the day, parking structures can then be repurposed to

80 create more affordable housing or green spaces,
which can make cities more liveable.

Self-driving cars have the potential both to
disrupt cities with nightmarish transportation
problems and to reinvigorate downtown areas by
85 replacing parking structures with spaces that can
raise the quality of living. Cities must begin
planning now for these fundamental changes in
urban transportation because the self-driving car
promises to be one of the biggest revolutions in
90 city life since the private automobile.

Figure 1

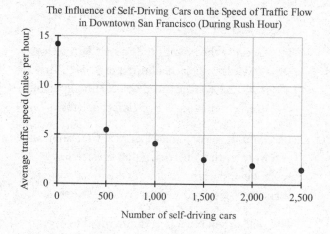

The Influence of Self-Driving Cars on the Speed of Traffic Flow in Downtown San Francisco (During Rush Hour)

Figure 2

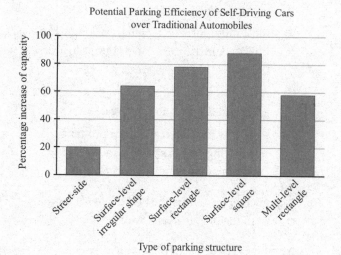

Potential Parking Efficiency of Self-Driving Cars over Traditional Automobiles

1. The primary purpose of the passage is to

   A) warn that the self-driving car will require even more parking structures in cities that already use too much land for parking.

   B) convince commuters to use public transit instead of privately owned self-driving cars.

   C) explain how the potential problems of traffic congestion and pollution associated with self-driving cars could be mitigated by their parking efficiency.

   D) urge city officials to act immediately to prevent all of the difficulties the self-driving car will likely create.

2. Which choice best describes the overall structure of the passage?

   A) An analysis of some problems the self-driving car might cause, details of a possible solution, and an appeal

   B) An explanation of the self-driving car, examples of difficulties it might cause, and a warning

   C) A rationale for the inevitability of the self-driving car, a list of problems, and a plan for avoiding the problems

   D) A definition of the self-driving car, reasons for its use, and a counterargument

3. The author uses the word "zombie" (line 23) in quotation marks to

   A) emphasize how too many self-driving cars could make city centers less lively.

   B) draw a contrast between electric cars and more exciting traditional gasoline-fueled cars.

   C) describe the sluggishness of electric self-driving cars that are cruising aimlessly.

   D) argue that people who rely on self-driving cars instead of driving themselves will become mindless.

4. As used in line 24, "programmed" most nearly means

   A) processed.

   B) registered.

   C) calculated.

   D) built.

5. In line 37, the word "demands" most nearly means

   A) appeals.

   B) petitions.

   C) commands.

   D) needs.

6. In the passage, the author makes which point about electric cars?

   A) If they are in groups of identical fleets, they are interchangeable and can pick up any passenger.

   B) If they are privately owned, they will make downtown business district parking problems worse.

   C) If they are programmed to save energy while cruising, they will drive intelligently to reduce traffic congestion.

   D) If they recharge on an electric grid based on a nonrenewable energy source, they increase pollution.

7. Which choice provides the best evidence for the answer to the previous question?

   A) Lines 22–25 ("Based . . . speeds")

   B) Lines 31–35 ("Even though . . . sources")

   C) Lines 60–62 ("Reducing . . . even more")

   D) Lines 66–69 ("A fleet . . . passenger")

8. Based on the passage and Figure 1, the author would most likely agree with which of the following statements?

   A) Even the addition of 1,000 self-driving cars in the downtown area of San Francisco during rush hour would significantly increase travel time.

   B) The increase in traffic congestion in downtown San Francisco would be negligible if the additional 2,000 self-driving cars were not electric.

   C) If they were not programmed to conserve energy when in cruising mode, the 2,000 self-driving cars added would not affect the average speed of traffic in downtown San Francisco.

   D) Because the average traffic speed drops less and less with each addition of 500 self-driving cars, the average speed will eventually stabilize, thus eliminating congestion problems.

9. Based on the passage and Figure 2, you can most readily infer that the reason that surface-level rectangular parking structures are more efficient than multi-level rectangular parking structures is

   A) self-driving cars need more room to open doors in multi-level rectangular parking structures than in surface-level rectangular parking structures.

   B) most multi-level rectangular parking structures require extra space for ramps to access the non-surface-level areas.

   C) privately owned self-driving cars need space to enter and exit the parking area.

   D) some city parking regulations prohibit self-driving cars from using multi-level rectangular parking structures.

10. Which choice provides the best evidence for the answer to the previous question?

    A) Lines 54–59 ("After . . . vehicle")

    B) Lines 69–72 ("In this . . . bumper-to-bumper")

    C) Lines 72–77 ("When . . . Toronto")

    D) Lines 77–81 ("With . . . liveable")

Answers and explanations follow on the next page. ▶ ▶ ▶

Answers and Explanations

The Method for SAT Reading Questions Practice Set

Sample Passage Map

P1: Concern: where self-driving car will park

P2: Problem #1: self-driving car will cause traffic congestion b/c it won't park. Problem #2: even *electric* self-driving car increases pollution if it drives all day.

P3: One solution: more parking structures BUT already too much space dedicated to parking; okay b/c self-driving car needs less space to park

P4: Fleets of identical self-parking cars mean even less parking space needed.

P5: City planners need to anticipate the effects of the self-driving car.

Purpose: To discuss some issues surrounding self-driving cars and their implications for cities

Main Idea: City planners should begin now to prepare for the advantages and challenges posed by self-driving cars.

1.   C
Difficulty: Medium

Strategic Advice: Step 1 of the Reading method is unpacking the question stem. The phrase "primary purpose" means that you'll want to consider not only the topic of the passage but also the author's reason or reasons for writing the passage.

Getting to the Answer: Step 2 of the Reading method is to research the answer. Your passage map should have identified the author's purpose, so check your notes. Step 3 is to predict the answer: the author's purpose is to explain the consequences of self-driving cars. Step 4 is to find the answer that matches your prediction. Choice **(C)** is closest and is correct.

Choice (A) misconstrues information in the passage and focuses on a detail in paragraph 4. Choice (B) distorts a detail in paragraph 4. Choice (D) is too narrowly focused; the passage is not primarily addressed to city officials. Additionally, (D) is too extreme because the author does not claim that the suggested solutions will prevent all of the difficulties that the self-driving car could create.

2.   A
Difficulty: Hard

Strategic Advice: Step 1 is to unpack the question stem. The phrase "overall structure of the passage" indicates that the correct answer will reflect the author's entire argument. Any choice that leaves out or misconstrues a part of the passage will be incorrect.

Getting to the Answer: Step 2 is to research the answer: look at your passage map and turn the specific ideas into abstractions. The first paragraph raises the issue: where will the cars park? The next paragraph describes possible problems that the self-driving car might create. The third paragraph introduces proposed solutions. The fourth paragraph provides an in-depth discussion of a potential solution. The last paragraph reinforces the importance of cities dealing with the issue. Step 3 is to predict an answer: the structure is problems with the self-driving car, details of a solution, and a recommendation. Step 4 is to find a match: **(A)** matches the prediction and is the correct answer.

Choice (B) is incorrect because it omits the solution offered by the passage. Additionally, the passage does not end merely with a warning. The author claims that the self-driving car, if cities plan appropriately, can reinvigorate downtown centers and improve the quality of life. Choice (C) is incorrect because the passage does not begin with a rationale for the inevitability of the self-driving car. Similarly, the passage does not begin with a definition of the self-driving car, so (D) is incorrect.

3.   C
Difficulty: Hard

Strategic Advice: Step 1, Unpack: the question asks why the author uses a certain phrase. Looking at the surrounding context is a good place to start.

Getting to the Answer: Step 2, Research: the second paragraph outlines how self-driving cars could add to traffic congestion. Self-driving electric cars would likely be programmed to drive very slowly to save energy while waiting to pick up their passengers. Step 3, Predict: these cars are called "zombie" cars because they travel very slowly and without any destination. Step 4, Find a match: **(C)** is correct.

Choice (A) is incorrect because the liveliness of city centers is not mentioned until the end of the passage. Choice (B) is incorrect because there is no mention of traditional gasoline-fueled cars. The passage also never mentions the effects that riding in an autonomous vehicle will have on a person, so (D) is incorrect.

4. D
Difficulty: Medium

Strategic Advice: Step 1: the question asks about the meaning of a word in context. The correct answer will make sense when substituted for the word "programmed" where it occurs in the passage.

Getting to the Answer: Step 2: the sentence that contains the word "programmed" is about self-driving electric cars and how they will most likely be designed to drive at slow speeds to conserve energy. Step 3: replace the quoted word with a word of your own that expresses the idea indicated by the surrounding context. "Designed" or "created" is a good prediction. Step 4: **(D)** is the best match.

Choices (A), (B), and (C) are incorrect because they alter the meaning of the sentence. Choices (A) and (C) are actions the self-driving car might take. The car might process information or calculate the best driving speed to save energy, but the sentence is about what action the makers of the car will take.

5. D
Difficulty: Easy

Strategic Advice: Step 1: the question asks about the meaning of a word in context. The correct answer will make sense when substituted for the word "demands" where it occurs in the passage.

Getting to the Answer: Step 2: the original sentence claims that electric cars will increase the energy requirements of power plants. Step 3: treat the quoted word as a blank and fill it in with a word that maintains the same meaning as the original sentence. "Requirements" is a good prediction. Step 4: **(D)** matches and is correct.

Choices (A), (B), and (C) do not fit the context of the sentence. Choices (A) and (B) are types of demands that people make on other people, not something that an object can require of another object. Choice (C) doesn't make sense in this context.

6. D
Difficulty: Medium

Strategic Advice: Step 1, Unpack: the question asks about something the author specifically said, so use your passage map to locate word-for-word support in the passage.

Getting to the Answer: Step 2, Research: the third paragraph discusses self-driving cars that are specifically *electric*, so use the information in that paragraph to evaluate the answer choices one by one. Step 3: the paragraph makes two points about electric cars: they will cruise slowly when empty to save power, and they will contribute to pollution when recharging on a grid powered by nonrenewable energy. Find the choice that contains one or both of these points. Choice **(D)** matches the second point and is correct. Choices (A) and (B) are incorrect because they are points that the author makes about self-driving cars, not electric cars. Choice (C) is incorrect because the author states the opposite; electric cars will increase traffic congestion.

7. B
Difficulty: Medium

Strategic Advice: Step 1: this question references the previous one, so use your work on the previous question to answer this one.

Getting to the Answer: Steps 2 and 3: the answer to the previous question was based on the author's claim in the third paragraph that "recharging [electric cars] often creates greenhouse gas pollution because most electric grids are based on power plants that use nonrenewable energy sources" (lines 32–35). Step 4: **(B)** is correct. None of the other answer choices mention electric cars and greenhouse gas pollution.

8. A
Difficulty: Hard

Strategic Advice: Step 1: the question asks an open-ended question based on the first figure that accompanies the passage. Consider tables and graphs as part of the author's argument. Note the title, labels, units, and other information. The figure shows that an increase in the number of self-driving cars will slow traffic flow in downtown San Francisco during rush hour.

Getting to the Answer: Step 2: check each answer against the graph and the text. In the text, the author uses the findings of an expert to show the extent to which self-driving cars will affect traffic flow: "the addition of just 2,000 autonomous vehicles would slow the average speed of traffic in downtown San Francisco to under 2 miles per hour" (lines 26–29). This information is corroborated by the graph. For (A), if 1,000 self-driving cars are added, the graph shows that the average speed would be about 4 miles per hour, which is a significant drop from 14 miles per hour. Step 3: you can reasonably assume that this drop in average traffic speed would add to travel time. Step 4: **(A)** is correct.

If you're unsure, you can eliminate the other choices one by one. Choice (B) is incorrect because the graph shows data on self-driving cars, not specifically *electric* self-driving cars. Choice (C) is incorrect because adding cars to downtown San Francisco during rush hour would still add to traffic congestion, though not as severely as if they were programmed to cruise at slow speeds. Choice (D) is a distortion of the information in the graph; for each addition of 500 self-driving cars, the rate at which the average traffic speed decreases is lower. However, the average traffic speed is still lower each time, so the problem of roadway congestion will only get worse as more self-driving cars are added.

9.   B

Difficulty: Hard

Strategic Advice: Step 1, Unpack: the question asks what the passage and Figure 2 can tell you about two specific configurations of parking structures. Use the ideas in the passage to understand the figures that accompany it.

Getting to the Answer: Step 2, Research: in the passage, the author states that fleets of identical self-driving cars can park more efficiently than privately owned self-driving cars because they are interchangeable and can park bumper to bumper; when a car is needed, one from the edge of the group will be used, so no extra lane space is needed between the cars. Step 3, Predict: multi-level parking structures have ramps so that cars can move between levels. Even fleets of identical self-driving cars would need these ramps, or lanes, to access the upper levels of the parking structures. Therefore, multi-level parking structures do not allow self-driving cars to park as efficiently as surface-level structures of the same shape. Step 4, Find a match: **(B)** is correct.

There is nothing in the passage or in Figure 2 that suggests that multi-level parking structures require more space for cars to open their doors, so (A) is incorrect. Choice (C) is incorrect because using only privately owned self-driving cars to measure the space saved over traditional automobiles would not account for the difference between surface-level and multi-level parking structures; both would need dedicated lanes to enter and exit. Choice (D) is incorrect because the author never suggests that some cities have regulations barring self-driving cars from using multi-level parking structures.

10.   B

Difficulty: Hard

Strategic Advice: Step 1: use your research from the previous question to answer this one.

Getting to the Answer: Step 2: the answer to the previous question is based on multi-level parking structures having ramps. Step 3: the fifth paragraph mentions that fleets of identical self-driving cars are able to park more efficiently because they do not need extra space to enter or exit the parking area like privately owned cars do. Step 4: **(B)** is correct.

Choice (A) is incorrect because the space saved by not needing to open and close the doors of autonomous vehicles would not be greater in ground-level parking areas than in multi-level parking structures. Choice (C) is incorrect because it does not provide any information about multi-level parking structures. Choice (D) is incorrect because it does not mention why self-driving cars require less parking.

CHAPTER 3

Reading Question Types

Learning the test maker's code language can go a long way toward improved accuracy on the Reading section. There are six recurring Reading question types. You can tell from the phrasing of the question itself what kind of question you're dealing with—and what kinds of trap answers you are likely to see for that particular question. Here are the six question types:

1. **Global**—asks about the big picture
2. **Detail**—asks about facts explicitly stated in the passage
3. **Inference**—asks about ideas that are unstated but strongly implied
4. **Command of Evidence**—asks for evidence (lines from the passage) to support the answer to a previous question
5. **Function**—asks why the author wrote specific parts of the text
6. **Vocabulary-in-Context**—asks for the meaning of a word as it is used in the passage

The following table describes how you can recognize these question types, the form the correct answer will take, and common wrong answer patterns.

Question Type	Wording	Correct Answer	Common Incorrect Answers
Global	"main idea" "purpose of the passage" "theme"	must take the entire passage into account	will often provide details from the passage or even a summary of some, but not all, of the passage
Detail	"states" "indicates" "asserts" "according to"	must be stated explicitly in the passage	provide facts not stated in the passage or distort facts from the passage
Inference	"implies" "suggests" "most likely to agree" "based on"	may not be explicitly stated, but can be concluded from information in the passage	provide facts not stated or implied in the passage or that are extreme in that they go beyond what the passage suggests
Command of Evidence	"provides the best evidence"	must support the correct answer to the previous question	may support incorrect answer choices to the previous question
Function	"primarily serves to" "purpose of . . . is to"	correctly states why the author chose to include that part of the passage	distort the function of that part of the passage
Vocab-in-Context	"most nearly means"	gives the definition of the word as it is used in the passage	give other common definitions of the word

Reading Question Types Drill

Practice identifying question types in the following drill. Answers are located in the "Answers and Explanations" section at the end of the chapter. Then put your new understanding to work in the question set that follows.

1. The description in the third paragraph (lines 27–30) primarily serves to

2. The narrator's reaction suggests that she is experiencing which strong emotion?

3. The main purpose of the passage is to

4. As used in line 16, "mischief" most nearly means

5. According to the passage, sunspots are most likely to form during which part of the solar cycle?

6. Which choice provides the best evidence for the answer to the previous question?

7. The main purpose of the question in the fourth paragraph is to

8. The passage indicates that which of the following has been true of philatelists' tools for the past half-century?

9. The author mentions the demise of the Federalist party primarily in order to

10. The author implies that Leonardo da Vinci left Milan for Venice because

Reading Question Types Practice Set

DIRECTIONS: Take as much time as you need on these questions. Work carefully and methodically. There will be an opportunity for timed practice in chapter 6.

Questions 1–10 refer to the following passage.

This passage discusses the discovery of J0740+6620, the most massive neutron star yet identified.

Is it *possible* for a star to be *impossibly* large? This is a question that astronomers are pondering as they examine a massive neutron star located about 4,600 light-years from Earth that seems to
5 be larger than the previously calculated theoretical maximum mass. While astronomers have known about neutron stars—compressed remains of stars that were once supernovas—for decades, there is much about the nature of their
10 interiors that remains a mystery. Is the core of a neutron star a spongy gel of quarks, technically known as a quark-gluon plasma, or a solid lump of matter filled with particles called kaons? And what is the upper limit of the mass of a
15 neutron star?

At one time, it was believed that a neutron star has a mass between 1.4 and 2.0 times the mass of the sun; anything over that mass had to be a black hole. In more recent decades, however,
20 some astronomers argued that the threshold could be as high as 3.0 times the mass of our sun. The upper limit is currently believed to be less than that but is still not empirically known.

The members of the NANOGrav Physics
25 Frontiers Center discovered the massive neutron star, known as J0740+6620, using the National Science Foundation's Green Bank Telescope in West Virginia. They identified J0740+6620 as the most massive neutron star ever measured,
30 squeezing over 2.17 times the the mass of Earth's sun into a sphere less than 30 kilometers across. With J0740+6620 pushing the theoretical upper limit of neutron star mass, is it time for researchers to rethink the calculations behind
35 that theoretical limit? One alternative to working with theoretical calculations is to use each massive neutron star discovered to help determine the true tipping point at which gravity

prevails over matter and dead stars become black
40 holes instead of neutron stars.

Since J0740+6620 is a pulsar, a highly magnetized rotating neutron star, existing in a binary system, in which two stars orbit a common center of mass, astronomers were able to
45 calculate the mass of the neutron star with a great deal of precision using a phenomenon known as the Shapiro delay. Pulsars spin at a phenomenal speed and with such amazing regularity that that astronomers use them as the
50 atomic clocks of the cosmos. As the pulsar passes its white dwarf companion, the white dwarf's distortion of space-time causes a delay, on the order of magnitude of 10 millionths of a second, in receiving the radio waves that come from the
55 pulsar. The length of this delay can be used to calculate the mass of the neutron star, with the range of the Shapiro delay being proportional to the mass of the neutron star.

Astronomer Scott Ransom of the National
60 Radio Astronomy Observatory (NRAO) posits that "the orientation of this binary star system created a fantastic cosmic laboratory." The 100-meter diameter collecting area, unblocked aperture, and unprecedented sensitivity of the
65 Green Bank Telescope were critical to researchers discovering the star system. It is hoped that further study of the system at the NRAO will provide researchers with more insight into the interesting properties of the interior of neutron
70 stars and the actual limits on the mass of a neutron star.

1. The primary purpose of the passage is to

   A) discuss the obstacles that astronomers face in calculating the maximum mass of neutron stars.

   B) argue that the Shapiro delay is the most accurate way to calculate the mass of neutron stars.

   C) describe how J0740+6620 will further astronomers' understanding of neutron stars.

   D) explain how astronomers determined the composition of neutron stars.

2. The first paragraph serves mainly to

   A) describe how a new celestial object was discovered.

   B) present an example that seems to contradict a theory.

   C) explain how the mass of a celestial object is calculated.

   D) predict how a new discovery will answer many questions.

3. As used in line 20, "threshold" most nearly means

   A) sill.

   B) opening.

   C) value.

   D) limit.

4. According to the passage, what is one hypothetical composition of the core of neutron stars?

   A) A substance composed of quarks and gluons

   B) The compressed remains of a black hole

   C) A binary system that includes a white dwarf

   D) A plasma of kaons and quarks

5. Which choice provides the best evidence for the answer to the previous question?

   A) Lines 6–10 ("While astronomers . . . mystery")

   B) Lines 10–13 ("Is the . . . kaons")

   C) Lines 41–47 ("Since J0740+6620 . . . Shapiro delay")

   D) Lines 66–71 ("It is hoped . . . star")

6. As used in line 60, "posits" most nearly means

   A) hypothesizes.

   B) assumes.

   C) asserts.

   D) decides.

7. Based on the information in the passage, the author likely believes which of the following about "the true tipping point" (line 38)?

   A) It can only be quantified after the masses of all identified neutron stars are known.

   B) It will need to be calculated via a binary star system to be truly accurate.

   C) It is less accurate than before due to the Shapiro delay phenomenon.

   D) It will continue to be refined with observation of each newly discovered massive neutron star.

8. The passage identifies which of the following as a characteristic of the Shapiro delay?

    A)   The distortion of space-time

    B)   The ability to use pulsars as atomic clocks

    C)   The microscopic shortening of radio waves

    D)   The means to determine neutron stars' masses

9. Which choice provides the best evidence for the answer to the previous question?

    A)   Lines 41–47 ("Since J0740+6620 . . . delay")

    B)   Lines 47–50 ("Pulsars spin . . . cosmos")

    C)   Lines 50–55 ("As the . . . pulsar")

    D)   Lines 55–58 ("The length . . . star")

10. What does the author suggest about the Green Bank Telescope?

    A)   The Green Bank Telescope was designed specifically to detect neutron stars.

    B)   The Green Bank Telescope is only used by astronomers from the National Radio Astronomy Observatory.

    C)   The Green Bank Telescope is able to detect cosmic phenomena that might be missed by other telescopes.

    D)   J0740+6620 would never have been discovered without the Green Bank Telescope.

Answers and Explanations

Reading Question Types Drill

1. Function question

2. Inference question

3. Global question

4. Vocab-in-Context question

5. Detail question

6. Command of Evidence question

7. Function question

8. Detail question

9. Function question

10. Inference question

Reading Question Types Practice Set

Passage Notes:

P1: New neutron star (NS) > theoretical max, NS interior—astr. know little

P2: Debate—max. mass of NS; true limit unknown

P3: Discovered J0—most massive NS—use massive ones to find upper limit

P4: Pulsar, binary system, "Shapiro delay"—used to calc. mass

P5: Scott Ransom—J0 star system helpful for learning more

Purpose: To describe the discovery of the massive neutron star, J0740+6620, and its implications.

Main Idea: J0740+6620 is causing astronomers to rethink the limits on the mass of stars.

1. C

Difficulty: Medium

Strategic Advice: The "primary purpose" phrasing in this question identifies it as a Global question. Many passages come with a purpose or main idea question. This is why you should write down the purpose and main idea of the passage immediately after reading it.

Getting to the Answer: The first two paragraphs of the passage discuss the discovery of a new neutron star (which turns out to be J0740+6620) and some of the

remaining questions surrounding neutron stars. The remaining three paragraphs discuss some of the specific details about neutron stars that can be learned from J0740+6620 and the potential for learning even more. Sum up the purpose of the entire passage as "explain how a specific discovery helps increase understanding of a wider field." Using this or a similar prediction as a guide leads to **(C)** as the correct answer.

While the obstacles involved in calculating the theoretical maximum mass of a neutron star are mentioned in the passage, there is an entire paragraph devoted to how the Shapiro delay phenomenon allows for a very precise mass calculation, which makes (A) incorrect. By that same logic, since the Shapiro Delay is only discussed in one paragraph, (B) is also incorrect. (Remember that the correct answer to a Global question must cover the entire passage.) Choice (D) is incorrect because the passage says astronomers do not know the composition of the interior of neutron stars.

2. B

Difficulty: Medium

Strategic Advice: A question that asks about the purpose of an entire paragraph is a Function question, so use your margin notes to make a prediction for the purpose of the paragraph.

Getting to the Answer: The answer to the previous question identified the purpose of the passage as a whole as describing "how J0740+6620 will further astronomers' understanding of neutron stars." How does the first paragraph contribute to that purpose? It introduces J0740+6620 and mentions how it is larger than expected. This is a good match with **(B)**, which is the correct answer.

Choice (A) is incorrect because how J0740+6620 was actually discovered does not appear until the third paragraph. The explanation of how the mass of a neutron star is calculated appears in the fourth paragraph, so (C) is also incorrect. Be careful with (D); the first paragraph only presents one question that might be answered by the discovery of J0740+6620. The idea that the star system might provide several insights is more clearly presented in the final paragraph of the passage.

3.   D

Difficulty: Medium

Strategic Advice: For all Vocab-in-Context questions, predict a word that would be a good replacement in context and find the best match among the answer choices.

Getting to the Answer: The context is providing numbers for the theoretical maximum mass of a neutron star in terms of how much larger it would be than our sun. A good prediction would be "boundary." Choice **(D)** is close in meaning to the prediction and is correct.

Both (A) and (B) are incorrect because they are related to the construction definition of "threshold," which is a door opening, specifically the wood or metal that usually sits underneath the door. Choice (C) might seem like a possibility, but a "threshold" is more than just a value; it is the upper or lower limit of a set of values.

4.   A

Difficulty: Easy

Strategic Advice: This Detail question, identified by the phrasing "According to the passage," is best approached by reviewing the margin notes to find the paragraph where the specific detail is discussed.

Getting to the Answer: The first paragraph mentions the debate about what the interiors of neutron stars could be made of (lines 10–13): "Is the core a spongy gel of quarks, technically known as a quark-gluon plasma, or a solid lump of matter filled with kaons?" Only **(A)** correctly states one of those options.

Choice (B) is incorrect because the first paragraph says that neutron stars are the "compressed remains of stars that were once supernovas" (lines 7–8); black holes are not mentioned at all. Binary systems are mentioned in conjunction with calculating the mass of neutron stars, not in conjunction with the composition of their cores, so (C) is also incorrect. Choice (D) is a distortion of one of the options mentioned in the first paragraph; if there are kaons present, the core will be "a solid lump" (line 12), and quarks are not mentioned in conjunction with kaons at all.

5.   B

Difficulty: Easy

Strategic Advice: Command of Evidence questions are best approached by reflecting on where exactly in the passage you found the information used to answer the previous question.

Getting to the Answer: The correct answer will be evidence that the interiors of neutron stars are fluid made up of quarks, which is only found in the second paragraph. Choice **(B)** is the specific sentence that addresses the debate on the interiors of neutron stars.

Choices (A) and (D) simply mention the interiors of neutron stars, while (C) is a trap answer choice based on the binary system answer in the previous question.

6.   C

Difficulty: Medium

Strategic Advice: The phrasing "most nearly means" indicates that this is a Vocab-in-Context question. Predict a good replacement for the word being tested in the given context.

Getting to the Answer: When Ransom "posits" that the binary star system discussed in the passage can be used as a "cosmic laboratory," he is advancing that idea for consideration by others. He is basically stating an idea. Using "states" as the prediction leads to **(C)** as the correct answer.

The incorrect choices might all be meanings of "posits" in different contexts, but they are off the mark here, which will be obvious if you consider their definitions. Choice (A), "hypothesizes," means "takes an educated guess." Choice (B), "assumes," means "takes for granted without solid evidence." Choice (D), "decides," means "chooses one of two or more options."

7.   D

Difficulty: Hard

Strategic Advice: The key words "likely believes" identify this as an Inference question, and a thorough understanding of the context is necessary to determine which of the choices actually has support in the passage.

Getting to the Answer: The "true tipping point" is defined as the point at which "gravity prevails over matter and dead stars become black holes instead of neutron stars," or the maximum mass that separates a neutron star from a black hole. The author writes that the discovery of each new massive neutron star will help in determining "the true tipping point." This idea fits best with **(D)**, which is the correct answer.

Choice (A) uses the extreme language "only" and "*all* identified neutron stars"; perhaps the tipping point will be determined after learning just a few more neutron stars' masses. The fourth paragraph states that binary star systems allow astronomers to calculate the mass of neutron stars "with a great deal of precision," but there is no indication that binary star systems are the *only* way to accurately calculate the mass of a neutron star, which makes (B) incorrect. Choice (C) is a distortion of what the passage says about the Shapiro delay; the passage indicates that the Shapiro delay phenomenon has actually led to more accurate mass calculations of neutron stars.

8. D

Difficulty: Hard

Strategic Advice: The question stem says that "the passage identifies" something specific, marking this as a Detail question. Use the margin notes to zero in on where the specific detail is mentioned in the passage.

Getting to the Answer: According to the margin notes, the Shapiro delay is the delay in our receiving radio waves from a pulsar in a binary system. The format of the question does not make it easy to make a prediction, so go through the choices one by one to see which choice has support in the passage.

"Space-time" is mentioned in the third sentence in the paragraph, and it is made clear that the distortion of space-time *causes* the Shapiro delay, but is not a characteristic of it; (A) is incorrect. "Atomic clocks" are good key words to use to check (B), but that specific reference to pulsars' speed and regularity is not a characteristic of the Shapiro delay, making (B) incorrect. When it comes to radio waves, the third sentence of the paragraph says that there is a "delay, on the order of magnitude of 10 millionths of a second, in receiving the radio waves," but this does not mean that the radio waves themselves are actually shorter; (C) is also incorrect. Choice **(D)** is correct because the Shapiro delay provides a means to calculate the mass of the neutron star because of the proportional relationship between the delay and the mass of the neutron star.

9. D

Difficulty: Medium

Strategic Advice: Command of Evidence questions should be considered in tandem with one another; if you can correctly answer the first question, then it is a simple matter of locating the evidence you used in the answer choices.

Getting to the Answer: The correct answer will be evidence that there is a proportional relationship between the length of the Shapiro delay and the mass of a neutron star. Choice **(D)** is the correct answer.

Choice (A) points to the usefulness of the Shapiro delay, but not the specific "proportional" aspect that answers the previous question. Choice (B) describes pulsars, while (C) explains what causes the delay but again does not make the connection to the proportionality.

10. C

Difficulty: Hard

Strategic Advice: Another frequently occurring indicator of an Inference question is the key word "suggest." Watch out for answer choices that use extreme language or do not have direct support in the passage.

Getting to the Answer: The Green Bank Telescope is referenced in the third paragraph and in the final paragraph. The reference in the third paragraph points out that the Green Bank Telescope was used by the astronomers who discovered J0740+6620, while the final paragraph mentions some specifics about the Green Bank Telescope that allowed the astronomers to discover J0740+6620. The only choice that is supported by those references is **(C)**.

While the Green Bank Telescope has features that are helpful to discovering neutron stars, there is no support for the idea that it was solely designed for that task, so (A) is incorrect. Be careful with (B); the passage says the astronomers who used the Green Bank Telescope to discover J0740+6620 were from the NANOGrav Physics Frontiers Center, not the National Radio Astronomy Observatory. Finally, beware of the extreme language in (D); even though J0740+6620 was discovered with the Green Bank Telescope, there is nothing to support that J0740+6620 would have *never* been discovered without it.

CHAPTER 4

Paired Passages

In every SAT Reading section, there is always exactly one pair of shorter passages that takes the place of a single longer passage. The two passages share the same topic (although they'll each have their own take on the subject matter). The combined length of the paired passages is approximately the length of most single passages, so you don't have much, if any, extra reading to do.

Use these steps to tackle paired passages:

1. Read Passage 1 and answer the questions about Passage 1.
2. Read Passage 2 and answer the questions about Passage 2.
3. Answer questions about both passages.

Read and map paired passages as you would a single long passage, and then:

- Watch for similarities and differences of opinion between the two authors.
- Expect several questions in the set that ask about both passages. (These usually appear at the end of the set.)

Paired Passages Practice Set

> **DIRECTIONS:** Take as much time as you need on these questions. Work carefully and methodically. There will be an opportunity for timed practice in chapter 6.

Questions 1–10 refer to the following passages.

Passage 1 is excerpted from a speech delivered by President Woodrow Wilson to Congress in 1917. Passage 2 is excerpted from a speech delivered by Senator George Norris later that same week. Both speeches occurred prior to the entry of the United States into World War I against Germany and the Central Powers.

Passage 1

The present German submarine warfare against commerce is a warfare against mankind. It is a war against all nations. American ships have been sunk, American lives taken, in ways
5 which it has stirred us very deeply to learn of, but the ships and people of other neutral and friendly nations have been sunk and overwhelmed in the waters in the same way. There has been no discrimination. The challenge is to all mankind.
10 Each nation must decide for itself how it will meet it. The choice we make for ourselves must be made with a moderation of counsel and a temperateness of judgment befitting our character and our motives as a nation. . . . Our motive will not be
15 revenge or the victorious assertion of the physical might of the nation, but only the vindication of right, of human right, of which we are only a single champion. . . .

Neutrality is no longer feasible or desirable
20 where the peace of the world is involved and the freedom of its peoples, and the menace to that peace and freedom lies in the existence of autocratic governments backed by organized force which is controlled wholly by their will, not by
25 the will of their people. . . .

We are glad, now that we see the facts with no veil of false pretense about them, to fight thus for the ultimate peace of the world and for the liberation of its peoples, the German peoples
30 included: for the rights of nations great and small and the privilege of men everywhere to choose their way of life and of obedience. The world

must be made safe for democracy. Its peace must be planted upon the tested foundations of political
35 liberty. We have no selfish ends to serve. We desire no conquest, no dominion. We seek no indemnities for ourselves, no material compensation for the sacrifices we shall freely make. . . .

It is a distressing and oppressive duty, gentlemen
40 of the Congress, which I have performed in thus addressing you. . . . It is a fearful thing to lead this great peaceful people into war, into the most terrible and disastrous of all wars, civilization itself seeming to be in the balance.

Passage 2

45 There are a great many American citizens who feel that we owe it as a duty to humanity to take part in this war. . . . Men are often biased in their judgment on account of their sympathy and interests. To my mind, what we ought to have
50 maintained from the beginning was the strictest neutrality. If we had done this, I do not believe we would have been on the verge of war at the present time. . . .

I have no quarrel to find with the man who
55 does not desire our country to remain neutral. While many such people are moved by selfish motives and hopes of gain, I have no doubt but that in a great many instances, through what I believe to be a misunderstanding of the real
60 condition, there are many honest, patriotic citizens who think we ought to engage in this war and who are behind the President in his demand that we should declare war against Germany. I think such people err in judgment and to a great extent
65 have been misled as to the real history and the true facts by the almost unanimous demand of the great combination of wealth that has a direct financial interest in our participation in the war. . . . We are going to run the risk of sacrificing
70 millions of our countrymen's lives in order that other countrymen may coin their lifeblood into money.

1. A major theme of Passage 1 is that the United States is

    A)   the best example of a democracy.

    B)   at risk of ceasing to be a democracy. ✗

    C)   part of a larger community of nations.

    D)   apprehensive about going to war.

2. As used in line 35, "ends" most nearly means

    A)   conclusions.

    B)   intentions.

    C)   masters.

    D)   outcomes.

3. Which of the following does Wilson indicate is a reason for entering the war?

    A)   The necessity of freedom for the German people

    B)   The superiority of German submarines to American ships

    C)   The unique position of the United States in world politics

    D)   The sound judgment of the United States government

4. Which choice provides the best evidence for the answer to the previous question?

    A)   Lines 1–2 ("The present . . . mankind")

    B)   Lines 3–8 ("American . . . way")

    C)   Lines 19–25 ("Neutrality . . . people")

    D)   Lines 26–32 ("We are . . . obedience")

5. In the second paragraph of Passage 2, the main purpose of the first sentence ("I have no quarrel to find with the man who does not desire our country to remain neutral") is to

    A)   differentiate between attacking people and attacking an idea.

    B)   apply an idea expressed in the first paragraph to a different subject.

    C)   admit the limited value of neutrality.

    D)   express well wishes for President Wilson.

6. Based on the second passage, it can be inferred that when Norris delivered his speech, the United States had already

    A)   profited greatly from the war.

    B)   begun favoring one side in the war.

    C)   lost allies.

    D)   rallied behind its president.

7. Which choice best states the relationship between the two passages?

    A)   Both passages advocate for the same course of action, but Passage 2 refutes the evidence of Passage 1.

    B)   Passage 2 criticizes the advocates of the primary argument made in Passage 1.

    C)   Passage 1 and Passage 2 suggest a common strategy for achieving different goals.

    D)   Passage 1 and Passage 2 interpret circumstances differently and arrive at different conclusions.

8. Based on Passage 1, Wilson would likely have reacted to Norris's remark that "We are going to run the risk of sacrificing millions of our countrymen's lives in order that other countrymen may coin their lifeblood into money" (lines 69–72) with

    A)   agreement, because war requires a great deal of sacrifice.

    B)   uncertainty, because the outcome of the war is difficult to predict.

    C)   anger, because Norris is likely exaggerating the potential casualties.

    D)   disagreement, because the United States would not enter the war for financial reasons.

9. Which choice provides the best evidence for the answer to the previous question?

    A)   Lines 14–18 ("Our motive . . . champion")

    B)   Lines 35–38 ("We have . . . make")

    C)   Lines 39–41 ("It is . . . addressing you")

    D)   Lines 41–44 ("It is . . . balance")

10. Based on the passages, Wilson and Norris would both most likely agree with which of the following statements?

   A) Abstract ideals are sometimes more important than human lives.

   B) Citizens live better lives under democracies than autocracies.

   C) Strong moral character is compatible with a willingness to go to war.

   D) The health of nations is intertwined.

Answers and Explanations

Paired Passages Practice Set

Sample Passage Map

Passage 1

P1: American lives lost; challenge to all humanity; human right

P2: Neutrality won't work; against autocracy

P3: Fight for rights of all people incl Germans; no selfish ends

P4: Oppressive duty; civilization in balance

Purpose: To argue in favor of the U.S. joining the war

Main Idea: Entire world must be made "safe for democracy."

Passage 2

P1: Needed stricter neutrality; war was avoidable

P2: Some who want war simply mistaken; could lead to death of some, enrichment of others

Purpose: To argue against the U.S. joining the war

Main Idea: American involvement could benefit mon-eyed interests at the expense of life.

1. C

Difficulty: Medium

Strategic Advice: Based on the phrase "major theme," this is a Global question. Start by glancing at the main idea you wrote down: the entire world must be made safe for democracy.

Getting to the Answer: Throughout the passage, the United States is put into context as one of many nations in a worldwide conflict. Wilson relates that "the ships and people of other neutral and friendly nations have been sunk and overwhelmed in the waters in the same way" as America, and he says that the nation is only "a single champion" in the struggle for human rights. Choice **(C)** is correct.

Wilson does not state whether America is a superior example of a democracy, so (A) is incorrect. He does indicate that "civilization" is at risk and expresses concern over autocratic governments, but the specific idea that the United States could cease to be a democracy is never

discussed, so (B) is incorrect. Wilson states in the final paragraph that going to war is a "fearful thing," but this is not a theme throughout the passage, so (D) is incorrect.

2. B

Difficulty: Easy

Strategic Advice: The phrase "most nearly means" indicates that this is a Vocab-in-Context question. Use context to predict an appropriate equivalent for the word.

Getting to the Answer: Wilson states: "We have no selfish ends to serve. We desire no conquest, no dominion." He is discussing the "desires" that the United States has for war; use this as your prediction. Choice **(B)** matches this prediction.

Choices (A) and (D) are other possible meanings of "ends," but do not fit the context. Although it might make sense to say that "we have no selfish masters to serve," the following sentence makes it clear that Wilson is discussing intentions, not "masters," so (C) is incorrect.

3. A

Difficulty: Medium

Strategic Advice: Given the word "indicate," this is a Detail question. Use the clues in the question stem, as well as your passage map, to guide your research.

Getting to the Answer: One reason Wilson cites for going to war is in the third paragraph: "the ultimate peace of the world [and] the liberation of its peoples, the German peoples included." Choice **(A)** is correct.

Wilson never compares submarines to American ships, so (B) is incorrect. He emphasizes how America is one of many nations rather than how it is unique in the world, so (C) is incorrect. He does discuss the need for sound judgment in the first paragraph, but this is not itself a reason for going to war, so (D) is incorrect.

4. D

Difficulty: Easy

Strategic Advice: Given the phrase "provides the best evidence," this is a Command of Evidence question. The part of the passage you used to answer the previous question should be your prediction for this one.

Getting to the Answer: The answer to the previous question was found in the phrase "the ultimate peace of the world and for the liberation of its peoples, the German peoples included" in the third paragraph. This is contained in **(D)**.

5. A

Difficulty: Medium

Strategic Advice: The word "purpose" means that this is a Function question, so use your margin notes and context to determine what role the sentence plays in the paragraph.

Getting to the Answer: In context, Norris explains that although he has "no quarrel" or argument with some of the *people* in favor of the war, he believes that they have been misled. Though he is not against these *people*, he is against their *ideas*. Choice **(A)** is correct.

The sentence does not introduce a new subject, so (B) is incorrect. Norris seems to believe that neutrality is quite valuable, so (C) is incorrect. Norris does not go so far as to wish Wilson well—and the sentence does not refer to him specifically—so (D) is incorrect.

6. B

Difficulty: Hard

Strategic Advice: Given the word "inferred," this is an Inference question. When it's difficult to make a specific prediction, check the answer choices one by one against your margin notes.

Getting to the Answer: Norris is concerned about greedy parties profiting from the war, but this does not mean that this has already happened, so (A) is incorrect. Norris writes in the first paragraph that "we ought to have maintained from the beginning [. . .] the strictest neutrality," implying that America has *not* been strictly neutral up to that point. Choice **(B)** is correct.

There is no discussion of losing allies, so (C) is incorrect. Norris admits that "there are many honest, patriotic citizens who think we ought to engage in this war and who are behind the President," but it would be extreme to infer that the nation as a whole had rallied behind Wilson, so (D) is incorrect.

7. D

Difficulty: Medium

Strategic Advice: The question asks about the relationship between the entire passages, so it is Global. Consult your margin notes and compare the purpose and main idea of each passage to assess the passages' big picture relationship.

Getting to the Answer: In Passage 1, Wilson discusses the need to go to war in order to secure "freedom" throughout the world, asserting that America's motives are pure. Norris argues that America should have been more careful to stay neutral in the first place and expresses concern that the war may be a pretext to enrich certain individuals. The writers have both different conclusions and different interpretations of circumstances, so **(D)** is correct.

The passages do not share a goal or strategy, so (A) and (C) are incorrect. Passage 2 does criticize some proponents of the war, but it shelters others from blame, so (B) does not fit.

8. D

Difficulty: Medium

Strategic Advice: The question asks you to speculate about how Wilson would react to something, so this is an Inference question. Your answer still must be supported by specific evidence in the passage.

Getting to the Answer: Norris holds that the loss of life may only serve to enrich certain individuals. Wilson writes in the third paragraph of Passage 1: "We have no selfish ends to serve. We desire no conquest, no dominion. We seek no indemnities for ourselves, no material compensation," indicating that he does not believe greed to be a factor. Choice **(D)** is correct.

Wilson would not agree with the statement, so (A) does not fit. It isn't necessary to know the outcome of the war to have an opinion on whether lives will be exchanged for money, so (B) is incorrect. He never makes a prediction about the specific number of casualties, so (C) is incorrect.

9.   B

Difficulty: Medium

Strategic Advice: Keep the location of your research from the previous question in mind to answer this Command of Evidence question.

Getting to the Answer: The previous question was answered using the text in **(B)**, the correct answer.

10.   C

Difficulty: Hard

Strategic Advice: You are asked which statement both writers would likely agree with, so this is an Inference question. Since the writers must agree, make sure that you can support the correct answer with evidence from each passage. There are no clues in the question stem to direct your research, so you may find it easiest to go through the answer choices one at a time.

Getting to the Answer: Wilson would likely agree that abstract ideals (like "liberty") may be more important than human lives at times. However, Norris never prioritizes ideals over lives, so (A) is unsupported and therefore incorrect.

While Norris *could* agree with (B), he never discusses how anyone lives under autocracies, so this answer is incorrect as well.

Choice **(C)** is correct because both writers provide evidence to support it. Wilson explains that the choice to go to war can be made with "a temperateness of judgment befitting our character and our motives as a nation." Further, although Norris is against going to war, he references "honest, patriotic citizens who think we ought to engage in this war."

Wilson appears to support (D), since he discusses how "the challenge is to all mankind," but Norris never discusses how the health of one nation impacts another, so this answer is incorrect.

CHAPTER 5

Literature Passages

Exactly one passage in each SAT Reading section is a Literature passage: an excerpt from a novel or short story. The Literature passage is typically the first passage in the section, but that doesn't mean you have to tackle it first. Skip it and come back to it if you prefer science or social studies passages.

Read and map Literature passages as you would a science or social studies passage, and then:

- Read for what motivates the characters.
- Read for tone.

Though you should still take notes, unlike for other passage types, it doesn't make sense to think through the author's purpose and main idea after reading a Literature passage. Just get a sense of the primary action and characters and go straight to the question set.

The SAT does not typically test symbolism, though you may see questions about how the author creates a given effect or mood.

Literature Passages Practice Set

DIRECTIONS: Take as much time as you need on these questions. Work carefully and methodically. There will be an opportunity for timed practice in chapter 6.

Questions 1–10 refer to the following passage.

The following passage is adapted from a British novel published in the 1920s that tells the story of an American lecture tour by Mrs. Horace Hignett, a British writer and psychic, and her adult son, Eustace.

Through the curtained windows of the furnished apartment which Mrs. Horace Hignett had rented for her stay in New York, rays of golden sunlight peeped in like the foremost spies of some advancing army.
5 It was a fine summer morning. The hands of the Dutch clock in the hall pointed to thirteen minutes past nine, those of the ormolu clock in the sitting-room to eleven minutes past ten, those of the carriage clock on the bookshelf to fourteen minutes to six. In
10 other words, it was exactly eight, and Mrs. Hignett acknowledged the fact by moving her head on the pillow, opening her eyes, and sitting up in bed. She always woke at eight precisely.

Mrs. Hignett, *the* Mrs. Hignett, the world-famous
15 writer on Theosophy, had come over to America on a lecturing tour.

The year 1921, it will be remembered, was a trying one for the inhabitants of the United States. Every boat that arrived from England brought a fresh
20 swarm of British lecturers to the country. Novelists, poets, scientists, philosophers, and plain, ordinary bores; some herd instinct seemed to affect them all simultaneously. It was like one of those great race movements of the Middle Ages. Men and women
25 of widely differing views on religion, art, politics, and almost every other subject: on this one point, the intellectuals of Great Britain were single-minded, that there was easy money to be picked up on the lecture platforms of America and that they might just
30 as well grab it as the next person.

Mrs. Hignett had come over with the first batch of immigrants, for, spiritual as her writings were, there was a solid streak of business sense in this woman, and she meant to get hers while the getting
35 was good. She was halfway across the Atlantic with a complete itinerary booked before 90 percent of the poets and philosophers had finished sorting out their clean collars and getting their photographs taken for the passport.

40 She had not left England without a pang, for departure had involved sacrifices. More than anything else in the world, she loved her charming home, Windles, in the county of Hampshire, for so many years the seat of the Hignett family. Windles
45 was as the breath of life to her. Its shady walks, its silver lake, its noble elms, the old gray stone of its walls—these were bound up with her very being. She felt that she belonged to Windles, and Windles to her. Unfortunately, as a matter of cold, legal
50 accuracy, it did not. She did but hold it in trust for her son, Eustace, until such time as he should marry and take possession of it himself. There were times when the thought of Eustace marrying and bringing a strange woman to Windles chilled Mrs. Hignett to
55 her very marrow. Happily, her firm policy of keeping her son permanently under her eye at home and never permitting him to have speech with a female below the age of fifty had averted the peril up till now.

60 Eustace had accompanied his mother to America. It was his faint snores which she could hear in the adjoining room, as, having bathed and dressed, she went down the hall to where breakfast awaited her. She smiled tolerantly. She had never desired
65 to convert her son to her own early rising habits, for, apart from not allowing him to call his soul his own, she was an indulgent mother. Eustace would get up at half-past nine, long after she had finished breakfast, read her mail, and started her duties for
70 the day.

1. Which choice best summarizes the passage?

    A) The precise qualities of a character's habits are described while she visits the United States.

    B) A character's personality traits are revealed during her visit to the United States.

    C) A character's relationship with her grown son is strengthened while they tour the United States.

    D) A character's plans for making money on her trip to the United States are detailed.

2. The author regards Mrs. Hignett as

    A) unrealistically determined to make her fortune.

    B) unfortunately indulgent toward her son.

    C) comically resolute in the pursuit of her own desires.

    D) uniquely inflexible in her habits.

3. The author implies that Mrs. Hignett's primary motivation in coming to the United States is to

    A) promote an interest in her writings.

    B) earn money through lecturing.

    C) secure a suitable mate for Eustace.

    D) escape her home in England.

4. Which choice provides the best evidence for the answer to the previous question?

    A) Lines 14–16 ("Mrs. Hignett . . . tour")

    B) Lines 33–35 ("there was . . . good")

    C) Lines 40–44 ("She had . . . family")

    D) Lines 50–52 ("She did . . . himself")

5. In line 18, "trying" most nearly means

    A) attempting.

    B) agonizing.

    C) striving.

    D) aggravating.

6. According to the passage, the primary reason British lecturers came to the United States in 1921 was to

    A) copy a trend first established in the Middle Ages.

    B) promote their various philosophies and religions.

    C) earn money by speaking to American audiences.

    D) practice their lecturing skills in front of large groups.

7. Which choice provides the best evidence for the answer to the previous question?

    A) Lines 19–20 ("Every . . . country")

    B) Lines 23–24 ("It was . . . Middle Ages")

    C) Lines 24–26 ("Men . . . subject")

    D) Lines 26–30 ("on this . . . person")

8. In line 19, "fresh" most nearly means

    A) insolent.

    B) pristine.

    C) additional.

    D) unspoiled.

9. The main purpose of the fifth paragraph (lines 40–59) is to

    A) demonstrate Mrs. Hignett's selfish desire to retain control of her family home.

    B) provide a physical description of the Hignett family home, Windles.

    C) convey Mrs. Hignett's willingness to sacrifice her home in order to accomplish her goals.

    D) reveal Mrs. Hignett's belief that no woman is an acceptable mate for her son, Eustace.

10. Mrs. Hignett's attitude toward Eustace could best be described as

    A) controlling.

    B) disappointed.

    C) tolerant.

    D) detached.

Answers and Explanations

Literature Passages Practice Set

Sample Passage Map

P1: Mrs. H wakes at 8am; clocks

P2: lecturing tour

P3: 1921, many British lecturers

P4: Mrs. H: strong businesswoman

P5: difficult to leave home; Windles actually belongs to Eustace; keep him from marrying

P6: Mrs. H controlling of E on big issues but indulgent on small issues

1.   B

Difficulty: Medium

Strategic Advice: Remember that the correct answer for a Global question must take the entire passage into account, not just part of the passage.

Getting to the Answer: Use your passage map to determine the overall theme of the passage. In every paragraph but the third, the author reveals some aspect of Mrs. Hignett's character and personality; **(B)** matches this and is correct. Choice (A) is incorrect because while the passage does describe Mrs. Hignett's rising habits and morning routine, these are details, not a summary of the entire passage. Choice (C) is incorrect because there is no evidence that anything about Mrs. Hignett's relationship with her son changes. Finally, (D) is incorrect because while Mrs. Hignett's motivation for her lecturing tour is to make money, the passage never details her plans for doing so.

2.   C

Difficulty: Medium

Strategic Advice: There is no specific research clue for this Inference question, but Mrs. Hignett is the primary character, so think about the tone of the passage as a whole.

Getting to the Answer: The author seems to be poking fun at Mrs. Hignett. The passage says that she came to the U.S. to make "easy money" lecturing and that she

prevented her son from marrying in order to keep possession of her house. Although this doesn't paint a very pretty picture, the tone of the passage is light and humorous. Choice **(C)** is correct. Choice (A) is incorrect because although Mrs. Hignett is determined to make money, she has "a solid streak of business sense," so it's not an "unrealistic" aim. Choice (B) is incorrect because Mrs. Hignett is actually quite bossy. Note that the author is being ironic when he says that "apart from not allowing him to call his soul his own, she was an indulgent mother." That means that concerning issues that really matter, she's not at all "indulgent." Choice (D) is incorrect because although Mrs. Hignett seems somewhat "inflexible" (she always wakes up at the same time, for example), there's no indication that this is unique. Many other people are also somewhat inflexible.

3.   B

Difficulty: Low

Strategic Advice: Use your passage notes to locate the part of the passage to research.

Getting to the Answer: Your passage notes should indicate that the correct answer can be found in paragraphs 2, 3, and 4. Paragraph 2 introduces the fact that Mrs. Hignett is on a lecturing tour, but it does not mention her motivation for making this tour. In paragraph 3, it becomes apparent that she is one of a group of lecturers who are trying to make money in the United States, and in paragraph 4, we learn that Mrs. Hignett is one of the first of this group to arrive. So earning money is Mrs. Hignett's motivation, and **(B)** is correct. Choice (A) is incorrect because although Mrs. Hignett might want people to be interested in her writings, the author only mentions "easy money" as a motivation. Choice (C) is incorrect because Mrs. Hignett seems determined to *prevent* Eustace from marrying. Choice (D) is incorrect because Mrs. Hignett's leaving her home was a "sacrifice."

4. B

Difficulty: Medium

Strategic Advice: Use the location from your prediction for the previous question to find the answer. It must come from somewhere in paragraphs 2 through 4.

Getting to the Answer: Mrs. Hignett's primary motivation is strongly suggested in lines 33–35, which matches **(B)**. None of the other choices correctly indicates Mrs. Hignett's motivation. Note that (A) is incorrect because while it introduces Mrs. Hignett's lecture tour, it does not directly support the correct answer to the previous question, which includes the idea of earning money.

5. D

Difficulty: Medium

Strategic Advice: For Vocabulary-in-Context questions, mentally substitute a blank for the word the question asks about and fill the blank with a different word. That word becomes your prediction. Then look through the choices for a match.

Getting to the Answer: The author describes the year 1921 as a "trying one" for the inhabitants of the United States since the country was "swarmed" with a variety of British lecturers, including some described as "plain, ordinary bores." Thus, the author uses "trying" to describe something "unpleasant" or "bothersome." Choice **(D)** matches this prediction. Choice (A) is a verb that does not match the context of describing a year. Choice (C) is incorrect for the same reason. Choice (B) is too extreme: while the year might have been annoying, the conditions described are not bad enough to create agony.

6. C

Difficulty: Medium

Strategic Advice: Your passage notes should point you to the third paragraph, which discusses the arrival of a multitude of British lecturers in the United States. Go there to look up the answer.

Getting to the Answer: The last sentence of the paragraph states that "on this one point, the intellectuals of Great Britain were single-minded, that there was easy money to be picked up on the lecture platforms of America." This points to **(C)** as the correct answer. Choice (A) is a distortion. The "great race movements of the Middle Ages" are mentioned as being similar to the influx of lecturers in 1921, but the lecturers' motivation is not to copy those movements. Choice (B) is incorrect because while the author mentions that the lecturers have a wide variety of views, only earning money is identified as the lecturers' motivation. Choice (D) is incorrect because it is not mentioned in the passage.

7. D

Difficulty: Low

Strategic Advice: Use the location from your prediction for the previous question to find the answer. It must come from the end of the third paragraph.

Getting to the Answer: The lecturers' motivation is stated in the last few lines of the third paragraph; that matches **(D)**. None of the other choices indicates the correct motivation—earning money.

8. C

Difficulty: Medium

Strategic Advice: For Vocabulary-in-Context questions, think about the meaning of the word as it is used in the sentence and come up with a synonym that would work just as well. That synonym is your prediction. Scan the choices for a match.

Getting to the Answer: The cited line states that "Every boat that arrived from England brought a *fresh* swarm of British lecturers to the country." In other words, every boat brought *more* or *new* British lecturers. This matches **(C)**. Choice (A) is incorrect because "insolent" means "impolite." It is a synonym of a different meaning of the word "fresh." Choices (B) and (D) are incorrect for a similar reason: they are also alternate meanings of "fresh," but nothing indicates that the newly arriving lecturers were, in contrast to the previous lecturers, less polluted or damaged.

9. A

Difficulty: High

Strategic Advice: Review the information in the fifth paragraph, then think about why the author chose to include that information.

Getting to the Answer: The fifth paragraph states that Mrs. Hignett loves her home "More than anything else in the world." It then goes on to describe the home's legal status: she holds the home in trust for her son, who will become the owner when he gets married. However, Mrs. Hignett is preventing her son from ever marrying in order to keep control of the home. The author seems to be hammering home the point that Mrs. Hignett is putting her own desire to control Windles above the welfare of her son, making **(A)** the correct answer. Choice (B) is incorrect because while there are some physical descriptions of the home in the paragraph, such description is not the author's primary purpose for including the paragraph. Choice (C) is incorrect because while Mrs. Hignett is willing to travel away from her beloved home to earn money, she has no intention of "sacrificing" the home in the sense of giving it up permanently. Choice (D) is a distortion; Mrs. Hignett is preventing Eustace from marrying to retain control of her home, not because of her judgement of the suitability of any potential spouse.

10. A

Difficulty: Medium

Strategic Advice: Eustace comes up in the last two paragraphs, so focus your research there.

Getting to the Answer: The author notes that Mrs. Hignett kept her son "permanently under her eye" and never allowed him "to call his soul his own," so she's quite bossy. This matches **(A)**. Choice (B) is incorrect because although Mrs. Hignett feels the need to watch Eustace constantly, nothing in the passage indicates that she's disappointed with anything that he's done. Choice (C) is incorrect because the writer employs irony when he states that "apart from not allowing him to call his soul his own, she was an indulgent mother." This actually means that she controls his life. Choice (D) is incorrect because Mrs. Hignett keeps Eustace "permanently under her eye." That's hardly detached.

CHAPTER 6

Reading Practice Sets

Reading Practice Set 1

DIRECTIONS: For testlike practice, give yourself 13 minutes to complete this question set. Be sure to study the explanations, even for questions you got right.

Questions 1–11 refer to the following passage.

This passage is adapted from an article in a popular science magazine.

While there are thousands of species of birds that make an annual two-way migration of thousands of miles, only one type of migratory butterfly rivals the distances traversed by
5   migratory birds: the monarch. The behaviors that make possible the long migration from monarchs' northern breeding sites in Canada to their overwintering sites in Mexico—a journey of over 3,000 miles—are not fully understood, but in
10 recent years, researchers have shed light on certain aspects of monarchs' flight patterns and roosting behaviors.

Monarchs use environmental clues to determine exactly when they need to travel to a
15 warmer climate. Throughout their migration, monarchs use navigational aids and weather-based phenomena such as air thermals to facilitate their travel. An air thermal is a column of rising air caused by the uneven heating of the
20 earth. Following a circular motion, a monarch rides a thermal to its maximum height, then glides in a southerly direction until it hits another thermal that it can ride upward again. This use of thermals contributes to a noticeable pattern in
25 the relative heights at which monarchs fly throughout the day during migration season: in the early morning, they fly close to the ground to absorb radiant heat from the earth; during

midday, they travel farther by riding the
30 thermals, sometimes to heights of greater than 10,000 feet; and as the air cools in the evening, they fly close to the ground in search of a safe place to roost for the night.

Roosting is still not fully understood by
35 scientists, but they have identified monarchs' preferred roosting environments. The trees chosen for roosting sites must provide suitable protection from the wind, be structured in a way that facilitates clustering, and be close to a nectar
40 source. Early in the journey, in northern climates, this usually means selecting conifers; as monarchs get closer to their southern destination, they will often roost in oak or pecan trees, especially if the trees are close to a stream. While monarchs
45 migrate alone—unlike birds, which migrate in flocks—they cluster together when roosting overnight. Scientists have yet to discover whether monarchs seek each other out or merely gravitate toward the same microclimate for their evening
50 rest.

Although monarchs travel alone, it is clear that there are distinct pathways they follow on their migration. By tagging monarchs at the beginning of their migration and tracking them as they fly
55 south, researchers have been able to identify two major flyways: an "eastern flyway" that may end in Florida or Mexico, and a "central flyway" that ends in Mexico. This research has pointed to the need for more conservation efforts to be directed

60 toward the monarchs that follow the "eastern
flyway" because of the greater difficulties
associated with that route, including longer
distances, westerly winds, and unexpected
weather events originating in the Atlantic Ocean
65 and the Gulf of Mexico.

Once in Mexico, hundreds of millions of
monarch butterflies flock together in the oyamel
fir trees of Michoacán and Mexico states. One
particular site, which covers about 200 square
70 miles, is so valuable to the monarch population
that it was designated a World Heritage Site in
2008. Additionally, the Mexican government has
designated several monarch sanctuaries, including
the Piedra Herrada and Cerro Pelón sanctuaries
75 in Mexico state and El Rosario and Sierra
Chincua sanctuaries in Michoacán.

In the communities near monarch
overwintering sites, the return of the monarchs is
celebrated. In fact, at the end of the peak season
80 for monarchs, late January and February, there
is a week-long cultural festival, Festival Cultural
de la Mariposa Monarca. Each year tens of
thousands of people come to see the monarchs;
they are drawn to the monarchs in the same way
85 that the monarchs are inexorably drawn, in ways
that scientists still do not fully understand, to
their Mexican winter home.

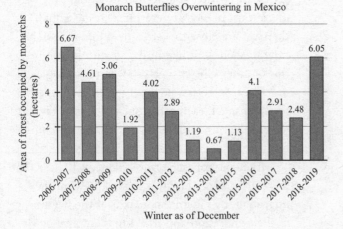

Monarch Butterflies Overwintering in Mexico

1. The author mentions "migratory birds" (line 5)
   to highlight

   A) the similarities between bird and butterfly
      migration.

   B) the rarity of long migrations in butterfly
      species.

   C) the thousands of bird species that migrate
      to Mexico.

   D) birds' use of air thermals to aid their
      navigation.

2. As used in line 18, "facilitate" most nearly means

   A) explicate.

   B) expedite.

   C) shorten.

   D) aid.

3. The author would most likely agree with which of
   the following statements about air thermals?

   A) Air thermals do not exist in the morning.

   B) Air thermals reach their maximum height in
      the morning.

   C) Air thermals determine the time of day when
      monarchs make the most daily progress on
      their journey.

   D) Air thermals grow stronger as the monarchs
      move in a southerly direction.

4. Which choice provides the best evidence for the
   answer to the previous question?

   A) Lines 15–18 ("Throughout . . . travel")

   B) Lines 18–20 ("An air . . . earth")

   C) Lines 20–23 ("Following . . . again")

   D) Lines 23–33 ("This use of . . . night")

5. The passage suggests the primary reason trees selected for roosting vary at different points in the journey is that

   A) the tree species that best fit the needs of migrating monarchs change as the monarchs travel south.

   B) for part of the journey monarchs migrate alone and for the rest of the journey they migrate in a flock.

   C) the microclimate needed by migrating monarchs changes as they travel south.

   D) the trees that grow closest to the water change over the course of the journey.

6. Which choice provides the best evidence for the answer to the previous question?

   A) Lines 34–36 ("Roosting . . . environments")

   B) Lines 36–40 ("The trees . . . source")

   C) Lines 44–47 ("While monarchs . . . overnight")

   D) Lines 47–50 ("Scientists have . . . rest")

7. As used in lines 48–49, "gravitate toward" most nearly means

   A) are drawn to.

   B) circle around.

   C) fall into.

   D) wander near.

8. According to the passage, the World Heritage Site designation (lines 70–72) was assigned to

   A) an area with a large concentration of oyamel fir trees.

   B) a monarch butterfly sanctuary.

   C) a physical location that is important to a particular species.

   D) a nature preserve in Mexico that is governed by other nations.

9. According to the passage, what is the purpose of the Festival Cultural de la Mariposa Monarca?

   A) To provide the funding for the monarch sanctuaries

   B) To celebrate the increase in the monarch population

   C) To generate tourism at the World Heritage Site

   D) To commemorate the return of the monarchs

10. The graph following the passage offers evidence that the area of forest occupied by overwintering monarchs

    A) fully rebounded in 2019 to the area occupied in 2006.

    B) declined sharply between 2008 and 2010.

    C) will never exceed 7 hectares.

    D) exceeded 4 hectares for the majority of 2006 to 2019.

11. Based on the graph and the passage, the author would most likely attribute the small area of forest occupied from 2013 to 2014 to

    A) a large number of severe weather events in the Atlantic Ocean and in the Gulf of Mexico.

    B) unusually high winds in western Mexico.

    C) a reduction in funding for World Heritage sites.

    D) extremely cold temperatures on the west coast of North America.

Reading Practice Set 2

DIRECTIONS: For testlike practice, give yourself 13 minutes to complete this question set. Be sure to study the explanations, even for questions you got right.

Questions 1–11 refer to the following passage.

This passage describes a series of behavioral experiments performed on Capuchin monkeys.

Recent experiments with nonhuman primates show that humans might actually be able to learn some financial lessons from their closest genetic relatives. Laurie Santos, a professor of
5 cognitive science and psychology at Yale University, recently created a series of experiments that created a market economy for monkeys. Researchers trained a group of six Capuchin monkeys to exchange metal tokens for
10 food, and in the first experiments, the monkeys showed basic economic rationality, preferring to buy from researchers whose "shops" gave more grapes for fewer tokens and snatching loose, unclaimed tokens off the ground.
15 Santos's later experiments showed more complicated economic behaviors when, for example, the monkeys faced the following situation. At one shop, a token was always worth two grapes. At another shop, a token would yield
20 one grape half of the time and three grapes half of the time. Imagine a situation in which you are given two options: you can either have $20 for free, or you can gamble and have a 50-50 chance to receive either $10 or $30. What would you do?
25 Most people would rather receive $20 instead of risking $10 for the possibility of gaining $10, and the monkeys did the same thing: they preferred getting two grapes for the price of one token instead of spending one token for the unknown
30 outcome of getting either one grape or three grapes. Their behavior is an example of risk aversion, which in an economic setting was previously thought to be a uniquely human behavior.
35 In a variation of the previous experiment, the monkeys continued to exhibit complex economic behavior. This time, the monkeys were given three grapes and had to choose between a

100 percent chance of losing one grape and a
40 50 percent chance of keeping all three grapes and 50 percent chance of losing two grapes. Again, the monkeys' behavior aligned with humans': they risked losing more in order to keep more of what they were initially given. This choice is
45 remarkably sophisticated and shows that the monkeys act in ways similar to how humans respond to complex economic decisions. Essentially, like humans, monkeys are prone to riskier behavior when they face the threat of
50 losing what they have.
From an economist's point of view, however, the two outcomes yield exactly the same results and do not warrant a change in behavior. It doesn't matter whether you begin with two
55 grapes or three grapes—the probability of both scenarios is the same: a 100 percent chance of two grapes or a 50 percent chance of one grape and 50 percent chance of three grapes will still "balance out" to two grapes in the long term.
60 The cold math of the situation, though, is not reflected in the behavior of the monkeys in the experiment, or of humans' experience in the real world. Receiving $30 and losing $10 does not feel the same as receiving and keeping $20,
65 even though the outcome, having $20, is the same. The contradiction in the monkeys' behavior reveals some biologically ingrained economic irrationality, a lack of consistency that humans share.
70 The experiments, therefore, do not merely support the idea that monkeys have human-like reasoning abilities; they suggest that humans might be able to improve their own economic intuitions by learning to avoid the mistakes that
75 both they and the monkeys make. The findings, moreover, support a reconsideration of a classical model of economics that assumes all individuals are acting rationally. Financial advisers and companies that want to encourage their clients

80 and employees to save more money earlier are
using the results of these experiments to engineer
situations that promote less risky economic
behavior. Normally, if primates were to mimic
complex human behavior, researchers would
85 herald their capacity for intelligence, but in this
case, it is humans who would do better to
unlearn some of the inclinations they share with
other primates.

1. The main purpose of the passage is to

   A) explain the findings of several experiments with
      monkeys and their implications for humans.

   B) outline methods based on experiments with
      monkeys that humans could use to improve
      their economic intuitions.

   C) argue that humans' economic intuitions are no
      more advanced than a monkey's.

   D) show some ways that monkeys have more
      advanced cognitive abilities than previously
      thought.

2. The author would most likely describe taking
   money that has fallen on the ground and appears to
   have no owner as what kind of behavior?

   A) Unethical

   B) Instinctual

   C) Aggressive

   D) Rational

3. Which choice provides the best evidence for the
   answer to the previous question?

   A) Lines 8–14 ("Researchers . . . ground")

   B) Lines 21–24 ("Imagine . . . $30")

   C) Lines 44–47 ("This choice . . . decisions")

   D) Lines 70–75 ("The experiments . . . make")

4. Which choice best supports the claim that monkeys, like humans, generally want to avoid risk?

   A) Lines 25–31 ("Most people . . . grapes")

   B) Lines 35–37 ("In a variation . . . behavior")

   C) Lines 41–44 ("Again . . . given")

   D) Lines 48–50 ("Essentially . . . have")

5. The question in line 24 ("What would you do?")
   primarily serves to

   A) show that the rational response is to accept
      $20 and avoid receiving only $10.

   B) admit that the researchers thought most
      people would gamble for the chance to get $30.

   C) make the description of the experiment more
      concrete for the reader.

   D) strengthen the argument that monkeys and
      humans share some economic irrationality.

6. As used in line 32, "setting" most nearly means

   A) placement.

   B) situation.

   C) location.

   D) preparation.

7. In line 60, "cold" most nearly means

   A) frigid.

   B) unemotional.

   C) unprofessional.

   D) academic.

8. The author claims that which of the following
   behaviors is an example of economic irrationality?

   A) Choosing to lose a small amount of money
      instead of risking losing a large amount of
      money

   B) Risking losing more money when it is certain
      that some amount of money will be lost

   C) Making economic choices based on the
      probability of the final outcome

   D) Making different economic choices in two
      scenarios that are mathematically identical

9. Which choice provides the best evidence for the
   answer to the previous question?

   A) Lines 37–41 ("This time . . . grapes")

   B) Lines 53–59 ("It doesn't . . . term")

   C) Lines 63–65 ("Receiving . . . same")

   D) Lines 66–69 ("The contradiction . . . share")

10. It can most reasonably be inferred from the passage that the author believes that a classical model of economics is

   A) fundamentally broken and ought to be discarded and replaced with a new economic model.

   B) full of logical fallacies, all of which can be resolved with the conclusions of Santos's experiments.

   C) incompatible with some of the findings of Santos's experiments described in the passage.

   D) still the best framework for predicting economic trends in spite of Santos's conclusions.

11. Based on the passage, which of the following hypothetical situations would be most likely to result in an investor's making a risky economic decision?

   A) The investor must decide whether to sell or keep an asset when there is a high probability that the asset's value will increase.

   B) The investor must decide whether to sell or keep an asset when there is a low probability that the asset's value will increase.

   C) The investor must decide whether to sell or keep an asset when there is a low probability that the asset's value will decrease.

   D) The investor must decide whether to sell or keep an asset when there is a high probability that the asset's value will decrease.

Reading Practice Set 3

DIRECTIONS: For testlike practice, give yourself 13 minutes to complete this question set. Be sure to study the explanations, even for questions you got right.

Questions 1–11 refer to the following passage.

This passage describes a new application of Selye's theory of stress.

In 1936, Hans Selye published a paper entitled, "A Syndrome Produced by Diverse Nocuous Agents," which describes an organism's response to stress. Selye, a young endocrinologist at the

5 time, made his discovery by accident while searching for a new hormone. When he injected lab rats with varying amounts of ovarian extract, all of his test subjects displayed similar symptoms, the severity of which depended on the

10 amount of hormonal extract with which they were injected. Curiously, these same symptoms appeared even when he injected the animals with placental or pituitary extract, which made Selye begin to have doubts about whether he was

15 actually on the verge of discovering a new hormone. His suspicions were confirmed when the rats displayed the same symptoms even when injected with a toxic inorganic liquid. Although he was initially disappointed by these baffling

20 results, Selye reinterpreted the results of his study and became a pioneer in the scientific study of stress.

Selye's general adaptation syndrome, which offers a broad explanation of an organism's

25 response to stress, consists of three stages. Stage 1 is alarm or shock: hormones such as epinephrine and cortisol are released, blood pressure is elevated, and the classic "fight or flight" response is triggered. In this stage, the body prepares to

30 deal with the stress the best it can, either by confronting it directly or by running away. Stage 2 is adaptation or resistance: if the stress was not great enough to overwhelm the organism completely, the body responds to the stress by

35 conditioning itself to encounter a similar type of stress in the future. Epinephrine, cortisol, and blood pressure all return to normal levels, and the recovery process begins. If the stress is of

sufficient magnitude, or if the body lacks

40 adequate resources with which to repair itself, the body enters stage 3: exhaustion. The adaptive capacity of the organism is overwhelmed, and prolonged exposure to this stress may result in death. Selye himself offers the following pithy

45 summary of his discovery: "Every stress leaves an indelible scar, and the organism pays for its survival after a stressful situation by becoming a little older."

In recent years, there has been a burgeoning

50 interest in applying Selye's theory to the field of exercise science. In this scenario, exercise is the stress, and workouts are designed to disrupt biological equilibrium but to not overwhelm the recovery abilities of the athlete. After the athlete

55 recovers, he or she displays a performance improvement.

On the surface, this application is simple and readily understandable. However, anyone who has trained for any length of time recognizes the

60 principle of diminishing returns. In the beginning, improvement is easy, fast, and predictable. However, the longer you train for your chosen sport (swimming, weightlifting, martial arts, etc.), the more difficult and time-

65 consuming it becomes to improve. For example, a novice weightlifter may be able to add five pounds to his deadlift every workout for several weeks or months. However, this rate of increase is not sustainable indefinitely, for if it were, new

70 world records would be set at every competition. Clearly, there are additional factors at play.

What actually occurs in practice is considerably less straightforward than Selye's theory would suggest. As the athlete becomes

75 more advanced, greater and greater stress is necessary in order to force an adaptation, but at the same time, the need for recovery increases as well. In the beginning, an athlete can recover from a hard workout within 48 to 72 hours. In

80 contrast, elite Olympic athletes may require a
month or more for proper recovery. Training at
these levels requires the coach and athlete to
work together to stay in stages 1 and 2 of the
general adaptation syndrome and to avoid stage 3.

85 Indeed, the more advanced the athlete is, the
finer the line between doing too much and doing
too little.

Hormone	Function
Aldosterone	Promotes sodium and water retention and the excretion of potassium
Cortisol	Increases in times of stress; long-term elevation causes muscle weakness and osteoporosis
Glucagon	Causes glucose to be released from muscle and liver cells into the bloodstream
Growth Hormone	Stimulates growth and cell regeneration in all tissues
Insulin	Causes glucose to move from the bloodstream into muscle and liver cells
Thyroxine	Regulates basal metabolic rate

1. The primary purpose of the passage is to

    A) describe an unexpected finding and its application to another field.

    B) propose a novel research program for studying stress.

    C) outline a common syndrome and list its symptoms.

    D) summarize the findings of a seminal research project.

2. As used in line 35, "conditioning" is closest in meaning to

    A) setting.

    B) applying.

    C) preparing.

    D) influencing.

3. The third paragraph (lines 49–56) serves mainly to

    A) refute a commonly held notion.

    B) introduce a qualification with which the previous two paragraphs must be interpreted.

    C) summarize what has been stated thus far.

    D) provide a transition between the two major parts of the passage.

4. According to Selye, a stressful event causes an organism to

    A) become less resilient than it was before, if the stress is mild.

    B) become more resilient than it was before, if the stress is severe.

    C) remain unchanged, if the stress is severe.

    D) become either more or less resilient, depending on the severity of the stress.

5. Which choice provides the best evidence for the answer to the previous question?

    A) Lines 6–11 ("When . . . injected")

    B) Lines 25–29 ("Stage 1 . . . triggered")

    C) Lines 31–36 ("Stage 2 . . . future")

    D) Lines 41–44 ("The adaptive capacity . . . death")

6. An assumption made by Selye about ovarian, placental, and pituitary extracts is that

    A) pituitary extracts are toxic to rats.

    B) different hormonal extracts would have different effects

    C) the hormones in ovarian extracts are substantially different from those in placental extracts but similar to those in pituitary extracts.

    D) the hormones in ovarian extracts are substantially different from those in pituitary extracts but similar to those in placental extracts.

7. Based on the information in the passage and the table, which hormone is most likely secreted in stage 2 of general adaptation syndrome?

    A) Cortisol

    B) Epinephrine

    C) Glucagon

    D) Growth hormone

8. As used in line 86, "finer" most nearly means

    A) thinner.

    B) better.

    C) more excellent.

    D) clearer.

9. A biological process is called "anabolic" if it builds up organs and tissues. It is called "catabolic" if it breaks down organs and tissues. Based on the information in the passage and the table, which of the following hormones is likely to be catabolic in its effects?

    A) Thyroxine

    B) Aldosterone

    C) Cortisol

    D) Insulin

10. Which of the following is most consistent with the information in paragraph 4 (lines 57–71)?

    A) An athlete who has been training for one month becomes injured and does not improve in the second month.

    B) An athlete who has been training for one month improves marginally in the second month.

    C) An athlete who has been training for 10 years improves marginally in the next year.

    D) An athlete who has been training for 10 years adjusts her diet and starts to see a performance increase in the next year.

11. The passage most strongly suggests that stress

    A) may actually be beneficial to the organism experiencing it.

    B) must be inversely related to an athlete's level of training advancement.

    C) is less important than recovery in athletic training.

    D) invariably leads to exhaustion, from which recovery may or may not be possible.

Answers and Explanations

Reading Practice Set 1

Sample Passage Map

P1: Only long-distance migratory butterfly: monarch

P2: Use air thermals, time of day

P3: Roosting, choosing trees

P4: "Eastern" and "central" flyways

P5: Monarch sanctuary locations in Mexico

P6: Festival Cultural de la Mariposa Monarca

Purpose: To explain what is known about the migration and roosting patterns of monarch butterflies

Main Idea: Scientists continue to increase their knowledge about an iconic butterfly species.

1. B

Difficulty: Medium

Strategic Advice: The phrasing "The author mentions . . . to highlight" indicates that this is a Function question, so determine *why* the author has chosen to include this detail.

Getting to the Answer: The author contrasts the "thousands" of bird species that perform long migrations with the "one" butterfly species that does so. A good prediction would be that the migratory birds are mentioned to show how few butterfly species migrate thousands of miles: only one. That prediction matches **(B)**.

The passage only indicates that many bird species and monarchs migrate; there are no similarities mentioned beyond that, so (A) is incorrect. Be careful with (C): the passage does say that thousands of bird species migrate, but their destination is never mentioned. Choice (D) is incorrect because air thermals are only mentioned in connection with butterfly migration.

2. D

Difficulty: Easy

Strategic Advice: The phrasing "most nearly means" always indicates a Vocab-in-Context question. The best approach is to examine the context, predict a replacement word, then find the best match among the answer choices.

Getting to the Answer: The original context explains how monarchs use "weather-based phenomena" in their travels. A good prediction to replace the word would be "help" or "assist," which matches **(D)**.

Choice (A), which means "to explain," does not make sense in the context of the sentence. Choice (B) means "to make something happen faster." Choices (B) and (C) are incorrect because there is nothing in the context to indicate that the air thermals make the actual journey to Mexico any faster or shorter.

3. C

Difficulty: Hard

Strategic Advice: Looking for what the author would "most likely agree with" means that this is an Inference question. Use the key phrase "air thermals" to determine where to focus your research.

Getting to the Answer: Based on the passage map, "air thermals" are the focus of the second paragraph. Check the answer choices against the information in this paragraph.

Choice (A) is not fully supported by the passage: air thermals are caused by the uneven heating of the earth, and there is nothing in the passage to indicate that the earth is not unevenly heated during the morning. Choice (B) is incorrect because the passage does not mention anything about the height of air thermals in the morning. Choice **(C)** is correct because the passage says that monarchs "travel farther by riding the thermals" (lines 29–30). Choice (D) is incorrect because while the passage says that monarchs ride the thermals in a southerly direction, it does not say that the thermals grow stronger in that direction.

4. D

Difficulty: Medium

Strategic Advice: Always consider a Command of Evidence question in tandem with the preceding question.

Getting to the Answer: The reference for answering the preceding question was the sentence that mentions that monarchs ride air thermals at midday, so **(D)** is the correct answer.

The remaining choices, (A), (B), and (C), all make mention of air thermals, but not in connection with monarchs traveling on the thermals at midday.

5. A

Difficulty: Medium

Strategic Advice: The phrase "The passage suggests" is a sure sign of an Inference question. Use your notes to determine the best place in the passage to research the answer.

Getting to the Answer: Your passage notes should indicate that roosting is the topic of the third paragraph. The paragraph indicates that there are a number of factors that must be considered when choosing a roosting site. In addition, the paragraph mentions that monarchs choose conifers at the northern end of their migration route and pecan and oak trees as they move south. This suggests that monarchs choose those tree species native to different latitudes that meet their roosting needs. Choice **(A)** is correct.

Choice (B) is incorrect because the passage does not say that monarchs ever migrate as a flock. Be careful with the mention of a microclimate in (C). The passage states that scientists think monarchs *might* gravitate to the same microclimate, but that is never connected with the roosting tree choice. Choice (D) is incorrect because the passage only mentions monarchs' choosing oak and pecan trees close to the water, not whether all the trees chosen need to be close to water.

6. B

Difficulty: Medium

Strategic Advice: To answer a Command of Evidence question, return to the research you did for the preceding question.

Getting to the Answer: Which sentence was instrumental in answering the preceding question? The sentence that mentions the requirements that monarchs look for when deciding on a roosting tree. Choice **(B)** is correct.

Choice (A) provides a definition of roosting, (C) mentions how monarchs roost together at night, and (D) brings up the idea that monarchs might gravitate to the same microclimate, but none of those choices explain monarchs' choice of trees.

7. A

Difficulty: Medium

Strategic Advice: To answer a Vocab-in-Context question, predict a replacement word based on the context and find the best match among the answer choices.

Getting to the Answer: The context of the phrase is the scientists' theory that monarchs may look for the same microclimate to roost for the night. A good prediction would be "are attracted to," which matches **(A)**.

None of the other choices fully capture the idea implied in the passage: that monarchs are actively attracted to the microclimate and do not just happen to be near it.

8. C

Difficulty: Medium

Strategic Advice: When you see the indicator of a Detail question, the phrasing "According to the passage," use the margin notes to focus your research. The correct answer will be a slight paraphrase of what appears in the passage.

Getting to the Answer: The context of the line reference indicates that the World Heritage Site designation was received because the area is "so valuable to the monarch population." That best matches **(C)**, which is the correct answer.

The passage does not indicate that the oyamel fir trees are only on the World Heritage Site, so (A) is incorrect. Later in the fifth paragraph, it says the Mexican government has designated several other locations as monarch sanctuaries, which eliminates (B). Finally, (D) is unsupported by the passage; nothing indicates that the area described is "governed by other nations."

9. D

Difficulty: Easy

Strategic Advice: This is a Detail question because it starts with the phrase "According to the passage." Use your passage notes to focus your research.

Getting to the Answer: The final paragraph of the passage states that the Festival Cultural de la Mariposa Monarca is held at the end of the peak monarch season to celebrate their return. This matches **(D)**.

The passage mentions that the Mexican government has designated several monarch sanctuaries, but the passage never says where the funding comes from, so (A) is incorrect. Choice (B) might sound logical, but there is no support in the passage for an increase in the monarch population. The passage also does not say if the Festival Cultural de la Mariposa Monarca is held at the World Heritage Site or at some other location, so (C) is also incorrect.

10. B

Difficulty: Medium

Strategic Advice: Start by noting the axes, units, and trends in the graph and work through the answer choices to determine which one the graph supports.

Getting to the Answer: The graph shows how the hectares of forest occupied by monarchs varied each year from 2006 to 2019. While there is no overall trend in the data, there is a definite slump in the values from 2012 to 2015; the high points of the data are from 2006 to 2007 and 2018 to 2019.

Even though 2006 to 2007 and 2018 to 2019 are the high points in the data set, the values did not *fully* rebound because the 2006 to 2007 value, 6.67, is still greater than the 2018 to 2019 value, 6.05, so (A) is incorrect. From 2008 to 2010, the hectares occupied by monarchs dropped from 5.06 to 1.92, which is a sharp decline, so **(B)** is correct. The fact that there are no values above 7 hectares on the graph does not mean that the area can *never* exceed 7 hectares, so (C) can be eliminated. For the 13 winter seasons shown on the graph, the area of forest occupied by monarchs exceeds 4 hectares in 6 years. Six is less than half of 13, so (D) is incorrect.

11. A

Difficulty: Medium

Strategic Advice: Some questions will ask you to combine information from the graph with information in the passage and draw a conclusion. Treat questions like this as Inference questions.

Getting to the Answer: The number of hectares occupied by monarchs is exceptionally small in 2013–2014; in fact, it is the smallest value on the graph. What are some of the factors the author mentions that might affect the number of monarchs that overwinter in Mexico? In the fourth paragraph, the author mentions

that the "eastern flyway" should receive more conservation efforts because of the difficulties involved with traversing that path south. The author mentions some of the "difficulties associated with that route, including longer distances, westerly winds, and unexpected weather events originating in the Atlantic Ocean and the Gulf of Mexico." Choice **(A)** speaks specifically to some of those difficulties.

When the passage mentions the wind, it is in conjunction with the westerly winds causing difficulty in the "eastern flyway," which encompasses the coast near the Atlantic Ocean and the Gulf of Mexico, so (B) is incorrect. Neither a reduction nor an increase in funding for World Heritage sites is ever mentioned in the passage, which makes (C) incorrect. Finally, extremely cold temperatures on the west coast are not likely to affect the "central" and "eastern" flyways, so (D) is also incorrect.

Reading Practice Set 2

Sample Passage Map

P1: Experiment: monkeys make rational econ. decisions

P2: Like humans, monkeys display risk aversion when making decisions

P3: Monkeys, humans both risk more to keep more (complex decision making)

P4: Monkey, human decisions not always mathematically sound—"biologically ingrained econ. irrationality"

P5: Results may teach humans to make better econ. decisions

Purpose: To explain the results of an experiment on monkey's economic decision making

Main Idea: Monkeys make economic decisions in ways similar to humans, and those decisions are not always entirely rational.

1. A

Difficulty: Medium

Strategic Advice: Global questions, like this one, ask about the passage overall, so avoid answer choices that focus too much on one specific aspect of the passage.

Getting to the Answer: The majority of the passage describes the experiments that Santos performed with the monkeys. The first and last paragraph also draw a comparison between humans and the monkeys in the experiment. The author's purpose, therefore, is to describe these experiments and what significance they might have for humans. Choice **(A)** is a good fit and is correct.

Choices (B) and (C) focus too much on humans and are not representative of the passage, which is primarily about the monkeys in the experiments. Choice (D) is incorrect because the conclusion drawn from the experiments is not that monkeys are smarter than originally thought, but rather that humans make the same mistakes that monkeys make in a market economy.

2.   D
Difficulty: Medium

Strategic Advice: Find a situation in the passage that is similar to the scenario presented in the question stem, and use Santos's interpretation to understand it.

Getting to the Answer: Several paragraphs mention money, but they are always about receiving money, not specifically finding money on the ground. In the first paragraph, however, the metal tokens that the monkeys use as money are described in one early experiment to be "unclaimed" and on "the ground" (line 14). This situation is similar to the scenario in the question stem. When the monkeys grab these tokens, the author describes this behavior as "basic economic rationality" (line 11), so it is likely that she would describe the scenario in the question stem as economically rational behavior. Choice **(D)** is correct.

Choice (A) is incorrect because the topic of ethics is never raised in the passage. Although the author does call some behaviors economic intuitions and inclinations, the behavior in question, taking money off the ground, is described as rational; (B) is incorrect. Even though the author uses the word "snatch" to describe the manner in which the monkeys took the unclaimed tokens, the behavior is an example of economic rationality, not aggressiveness; (C) is also incorrect.

3.   A
Difficulty: Medium

Strategic Advice: Use your work from the previous question to find the relevant part of the passage.

Getting to the Answer: The answer to the previous question was about finding money on the ground. The passage gives this situation in the first paragraph, in lines 8–14. The correct answer is **(A)**.

4.   A
Difficulty: Medium

Strategic Advice: Most Command of Evidence questions ask about the previous question, but some stand alone, such as this one. Use the passage map to find the paragraph where the answer will likely be.

Getting to the Answer: The claim in the question stem is that monkeys and humans try to avoid risk in most situations. There are two main experiments described in the passage, one in the second paragraph and the other in the third paragraph. It is the experiment described in the second paragraph that concludes that humans and monkeys are risk averse. Choice (A) looks as if it supports the claim in the question stem, so keep it for the moment. Choice (B) mentions complex economic behavior but does not specify if this behavior is risk aversion. Eliminate (C) and (D) because neither is a good example of avoiding risk. Therefore, **(A)** is correct.

5.   C
Difficulty: Hard

Strategic Advice: Use the surrounding context to interpret the function of a specific word, phrase, or sentence.

Getting to the Answer: The author is asking readers to put themselves in the situation that is analogous to the first monkey experiment. The author appears to believe that most people will choose to keep $20 instead of risking it for either $10 or $30, just as the monkeys did. The question in line 24, therefore, improves readers' understanding of the experiment by including them in it in a concrete way. Choice **(C)** is correct.

Choice (A) is incorrect because it merely states what the common choice is and does not treat the question in line 24 as a genuine question posed to the reader. Choice (B) is incorrect because the passage does not suggest that the researchers initially thought one option was more likely than another. The concept of economic irrationality arises only after the second experiment (in the third paragraph) shows how humans and monkeys make different choices even when the probability of the outcomes is the same, so (D) is incorrect.

6. B

Difficulty: Easy

Strategic Advice: Replace the word in quotation marks with a word or phrase of your own that keeps the same meaning in the sentence. Use your own word or phrase as a prediction.

Getting to the Answer: The word "setting" here means something similar to "scenario." Choice **(B)** is correct. Choices (A), (C), and (D) are incorrect because it does not make sense in this sentence to talk about an economic "placement," an economic "location," or an economic "preparation."

7. B

Difficulty: Medium

Strategic Advice: Imagine the word in the question as a blank and fill it in. Find the best match in the answer choices.

Getting to the Answer: The author distinguishes between the feeling that people have in the second experiment that causes them to make a riskier choice and the probability of the outcomes in the first and second experiments. The author's point is that people would make the same choice in both experiments if they ignored how losing $10 feels and looked only at the math underlying the probabilities. Choice **(B)** is correct. Choice (A) is incorrect because it does not fit in the context of the sentence. Choices (C) and (D) are incorrect because the math behind the probabilities is not "unprofessional" or "academic"; it is merely an alternative to emotion.

8. D

Difficulty: Hard

Strategic Advice: "The author claims" signals a Detail question. Watch out for incorrect choices that provide details stated in the passage that do not actually answer the question.

Getting to the Answer: The author mentions "economic irrationality" in the last sentence of paragraph 4, which compares the choices that the monkeys made in the two experiments. The irrationality the author describes is making different decisions when presented with two scenarios that have the same outcome probability. Choice **(D)** is correct.

Choices (A) and (B) are incorrect because it is not a single decision in either experiment that the author claims to

be an example of economic irrationality, but rather it is the contradiction of making different choices when the outcomes have the same probability. Choice (C) is the opposite of the correct answer and would be an example of economic rationality, according to the author.

9. D

Difficulty: Medium

Strategic Advice: Use your work from the previous question to find the correct answer.

Getting to the Answer: The previous question is about economic irrationality, and only (D) mentions it specifically. Choice **(D)** is correct because it notes the contradiction in the monkeys changing their decision even in light of the probability of the outcome being the same.

Choice (A) is incorrect because it presents only the scenario, not the monkeys' choices. While (B) and (C) mention the probability and the outcome being the same, they do not mention the contradiction.

10. C

Difficulty: Medium

Strategic Advice: Avoid extreme interpretations of the passage when answering an Inference question.

Getting to the Answer: The author introduces the notion of a classical model of economics in the last paragraph and claims that Santos's experiments "support a reconsideration of a classical model of economics that assumes all individuals are acting rationally" (lines 76–78). The author concludes that humans' tendency not to act rationally in economically threatening situations is deeply ingrained because the monkeys behaved in similar ways. If Santos's experiments are at odds with the assumption that all individuals act rationally in economic contexts, then the experiments are also at odds with a classical model of economics. Choice **(C)** is correct.

Choice (A) is too extreme; the author does not want to discard the classical model of economics. Choice (B) is incorrect because the author implies only one problem with a classical model of economics: that it assumes all individuals act rationally. Moreover, a "reconsideration" does not imply that the results of Santos's experiments can resolve this problem. Choice (D) also goes too far in its assumptions about the author's positive outlook for a classical model of economics.

11. D
Difficulty: Hard

Strategic Advice: Evaluate the answer choices by looking for a situation that is analogous to a situation in the passage.

Getting to the Answer: In the third paragraph, the author states that people are prone to more risky economic behavior when faced with the threat of losing money. Choices (A) and (B) deal with the probability, strong or not, that an investment will *increase* in value, so eliminate them. According to the third paragraph, people are more likely to gamble when the threat of losing money appears to be more certain, but less likely to gamble when they feel there is less of a threat of loss. Eliminate (C) because when faced with little threat of losing money, the investor is more likely to make a rational economic decision about whether to sell. Choice **(D)** is correct; when faced with the greater threat of loss, an investor is more likely to make a risky decision.

Reading Practice Set 3

Sample Passage Map

P1: Selye, hormone injections, stress

P2: general adaptation syndrome, stages

P3: Apply to exercise science

P4: Diminishing returns, complexity

P5: Advanced athletes, balance

Purpose: To describe Hans Selye's research, which led to his theory of stress and its later adaptation to exercise

Main Idea: Selye's research into stress can provide helpful insights into exercise science.

1. A
Difficulty: Easy

Strategic Advice: Global questions ask about the passage as a whole. Common incorrect answer traps are often too narrow.

Getting to the Answer: This passage begins by outlining Hans Selye's unintended discovery of general adaptation syndrome and then discusses how this model is currently being applied to the field of exercise science. Choice **(A)** is correct.

Choice (B) is a distortion; Selye has already successfully created a research program for studying stress, and the passage does not propose a new one. Choices (C) and (D) are too narrow; while the passage does summarize Selye's findings and lists some typical symptoms of stress, these answer choices ignore the rest of the passage, which focuses on the general adaptation syndrome's applications to exercise science.

2. C
Difficulty: Medium

Strategic Advice: Context is critical in Vocab-in-Context questions. The SAT will often ask about words that have multiple different shades of meaning.

Getting to the Answer: Go back and read around the cited line. The passages states that "the body responds to stress by conditioning itself to encounter a similar stress in the future." Since the response is related to how the body will handle similar stress in the future, predict that the body is "readying" or "developing" itself. Choice **(C)** is correct.

Choices (A), (B), and (D) do not capture this idea of preparation.

3. D
Difficulty: Medium

Strategic Advice: The phrase "serves mainly to" indicates that this is a Function question. Your passage map is your best tool for obtaining a big picture view of the passage and how paragraph 3 fits in it.

Getting to the Answer: Paragraphs 1 and 2 outline Selye's discovery and provide an overview of general adaptation syndrome. Paragraph 3 discusses how Selye's theory can be applied to the field of exercise science. Paragraphs 4 and 5 both provide more detail about how this can be done. Thus, paragraph 3 is the "bridge" that connects the two major parts of the passage to each other. Choice **(D)** is correct.

Choice (A) does not match the tone of the passage; the passage never attempts to "refute" anything. Choice (B) is a distortion; while the third paragraph does represent a departure from the previous two paragraphs, it is not a "qualification," a statement in light of which the previous two paragraphs must be interpreted. The third paragraph does not necessitate a reinterpretation of the previous paragraphs but instead provides a modern application of Selye's theory. Choice (C) is also a distortion; the third paragraph represents a shift away from the previous topic, not a summary of it.

4.   D

Difficulty: Hard

Strategic Advice: The open-ended phrasing of the question stem identifies it as an Inference question. The correct answer will not be directly stated in the text, but it will logically follow from it.

Getting to the Answer: Recall the essence of Selye's theory, particularly stages 2 and 3. If the organism is able to recover from the stress, the organism becomes more resilient. If the stress is too great, the organism fails to adapt and may even die. If the stress is too small, equilibrium is not disrupted, and the organism is not forced to adapt. Choice **(D)** is correct.

Choice (A) is a distortion; a mild stress is not enough to overwhelm the organism and make it less resilient. Choice (B) is also a distortion; if the stress is too great, the organism can't adapt and actually becomes less resilient. Choice (C) is opposite; a severe stress may kill the organism.

5.   C

Difficulty: High

Strategic Advice: The answer to a Command of Evidence question must be direct and unambiguous. "Close" is not good enough.

Getting to the Answer: Look back at your answer to the previous question. You need to find evidence to support the idea that an organism will either become more or less resilient depending on the severity of the stress. Choice **(C)** summarizes this idea perfectly and is correct.

Choice (A) describes Selye's experiments with lab rats. Choice (B) outlines Stage 1 of general adaptation syndrome, alarm or shock. Choice (D) depicts Stage 3, exhaustion. None of these answer choices support the idea of an organism adapting to stress in different ways.

6.   B

Difficulty: Hard

Strategic Advice: The words "an assumption" are your clue that this is an Inference question. Look for an answer choice that is clearly supported, but not directly stated, by the passage.

Getting to the Answer: Paragraph 1 discusses Selye's experiments with different types of injections. Since he was surprised by his results and doubted that he had found a new hormone, you can infer that all the extracts were hormonal and that he expected different hormonal injections to have different effects. Choice **(B)** is correct.

Choice (A) is the opposite; nothing in the passage indicates that the rats were harmed from being injected with pituitary extracts. Choices (C) and (D) are also opposite; Selye was shocked that ovarian, placental, and pituitary extracts produced similar effects. He clearly expected them all to produce different effects.

7.   D

Difficulty: Medium

Strategic Advice: If necessary, go back to the passage and remind yourself what stage 2 of general adaptation syndrome consists of. Then find the answer choice that is consistent with this information.

Getting to the Answer: Stage 2 of general adaptation syndrome is adaptation or resistance. This is the phase in which the organism begins to rebuild itself from the stress. According to the passage, cortisol and epinephrine increase during stage 1 and decrease during stage 2, so rule out (A) and (B). According to the table, glucagon has to do with glucose metabolism. It is unclear whether this plays a role in recovery. Eliminate (C). Growth hormone, however, has to do with "cell regeneration," which is in line with the rebuilding of tissues. Choice **(D)** is correct.

8.   A

Difficulty: Easy

Strategic Advice: The words "most nearly means" are your clue that this is a Vocab-in-Context question.

Getting to the Answer: Read around the cited line for more context. The previous sentences discuss the delicate nature of training elite athletes, and the sentence with the underline states that there is a balance between doing too much and doing too little. Predict that "finer" means something like "smaller." Choice **(A)** is correct.

Choices (B), (C), and (D) do not make sense when plugged back into the original sentence. The sentence intends to convey that advanced athletes experience a more narrow margin for progress. This does not mean that one margin is "better" or "more excellent" than another. Similarly, the window of progress for advanced athletes is "smaller," not "clearer."

9.   C

Difficulty: Hard

Strategic Advice: The phrase "likely to be" signals that this is an Inference question.

Getting to the Answer: Check each answer choice systematically against the table. Thyroxine controls basal metabolism; there is no indication that it causes anything to break down, so (A) is incorrect. Aldosterone controls sodium, potassium, and water balance. Again, there is no indication that it causes tissue degradation, so (B) is incorrect. The table indicates that cortisol causes muscle weakness and osteoporosis. Weak muscles and bones can be inferred to be caused by tissue breakdown, so cortisol must be catabolic. Choice **(C)** is correct. For the record, the statement in the table that insulin drives glucose from the bloodstream into cells again does not suggest tissue degradation, so (D) is incorrect.

10.   C

Difficulty: Hard

Strategic Advice: The phrase "most consistent" marks this as an Inference question.

Getting to the Answer: Paragraph 4 describes how novices are able to make progress very rapidly at first but that things start to slow down the longer the athlete trains. Therefore, you would expect someone who has been training a long time to make very little improvement. Choice **(C)** is correct.

Choices (A) and (D) are incorrect because the passage never discusses the effects of injury and diet. Choice (B) is an understatement; when a novice first begins training, she can expect to see rapid and substantial improvement. Progress begins to slow when the athlete reaches more advanced levels.

11.   A

Difficulty: Medium

Strategic Advice: The words "strongly suggests" identify this as an Inference question.

Getting to the Answer: Paragraph 3 discusses the application of the stress/recovery/adaptation cycle to exercise science. Since coaches and athletes productively use this cycle to drive increases in performance, stress is not necessarily something that should always be avoided. Therefore, it may sometimes be a good thing. Choice **(A)** is correct.

Choice (B) is the opposite of what you need; the passage states that more advanced athletes need more, not less, stress to disrupt equilibrium. Choice (C) is incorrect because the passage never compares the relative importance of stress and recovery. Choice (D) is a distortion; while too much stress and inadequate recovery may lead to exhaustion, stress by itself does not cause exhaustion.

PART TWO

Writing and Language

CHAPTER 7

SAT Writing and Language

The Method for SAT Writing and Language Questions

The Writing and Language section of the SAT is 35 minutes long. You'll see four passages, each with 11 questions, for a total of 44 questions. The timing is brisk: you have an average of a little over 45 seconds per question. The method below will help you become efficient and accurate.

	SAT Writing and Language Method
Step 1	Identify the issue (use the choices if need be)
Step 2	Eliminate answer choices that do not address the issue
Step 3	Plug in the remaining answer choices and select the most *correct*, *concise*, and *relevant* one

Identifying the issue means figuring out what the question is testing. The Writing and Language section tests a limited number of grammar errors and style and logic issues. You should feel empowered in knowing that you can familiarize yourself with these recurring errors and issues and learn to spot and address them quickly and efficiently. We'll describe the issues that you're likely to see on test day and how to deal with them in the next few chapters.

Eliminating choices that do not address the issue will sometimes get you to the correct answer right away. Sometimes, though, there will be more than one choice left, in which case you'll proceed to the final step.

Correct, **concise**, and **relevant** means that the answer choice you select:

- Has no grammatical, structural, or punctuation errors.
- Is as short as possible while retaining the writer's intended meaning.
- Is relevant to the paragraph and the passage as a whole.

Correct answers must align with the intended meaning of the original sentence, paragraph, or passage and will not introduce any new grammatical errors.

Try using this method as you work through the following question set. Unlike in the Reading section, there is no need to read the entire passage before you attack the questions; just start reading and take the questions as they come.

The Method for SAT Writing and Language Questions Practice Set

DIRECTIONS: Take as much time as you need on these questions. Work carefully and methodically. There will be an opportunity for timed practice in chapter 13.

Questions 1–5 refer to the following passage.

The Ocean's Top Predator

A great deal of information exists about predator-prey interactions in marine ecosystems and how these interactions affect the distribution of prey populations. However, less is known about interactions among different top predators, how these interactions affect the behavior of the predators, and how these behaviors might affect prey species. Predation by one top predator on another can reduce competition for prey resources and confer benefits on the prevailing predator. Even in cases **1** where the actual rate of killing between different predators is low, the effects on the ecosystem can be profound.

One such example of this kind of inter-predator interaction has only recently been discovered. Great white sharks are one of the ocean's top predators, yet even great whites, it turns out, have predators to fear. In 1997, on a whale-watching trip near the Farallon Islands, off the coast of California, **2** two orcas were observed by tourists killing a great white. The orcas rammed the shark to death and then began to feed on it. At the time, predation by orcas on great whites was unknown. Since then, **3** however, people have observed a number of similar attacks by orcas on great whites.

In this area of the Pacific, great whites congregate seasonally to prey on juvenile elephant seals. In 2009, a research team from the Monterey Bay Aquarium was

1. A) NO CHANGE
    B) in which the actual rate of
    C) of the actual rate of
    D) the actual rate of

2. A) NO CHANGE
    B) tourists observed two orcas killing a great white.
    C) two orcas were observed killing a great white by tourists.
    D) tourists observed two orcas as they killed a great white.

3. A) NO CHANGE
    B) therefore,
    C) consequently,
    D) furthermore,

using radio tags to track 17 of these great whites around the Farallon Islands. The sharks congregate there each year between September and **4** <u>December. Their purpose is to feed on</u> the young seals that are entering the water for the first time. However, when a pod of orcas passed through, the sharks deserted the area within hours and stayed away for several months.

Wanting to know whether this avoidance behavior was usual and whether it was caused by the orcas, the research team examined survey data covering the years from 2006 to 2013 to compare the behavior of sharks with that of orcas. The researchers found that in years when orcas moved through the area, great whites rapidly **5** <u>retracted</u> and stayed away for many months. Significantly, incidents of predation by great whites on elephant seals dropped by an average of 62 percent in these years. Thus, it seems that the mere presence of orcas, and the fear sharks have of them, may significantly benefit the seals.

4. Which choice most effectively combines the sentences at the underlined portion?

A) December for the purpose of feeding on

B) December, where they feed on

C) December to feed on

D) December in order to feed on

5. A) NO CHANGE

B) rescinded

C) discarded

D) vacated

Answers and Explanations

The Method for SAT Writing and Language Questions Practice Set

1.   B

Difficulty: Medium

Strategic Advice: "Where" should only be used to refer to an actual location.

Getting to the Answer: First, identify the issue: "where" in this sentence is being used to describe a circumstance rather than a location, so it's incorrect. Next, eliminate choices that don't correct the answer; eliminate (A). The correct usage is "cases in which," as in (B). Neither (C) nor (D) creates a logical sentence, so you can eliminate them also. Plug in (B) to determine that it's correct, concise, and relevant. Choice **(B)** is correct.

2.   B

Difficulty: Hard

Strategic Advice: When there's a modifying phrase present, be sure it's placed to modify the logically correct element in the sentence.

Getting to the Answer: Identify the error. In this sentence, there are two different modifier errors: first, "on a whale-watching trip near the Farallon Islands" is illogically modifying "two orcas"; second, "killing a great white" seems to indicate that the tourists were killing the great white. Furthermore, the phrase "two orcas were observed by tourists" is in passive voice, which is frowned upon by the SAT. Eliminate (A). Choice (C) still contains a modifier error and is also in passive voice, so you can eliminate that, too. Choices (B) and (D) are both in active voice, but (D) contains the ambiguous modifier "as they killed the great white," since "they" might be referring to the orcas or the tourists. Quickly plug in **(B)** to make sure that it's correct, concise, and relevant, then choose it and move on.

3.   A

Difficulty: Medium

Strategic Advice: When a transition word or phrase is underlined, check out how the ideas on either side of the transition are logically related.

Getting to the Answer: Identify the issue: the idea expressed before the underlined transition word is that attacks by orcas on great whites were unknown; the idea after the transition is that these attacks have been observed repeatedly in recent years. Since these ideas are in contrast to each other, a contrast transition word is necessary, so **(A)** is correct. You can eliminate all of the other choices since they do not create the appropriate contrast.

4.   C

Difficulty: Medium

Strategic Advice: When combining two sentences, find the choice that creates a structurally sound sentence in the most concise way.

Getting to the Answer: The issue here is clearly identified in the question stem. Choice (A) is unnecessarily wordy. In (B), the modifier "where they feed on" incorrectly modifies "December." Choice (D) conveys the correct idea but, like (A), is unnecessarily wordy. Eliminate them. Choice **(C)** correctly and concisely joins the two sentences while maintaining the intended meaning.

5.   D

Difficulty: Medium

Strategic Advice: To determine the correct word, use the surrounding context to determine the logically intended meaning.

Getting to the Answer: The issue here is word choice. The end of the sentence, "and stayed away for many months," indicates that the great white sharks left the area. Choice (A), "retracted," or "drew in," does not match, so you can eliminate it. Likewise, the sharks did not (B), "rescind," or "repeal or annul," and they did not (C), "discard," or "get rid of." Eliminate these choices. Choice **(D)**, "vacated," correctly expresses the idea that the sharks left the area.

CHAPTER 8

Sentence Structure

Fragments and Run-Ons

A complete sentence must have both a subject and a verb and express a complete thought. If any one of these elements is missing, the sentence is a **fragment**. You can recognize a fragment because the sentence will not make sense as written. For example, *Drove to the pumpkin patch* is a fragment because there is no subject; the sentence doesn't say *who* drove to the pumpkin patch.

The fragment *While we drove to the pumpkin patch* is an example of a dependent clause: it has a subject (we) and a verb (drove), but it does not express a complete thought because it starts with a subordinating conjunction (while). You're left wondering what happened while we drove to the pumpkin patch. To fix this type of fragment, eliminate the subordinating conjunction (in this case, get rid of "while") or join the dependent clause to an independent clause using a comma (e.g., *While we drove to the pumpkin patch, a hail storm moved in and dented the car*). Subordinating conjunctions are words and phrases such as *since*, *because*, *unless*, *although*, and *due to*.

Unlike a dependent clause, an independent clause can stand on its own as a complete sentence. If a sentence has more than one independent clause, those clauses must be properly joined. If they are not, the sentence is a **run-on**: *Saurabh enjoys skiing, he skis a new trail every winter.* There are several ways to correct a run-on:

- Use a period. (*Saurabh enjoys skiing. He skis a new trail every winter.*)
- Use a semicolon or colon. (*Saurabh enjoys skiing; he skis a new trail every winter.*)
- Use a comma and a FANBOYS (for, and, nor, but, or, yet, so) conjunction. (*Saurabh enjoys skiing, so he skis a new trail every winter.*)
- Use a dash. (*Saurabh enjoys skiing—he skis a new trail every winter.*)
- Make one clause dependent by using a subordinating conjunction such as *since*, *because, unless, until, although, due to*, etc. (*Because Saurabh enjoys skiing, he skis a new trail every winter.*)

Try the drill that follows to gain proficiency in identifying and correcting fragments and run-ons. You can check your work by reviewing the "Answers and Explanations" section at the end of the chapter.

Fragments and Run-Ons Drill

1. My cousin loves nature and the <u>outdoors; so she</u> became a wildlife biologist.

   A) NO CHANGE

   B) outdoors so she

   C) outdoors, she

   D) outdoors, so she

2. The scientist Robert Hooke constructed one of the first Gregorian reflecting <u>telescopes. He, then</u> used the telescope to make astronomical discoveries, such as determining the rotation period of Mars.

   A) NO CHANGE

   B) telescopes, he then

   C) telescopes; he then,

   D) telescopes; he then

3. After winning numerous military victories in the sixteenth <u>century. King</u> Man Pa of the ancient kingdom of Arakan orchestrated the construction of a magnificent temple containing 80,000 representations of Buddha in the capital city of Mrauk U.

   A) NO CHANGE

   B) century, King

   C) century—King

   D) century, and King

4. While star charts are widely available on smart-phones and tablets, <u>but</u> most adults can only recognize a handful of constellations, such as Ursa Major and Orion.

   A) NO CHANGE

   B) and

   C) therefore,

   D) DELETE the underlined portion.

5. The history <u>professor wanting to accommodate students who had missed class due to inclement weather. She permitted</u> students to submit their research papers at a later date.

   A) NO CHANGE

   B) professor wanted to accommodate students who had missed class due to inclement weather, and permitted

   C) professor, wanting to accommodate students who had missed class due to inclement weather, permitted

   D) professor wanting to accommodate students who had missed class due to inclement weather; and she permitted

6. Historians of Afro-Eurasia have long maintained that villages <u>that were situated along the Silk Road trade routes and became</u> vibrant hubs of cross-cultural exchanges of knowledge.

   A) NO CHANGE

   B) that were situated along the Silk Road trade routes, which became

   C) situated along the Silk Road trade routes became

   D) situated along the Silk Road trade routes, they became

7. Health experts advocate near-daily cardiovascular <u>exercise and</u> also, they recommend resistance training at least twice a week.

   A) NO CHANGE

   B) exercise,

   C) exercise;

   D) exercise

8. The profitable company, an online retailer that emphasizes ethical business practices, <u>which requires</u> that new employees participate in extensive practice scenarios that build skills in empathizing with suppliers, customers, and co-workers.

   A) NO CHANGE

   B) requiring

   C) and it requires

   D) requires

Commas, Dashes, and Colons

Use **commas** to:

- Set off items in a list
- Set off parenthetical information
- Separate an introductory word or phrase from the rest of the sentence
- Separate independent clauses joined by a FANBOYS conjunction
- Separate a dependent clause from an independent clause that follows it

Use **dashes** to:

- Set off parenthetical information
- Separate independent clauses joined by a FANBOYS conjunction
- Introduce and/or emphasize a short phrase, quotation, explanation, example, or list
- Separate two independent clauses when the second clause explains, illustrates, or expands on the first sentence

Use **colons** to:

- Introduce and/or emphasize a short phrase, quotation, explanation, example, or list
- Separate two independent clauses when the second clause explains, illustrates, or expands on the first sentence

Note that there is some overlap in the functions of commas, dashes, and colons.

Try the following drill to help you learn these punctuation rules. You can check your work by reviewing the "Answers and Explanations" section at the end of the chapter. Then move on to the passage-based practice set to see how sentence structure and punctuation are tested on the SAT.

Punctuation Drill

1. Scientists released the first picture of a black <u>hole, an</u> extremely compact mass in space exhibiting an inescapable gravitational pull—by compiling data from numerous observatories around the world in 2019.

   A) NO CHANGE
   B) hole, which is an
   C) hole: an
   D) hole—an

2. Based on per capita consumption, Americans' favorite cheeses <u>include</u> mozzarella, cheddar, and Parmesan.

   A) NO CHANGE
   B) include—
   C) include:
   D) include;

3. English movie <u>director—Alfred Hitchcock directed</u> over 50 feature films in his long career.

   A) NO CHANGE
   B) director Alfred Hitchcock directed
   C) director, Alfred Hitchcock—directed
   D) director, Alfred Hitchcock, directed

4. The deadline was rapidly <u>approaching and the team still had two major tasks to complete,</u> revising the proposal and organizing a focus group.

   A) NO CHANGE
   B) approaching, and the team still had two major tasks to complete:
   C) approaching and the team still had two major tasks to complete:
   D) approaching, and the team still had two major tasks to complete

5. Wanting to do well at the <u>contest, and knowing that the competition would be fierce, Maya practiced tirelessly, and</u> carefully analyzed her performance during each practice session.

   A) NO CHANGE
   B) contest and knowing that the competition would be fierce, Maya practiced tirelessly and
   C) contest, and knowing that the competition would be fierce, Maya practiced tirelessly and
   D) contest and knowing that the competition would be fierce, Maya practiced tirelessly, and

6. In Maltravieso cave in <u>Spain, a stencil of a hand which has been dated to 64,000 years ago was</u> probably made by a Neanderthal rather than a biologically modern human.

   A) NO CHANGE
   B) Spain, a stencil of a hand, which has been dated to 64,000 years ago, was
   C) Spain, a stencil of a hand, which has been dated to 64,000 years ago was
   D) Spain a stencil of a hand which has been dated to 64,000 years ago, was

7. <u>Willingly, breaking a promise is</u> not only dishonorable but also destabilizing, fostering distrust among one's associates.

   A) NO CHANGE
   B) Willingly breaking a promise, is
   C) Willingly, breaking a promise, is
   D) Willingly breaking a promise is

8. <u>Consider the zipper, for example,</u> the design is so effective that it has been essentially unchanged since the early twentieth century.

   A) NO CHANGE
   B) Consider the zipper, for example:
   C) Consider: the zipper, for example,
   D) Consider the zipper for example

Sentence Structure Practice Set

DIRECTIONS: Take as much time as you need on these questions. Work carefully and methodically. There will be an opportunity for timed practice in chapter 13.

Questions 1–11 refer to the following passage.

The Buzz about Kazoos

Although plastic kazoos can be purchased for less than a **1** <u>dollar; they operate</u> on the same principle as more "professional" kazoos. Far from being mere children's toys, kazoos are genuine instruments of the membranophone class, which generate sound by vibrating a membrane. The modern kazoo's structure is simply a hollow **2** <u>tube, tapered at the end into which the player blows, with</u> a raised membrane placed about two-thirds of the way down the tube. The tube may be constructed of any solid **3** <u>material,</u> higher-quality kazoos are usually metal. Still, almost all kazoos— whether trinkets or professional instruments—have membranes of simple waxed paper. A kazoo's size correlates with the deepness of its pitch **4** <u>range. Kazoos meant to mimic:</u> the sound of tubas are nearly three feet in length.

The current kazoo design is of uncertain **5** <u>origin; though several</u> similar, recognizable patents for kazoo-like instruments were granted in the late 1800s and early 1900s. The Original American Kazoo Company, opened in **6** <u>New York in 1916, was the first to mass-produce kazoos</u> and still operates with similar machinery today. Instruments with a vibrating membrane, however, have

1. A) NO CHANGE
    B) dollar, they operate
    C) dollar, operating
    D) dollar, but they operate

2. A) NO CHANGE
    B) tube, tapered at the end into which the player blows with
    C) tube tapered at the end into which the player blows with
    D) tube, tapered at the end into which the player blows, with:

3. A) NO CHANGE
    B) material but
    C) material, but,
    D) material;

4. A) NO CHANGE
    B) range; kazoos, meant to mimic
    C) range; kazoos meant to mimic
    D) range, kazoos meant to mimic

5. A) NO CHANGE
    B) origin, though several
    C) origin, several
    D) origin though several

6. A) NO CHANGE
    B) New York in 1916 was the first to mass-produce kazoos,
    C) New York in 1916, was the first to mass-produce kazoos,
    D) New York. In 1916, was the first to mass-produce kazoos

existed for **7** centuries. Those from African ceremonial instruments to horizontally held mirlitons with onionskin membranes used since the 1500s in Europe.

One reason some musicians may not consider the kazoo a "real" instrument is due to the ease with which it can be played. Whereas playing brass instruments, for instance, requires a very specific **8** technique simply humming, or speaking, into a kazoo vibrates its membrane and produces its sound. The vibrations transform the player's vocalizations, **9** producing a distinct "buzzing" quality. Like singing, skillful kazoo playing requires rhythm and pitch-accuracy, but almost anyone can master the basic technique.

Despite the kazoo's apparent simplicity, it has featured widely in both American and international music. For instance, street quartets that perform during Carnival in Cádiz, Spain, use kazoos to accompany their skits and songs. Juvenile jazz **10** bands—which developed in the mining towns of England and Wales, typically play kazoos and simple percussion instruments. Across the Atlantic, kazoos have appeared in the last century in quintessentially American music, such as jazz and jug band tunes, musical theater numbers by Leonard Bernstein and Frank **11** Loesser; even a rock song by the Grateful Dead. Often, the instrument is chosen to add a homespun, comedic, or quirky quality to a song. Those seeking to add its unique timbre to their performances today can even purchase an electric kazoo, complete with tiny amplifier. The kazoo has, through its history, become a bit of an oxymoron in music—unconventional yet accessible, odd yet familiar.

7. A) NO CHANGE
   B) centuries: from
   C) centuries. From
   D) centuries, and from

8. A) NO CHANGE
   B) technique; simply humming or speaking into a kazoo vibrates
   C) technique, simply humming or speaking into a kazoo vibrates
   D) technique, simply humming or speaking into a kazoo, vibrates

9. A) NO CHANGE
   B) and produce
   C) they produce
   D) DELETE the underlined portion.

10. A) NO CHANGE
    B) bands, which developed
    C) bands developed
    D) bands

11. A) NO CHANGE
    B) Loesser; and even
    C) Loesser and, even
    D) Loesser, and even

Answers and Explanations

Fragments and Run-Ons Drill

1.   D

Both clauses in the sentence are independent, with the subject-verb pairs "cousin loves" and "she became." Choice **(D)** is correct because it joins the independent clauses with a comma and FANBOYS conjunction. Choice (A) incorrectly combines a semicolon with a FANBOYS conjunction, (B) omits the comma, and (C) creates a run-on by joining independent clauses with only a comma.

2.   D

The underlined portion connects two independent clauses, with the subject-verb pairs "Robert Hooke constructed" and "He . . . used." Choice **(D)** correctly joins the independent clauses with a semicolon. Choice (A) appropriately separates the clauses into two sentences, but it adds an unnecessary comma that separates the subject "he" from its verb. Choice (B) is a run-on because it joins independent clauses with only a comma. Choice (C), like (A), separates the subject "he" from its verb.

3.   B

As written, the first sentence is a fragment because it does not express a complete thought; eliminate (A). Choice **(B)** correctly uses a comma to join the dependent clause and independent clause. The punctuation in the other choices (a dash and a comma with a FANBOYS conjunction) would be correct only when joining one independent clause to another.

4.   D

The word "While" makes the first clause dependent. The second clause is independent, with the subject-verb pair "adults can." A comma by itself joins a dependent clause to an independent clause, so **(D)** is correct. The other choices add unnecessary conjunctions or transition words.

5.   C

As written, the first sentence does not express a complete thought; eliminate (A). Choice **(C)** is correct because it uses commas to set off the descriptive phrase "wanting . . . weather" and expresses a complete thought with the subject-verb pair "professor . . . permitted." Choice (B) adds an unnecessary comma between the verbs ("wanted" and "permitted") of its

compound predicate. Choice (D) is incorrect because a semicolon joins independent clauses, but the first part of the sentence does not express a complete thought.

6.   C

As written, the sentence does not express a complete thought. Choice **(C)** is correct because it follows the noun phrase "villages situated along the Silk Road trade routes" with the verb "became," thus expressing as a complete thought what "Historians . . . have long maintained." Choices (A) and (B) unnecessarily separate "villages" from "became" (with "and" and "which," respectively), and (D) inserts an extra, unnecessary subject ("they") into the clause.

7.   C

Both clauses in the sentence are independent, with the subject-verb pairs "experts advocate" and "they recommend." Choice **(C)** is correct because it links the independent clauses with a semicolon. While a comma and FANBOYS conjunction could join independent clauses, (A) omits the comma, and (B) omits the FANBOYS conjunction. Choice (D) omits all connecting punctuation.

8.   D

The sentence is a fragment as written because it does not express a complete thought; (A) is incorrect. Choice **(D)** is correct because it results in a sentence with the subject-verb pair "company . . . requires" that expresses a complete thought. Choice (B) creates a fragment. Choice (C) turns the part of the sentence after "and" into an independent clause, but the first part of the sentence is not an independent clause. Thus, a comma and FANBOYS conjunction cannot be used to join the parts.

Punctuation Drill

1.   D

The definition of a black hole is parenthetical information, so it should be set off from the rest of the sentence by a set of matching punctuation; **(D)** uses a set of dashes and is correct. Although commas could set off parenthetical information, (A) and (B) are incorrect because the non-underlined portion uses a dash. A colon could introduce a definition, but (C) is incorrect because the portion after the colon contains an additional phrase after the dash.

2. A

No punctuation should separate the verb "include" from its objects (the list of cheeses); **(A)** is correct. A dash or a colon, as in (B) and (C), could introduce a list only when following an independent clause. (For example, *Americans have three favorite cheeses: mozzarella, cheddar, and Parmesan.*) A semicolon, as in (D), joins independent clauses or separates items in lists that contain commas within their items.

3. B

Non-parenthetical information does not need to be set off by punctuation. Since there is more than one "English movie director," the name "Alfred Hitchcock" is necessary information; **(B)** is correct. The other choices are incorrect because punctuation around "Alfred Hitchcock" is unnecessary.

4. B

The sentence contains two independent clauses, with the subject-verb pairs "deadline was" and "team . . . had." Choices (A) and (C) omit punctuation between the clauses, resulting in run-ons. Choice (D) omits any punctuation before that final phrase of the sentence that describes the two tasks. Choice **(B)** correctly joins the independent clauses with a comma and FANBOYS conjunction and uses a colon to introduce the tasks.

5. B

The sentence begins with an introductory phrase ("Wanting . . . fierce") with two verbs joined by the conjunction "and": "Wanting" and "knowing." The independent clause of the sentence has the subject "Maya" and two verbs joined by the conjunction "and": "practiced" and "analyzed." A comma should separate the introductory phrase from the independent clause, but no commas should separate the verbs in each compound. Choice **(B)** is correct. The other answer choices all insert an unnecessary comma between one or both sets of verbs.

6. B

The sentence begins with the introductory phrase "In Maltravieso cave in Spain" and has the subject-verb pair "stencil . . . was." The phrase "which has been dated to 64,000 years ago" is parenthetical information. The introductory phrase should be followed by a comma, and the parenthetical phrase should be set off by a pair

of punctuation marks; **(B)** is correct. The other choices omit one or both commas around the parenthetical phrase, and (D) also omits the comma after the introductory phrase.

7. D

The entire noun phrase "Willingly breaking a promise" is the subject of the sentence. No comma is needed within this noun phrase, nor should the noun phrase be separated from its verb "is"; **(D)** is correct. Choices (A) and (C) include an unnecessary comma within the noun phrase, and (B) and (C) separate the sentence's subject and verb.

8. B

The sentence contains two independent clauses. The first has the implied subject "you" and the verb "Consider," and the second has the subject-verb pair "design is." The phrase "for example" should be joined to the first clause with a comma, so eliminate (D). Choices (A) and (C) are incorrect because two independent clauses cannot be joined by just a comma. Choice **(B)** correctly follows the first independent clause with a colon, as the second clause provides a reason for the suggestion in the first clause.

Sentence Structure Practice Set

1. B

Difficulty: Medium

Strategic Advice: When the clauses of a sentence are joined at the underline, check to see if there is a fragment or run-on issue.

Getting to the Answer: A semicolon can join two independent clauses; because the word "Although" makes the first clause of the sentence dependent, (A) is incorrect as written. Likewise, eliminate (D), since a comma and FANBOYS conjunction would join two independent clauses. Because the first clause of the sentence is dependent, the second clause must be independent, expressing a complete thought. Choice **(B)** is correct because it provides the second clause with a subject ("they") and verb ("operate") and joins it to the dependent clause with a comma. Choice (C) is incorrect because it removes the subject from the second clause, resulting in a sentence fragment.

2. A

Difficulty: Hard

Strategic Advice: Pairs of punctuation marks, such as commas or dashes, indicate parenthetical information. Make sure that parentheticals are properly punctuated and modify the correct word or phrase.

Getting to the Answer: The phrase "tapered at the end into which the player blows" is parenthetical information that describes the "hollow tube." As written, the phrase is correctly punctuated with a set of commas. Choice **(A)** is thus correct. Choices (B) and (C) are incorrect because neither uses a pair of punctuation marks to set off the parenthetical. Choice (D) adds an unnecessary colon that separates the preposition "with" from its object.

3. D

Difficulty: Medium

Strategic Advice: When the underlined portion connects clauses, determine whether each is dependent or independent. Then choose the punctuation that correctly connects those types of clauses.

Getting to the Answer: Both of the clauses in the sentence are independent; each expresses a complete thought with a subject and predicate verb. As written, connecting independent clauses with only a comma results in a run-on, so (A) is incorrect. Choice **(D)** is correct because a semicolon can be used to connect independent clauses. A FANBOYS conjunction can join independent clauses, but it must be accompanied by a comma, so (B) is incorrect. Choice (C) adds an unnecessary comma after "but."

4. C

Difficulty: Medium

Strategic Advice: The underlined portion includes parts of two sentences, so be on the lookout for potential issues with connecting clauses: fragments and run-ons.

Getting to the Answer: As written, the two independent clauses are appropriately separated into two sentences, but a colon can only be placed after an independent clause. Choice (A) is incorrect. Choice (D) uses only a comma to separate the independent clauses and results in a run-on, so (D) is incorrect. Both (B) and (C) appropriately use a semicolon to separate the independent clauses, but (B) inserts an unnecessary comma that

separates the subject "kazoos" from the verb "are." Choice **(C)** is correct.

5. B

Difficulty: Medium

Strategic Advice: When determining whether clauses are independent or dependent, look for subordinating words such as *although* and *while*.

Getting to the Answer: The first clause of the sentence is independent, expressing a complete thought. If the second clause started with the word "several," it would be independent, but, as written, the word "though" subordinates the clause. Choice **(B)** correctly joins the independent and dependent clauses with a comma. Choice (A) incorrectly joins a dependent clause and an independent clause with a semicolon. By eliminating the subordinating word "though," (C) creates a run-on with two independent clauses joined with only a comma. Choice (D) is incorrect because it has no punctuation at all between the clauses.

6. A

Difficulty: Hard

Strategic Advice: Check that the punctuation in any underlined portion matches the punctuation and wording of the rest of the sentence.

Getting to the Answer: The subject of the sentence is "Original Kazoo Company," and it has a compound predicate with verbs "was" and "operates." The phrase "opened in New York in 1916" is parenthetical information that describes the company. The sentence already uses a comma after "Company" to set off the phrase, so **(A)** is correct because it closes the parenthetical with a matching comma and adds no unnecessary punctuation. Both (B) and (C) add a comma after "kazoos," which incorrectly separates the subject "Original Kazoo Company" from its verb "operates." Choice (D) is incorrect because it attempts to separate the sentence into two, but the second sentence is a fragment since it lacks a subject.

7. B

Difficulty: Medium

Strategic Advice: Make sure that every clause that is punctuated as though it were an independent clause expresses a complete thought.

Getting to the Answer: As written, the second sentence is a fragment because it lacks a predicate verb (the verb "used" is part of a phrase describing "mirlitons"); (A) is incorrect. Eliminate (C) for the same reason. Likewise, (D) is incorrect because a comma and FANBOYS conjunction would join independent clauses. Choice **(B)** is correct because it appropriately uses a colon after an independent clause to introduce the examples of instruments with vibrating membranes that follow.

8. C

Difficulty: Hard

Strategic Advice: Identifying the parts of the sentence will enable you to determine whether a comma is needed.

Getting to the Answer: The word "Whereas" makes the first part of the sentence a dependent clause. The independent clause of the sentence has the subject "humming or speaking" and the verbs "vibrates" and "produces." To connect the clauses, there should be a comma after the last word of the dependent clause, "technique," so eliminate (A) and (B). Eliminate (D) because it places a comma between the subject of the independent clause and its verbs. Choice (C) joins the clauses with a comma without introducing unnecessary commas, so **(C)** is correct.

9. A

Difficulty: Hard

Strategic Advice: While the SAT values conciseness, make sure that deleting text does not change the meaning of a sentence or introduce a new error.

Getting to the Answer: The part of the sentence before the comma is an independent clause, expressing a complete thought. As written, the use of the *-ing* form of "producing" creates a descriptive phrase that modifies the rest of the sentence: The transformation of vocalizations produces the buzzing. Such a phrase is correctly set off from the rest of the sentence by a comma, so **(A)** is correct. Although the construction in (B) could potentially create a compound predicate of "transform . . . and produce," (B) is incorrect because a comma should not separate the verbs of a compound predicate. Choice (C) is incorrect because it turns the part of the sentence after the comma into an independent clause, resulting in a run-on with two independent clauses joined by only a comma. By deleting the underlined

portion, (D) changes the meaning of the sentence: "a distinct 'buzzing' quality" would describe "vocalizations," which are not "'buzzing'" themselves but become so due to the vibrations.

10. B

Difficulty: Hard

Strategic Advice: When setting off parenthetical information, use the same type of punctuation mark on both sides.

Getting to the Answer: The phrase "which developed in the mining towns of England and Wales" is additional information about the "Juvenile jazz bands." Since the phrase ends with a comma after "Wales," a matching comma should begin the phrase; **(B)** is correct. Choice (A) sets off the phrase but uses mismatched punctuation: a dash and a comma. The other choices may be tempting since they create a more concise wording, but they introduce new errors. Choice (C) turns "developed" into the predicate verb of the sentence, resulting in an incomplete thought. Choice (D) would separate the subject "Juvenile jazz bands" from its verb "play."

11. D

Difficulty: Medium

Strategic Advice: All lists—even complex ones—follow a predictable pattern: each item is in parallel form, the last item is preceded by a conjunction, and commas separate the list items. The only time semicolons must separate list items is if commas appear within any of the list items.

Getting to the Answer: The underlined portion contains the connection between the last two items in a list of American songs that feature kazoos. Each list item uses a word that means "song(s)" ("tunes," "numbers," and "song") with some adjective or prepositional phrase modifiers. Since no list items themselves contain commas, (A) and (B) are incorrect because a semicolon is not needed to separate list items. Choice (C) incorrectly places the comma after the conjunction "and." Choice **(D)** properly uses a comma and conjunction to separate list items and is correct.

CHAPTER 9

Agreement

For a sentence to be grammatically correct, certain elements within it have to be properly matched. Verbs must agree with their subjects, and verb tenses must be consistent and logical. Pronouns must agree with the nouns they stand in for. Modifiers must agree with the words they describe and must be placed logically. The words and phrases in compounds and lists must agree structurally—that is, they must be in parallel form.

Verbs

Verb errors are very commonly tested, so be sure to learn the following rules. Use the drill that follows to get comfortable with them. You can check your work by reviewing the "Answers and Explanations" section at the end of the chapter.

Subject-Verb Agreement

A verb must agree with its subject in person and number:

- Person (first, second, or third)
  - First: *I* **ask** *a question.*
  - Second: *You* **ask** *a question.*
  - Third: *She* **asks** *a question.*

- Number (singular or plural)
  - Singular: *The new rug* **follows** *a modern pattern.*
  - Plural: *The new rugs all* **follow** *the same modern pattern.*

The noun closest to the verb is not always the subject: *The chair with the lion feet is an antique.* The singular verb in this sentence, "is," is closest to the plural noun "feet." However, the verb's actual subject is the singular noun "chair," so the sentence is correct as written.

When a sentence includes two nouns, only the conjunction *and* forms a compound subject requiring a plural verb form:

- Plural: *Anastasia and Peyton* **are** *in the chess club.*
- Singular: *Either Anastasia or Peyton* **is** *in the chess club.*
- Singular: *Neither Anastasia nor Peyton* **is** *in the chess club.*

Collective nouns are nouns that name entities with more than one member, such as *group*, *team*, and *family*. Even though these nouns represent more than one person, they are grammatically singular and require singular verb forms:

- *The Chester Beatty Library's collection of manuscripts* **boasts** *several unique ancient Greek, Egyptian, and Iranian texts.*
- *The Han family* **is** *anticipating a strong arugula harvest.*

Verb Agreement Drill

1. According to a leading researcher, genetically modified foods, despite the popular belief to the contrary, <u>has</u> no measurable negative impact when consumed by humans.

    A) NO CHANGE

    B) have

    C) having

    D) is having

2. After weeks of rehearsing the audition piece, the singer was devastated to discover that her agent <u>gave</u> her the wrong sheet music to practice.

    A) NO CHANGE

    B) had given

    C) has been giving

    D) will have given

3. From the time of Auguste Rodin's first commissions in the late 1800s to present-day exhibitions of his works, art critics <u>have long debated</u> the merits and themes of the artist's sculptures, although *The Thinker* has become a familiar cultural image throughout the world.

    A) NO CHANGE

    B) long debate

    C) will long be debating

    D) are long debating

4. Sometimes a word for a color, such as "periwinkle" for a shade of blue and "chartreuse" for a shade of green, <u>become</u> commonly used in popular speech, even if a large portion of the population cannot correctly identify the hue by name.

    A) NO CHANGE

    B) becoming

    C) becomes

    D) became

5. The online retailer, which managed to become the world's largest seller of consumer merchandise in just a few short years, <u>employing</u> over 600,000 people in its many facilities.

    A) NO CHANGE

    B) employ

    C) employs

    D) have employed

6. There is an ongoing debate in the United States about whether the electoral college system should <u>have continued</u> in future presidential elections.

    A) NO CHANGE

    B) be continued

    C) continues

    D) have been continued

7. The first Olympic competition for tandem bicycling, cycling on vehicles designed to carry multiple riders, <u>were</u> in 1908, though the first patents for tandem bicycles had been filed in the 1890s.

    A) NO CHANGE

    B) had been

    C) being

    D) was

8. In the 1930s, after years of destructive cultivation practices by farmers, the topsoil of the southern plains became loose and dried out, which in turn <u>led</u> to the devastation of the Dust Bowl.

    A) NO CHANGE

    B) lead

    C) has led

    D) is leading

Pronouns

Pronouns are tested fairly frequently, so it's worth learning a few basic pronoun rules. Use the drill that follows to practice. Answers and explanations are at the end of the chapter.

Pronoun Forms

A pronoun is a word that takes the place of a noun. Pronouns can take three different forms, each of which is used based on the grammatical role it plays in the sentence:

- If the pronoun is the subject of the sentence, use a **subjective** pronoun such as *I*, *you*, *she*, *he*, *it*, *we*, *they*, or *who*.
- If the pronoun is an object within the sentence, use an **objective** pronoun such as *me*, *you*, *her*, *him*, *it*, *us*, *they*, or *whom*.
- If the pronoun indicates possession, use a **possessive** pronoun such as *my*, *mine*, *your*, *yours*, *his*, *her*, *hers*, *its*, *our*, *ours*, *their*, *theirs*, or *whose*.

For example: ***Our*** *neighbors invited* ***us*** *to visit* ***them***. ***They*** *served* ***us*** *tea and fabulous pumpkin pie.* The pronoun "our" is possessive, the pronouns "us" and "them" are objective, and the pronoun "they" is subjective.

Pronoun-Noun Agreement

A singular noun requires a singular pronoun; a plural noun requires a plural pronoun: *The selection of boomerangs was returned to its former location.* In this sentence, the singular pronoun "its" refers to the singular noun "selection." Alternatively, you could say, *The boomerangs were returned to their former location.* Now, the pronoun must be plural ("their") to match the plural subject ("boomerangs").

Pronoun Ambiguity

A pronoun is ambiguous if the noun it stands in for is either missing or unclear. When you see an underlined pronoun, make sure you can identify the noun, called its **antecedent**, to which it refers. For example: *Janelle walked with Shirley to the post office, where* ***she*** *bought the latest commemorative stamps.* In this sentence, it isn't clear whether the pronoun "she" refers to Janelle or Shirley. Fixing the ambiguity in this case requires getting rid of the pronoun: *Janelle walked with Shirley to the post office, where* ***Janelle*** *bought the latest commemorative stamps.*

Pronoun Agreement Drill

1. The athletes <u>whom</u> finish the obstacle course in under two minutes will advance to the next round of competition.

   A) NO CHANGE

   B) who

   C) which

   D) DELETE the underlined portion.

2. Several students were allowed to bring their pets to class for show and tell, but <u>they</u> quickly became rambunctious and started acting wildly.

   A) NO CHANGE

   B) the animals

   C) all the children's pets

   D) them

3. The nurses <u>which</u> worked extra hours during the emergency should be compensated with a bonus in addition to their normal overtime pay.

   A) NO CHANGE

   B) whom

   C) whose

   D) who

4. The main thing I've always noticed about the twins is that <u>they're very different in their</u> musical preferences.

   A) NO CHANGE

   B) they're very different in there

   C) there very different in their

   D) there very different in they're

5. The museum lost an invaluable source of scientific knowledge when a thief stole hundreds of rare bird skins from <u>their</u> collection.

   A) NO CHANGE

   B) his

   C) they're

   D) its

6. Kokoro, <u>whose</u> favorite opera is *La Traviata*, has tickets to attend a live performance at the community theater in December.

   A) NO CHANGE

   B) whom

   C) her

   D) who's

7. The newly introduced, invasive insects were threatening the delicate ecosystem of the forest. The conservationists strategized about how to minimize <u>their</u> impact on the local wildlife.

   A) NO CHANGE

   B) the non-native insects'

   C) its

   D) whose

8. That the strawberries have a very short shelf life <u>which</u> ensures that the chef features them in the daily salad special the same day the berries are delivered to the restaurant.

   A) NO CHANGE

   B) when

   C) that

   D) DELETE the underlined portion.

Modifiers and Parallelism

Modifiers and parallelism are not tested as frequently as verbs and pronouns. Here are some basic rules to keep in mind in case you do see a modifier or parallelism question or two on test day.

Modifier Placement

A **modifier** is a word or phrase that describes, clarifies, or provides additional information about another part of the sentence. Modifier questions require you to identify the part of a sentence being modified and use the appropriate modifier in the proper place.

In order to be grammatically correct, the modifier must be placed as close to the word it describes as possible. Use context clues in the passage to identify the correct placement of a modifier; a misplaced modifier can cause confusion and is always incorrect on test day.

Note that a common way the SAT tests modifiers is with modifying phrases at the beginning of a sentence. Just like any other modifier, the modifying phrase grammatically modifies whatever is right next to it in the sentence. For example: *While biking to the library, mud spattered Arlene.* The initial phrase, "While biking to the library," grammatically modifies "mud," creating a nonsense sentence; mud can't bike to the library. The writer meant that Arlene was biking to the library, so the sentence should read: *While biking to the library, Arlene was spattered by mud.*

Modifier Agreement: Adjectives and Adverbs

Use adjectives only to modify nouns and pronouns. Use adverbs to modify everything else.

- **Adjectives** are single-word modifiers that describe nouns and pronouns: *Diomo ran an **effective** mayoral campaign.*
- **Adverbs** are single-word modifiers that describe verbs, adjectives, or other adverbs: *Diomo **effectively** ran a mayoral campaign.*

Note that nouns can sometimes be used as adjectives. For example, in the phrase *the fashion company's autumn line,* the word "fashion" functions as an adjective modifying "company," and the word "autumn" functions as an adjective modifying "line."

Parallelism

Parallelism means that two or more words or phrases have the same structure. The following must be in parallel form:

- **Lists** must be parallel: *A triathlon requires **swimming**, **cycling**, and **running**.*
- **Compounds** must be parallel: *Crickets are known **to chirp** loudly and **to leap** great distances for their size.*
- **Comparisons** must be parallel: *Toads croak more loudly **in the garden** than **in the pond**.*

Now put it all together. The following practice set contains questions based on the various grammar rules in this chapter.

Agreement Practice Set

DIRECTIONS: Take as much time as you need on these questions. Work carefully and methodically. There will be an opportunity for timed practice in chapter 13.

Questions 1–11 refer to the following passage.

Traditional Polynesian Wayfaring

The Polynesian triangle comprises over 800,000 square miles and approximately 1,000 islands in the Pacific Ocean. Starting in the eighteenth century, European navigators wondered how the initial populations **1** traversed thousands of miles of open waters to first settle each of the inhabited dots of land throughout the ocean. Attempts by Westerners to understand the sophisticated methods of traditional Polynesian wayfaring **2** beginning at the time of the earliest contacts between the cultures. The Polynesian navigator Tupaia met the British captain James Cook in 1768 and created a famous map of over 100 islands within several thousand miles of the island of Ra'iatea, though **3** he had personally traveled to only about a dozen of the islands. However, outsiders to Polynesia have struggled to comprehend the vast geographic knowledge of traditional navigators such as Tupaia due to differences in **4** their conceptual interpretation of the world.

European navigators developed an understanding of physical geography based on a bird's-eye view of maps. Alternately, traditional Polynesian navigators, visualizing the boats on which they traveled as remaining stationary while the islands and heavens shifted around their canoes, instead conceived of **5** them as geographic reference points. At least some Polynesian navigators made use of an *ekat*, or a system using a reference island, which could be real or

1. A) NO CHANGE
   B) will have traversed
   C) had traversed
   D) traversing

2. A) NO CHANGE
   B) begin
   C) which had begun
   D) began

3. A) NO CHANGE
   B) Tupaia
   C) himself
   D) the Polynesian navigator himself

4. A) NO CHANGE
   B) there conceptual interpretation
   C) there conceptual interpretations
   D) their conceptual interpretations

5. A) NO CHANGE
   B) their selves
   C) himself
   D) themselves

imaginary, conceptualized as off to one side of the intended pathway from one island to another. These differing perspectives complicated each **6** culture's attempts to comprehend the techniques of the other, but the Polynesian approach led to a flourishing localized navigational knowledge on each island that was handed down through oral traditions. The use of material navigation aids—instruments, charts, and maps—is significantly less common among Polynesian navigators than **7** that of their European counterparts.

Expert sailors, the Polynesian navigators incorporated a host of cues learned from experience on the oceans and the accumulated knowledge of their cultures. The resulting systems of accurate wayfaring, partly technical and partly intuitive, **8** have eluded precise explanation to outsiders. Applying their knowledge of changes in positions of stars in the night sky through the seasons and over distances traveled, **9** elaborate star paths were developed by navigators to guide their journeys between islands. Polynesian navigators' knowledge of ocean swells, bird flight patterns, and wind currents supplemented astronomical and *ekat* methods of navigation. Among both historical and modern Polynesians, the slowed movement of clouds over landmasses, which typically corresponds with a darkening of clouds' colors over lagoons, **10** have been used to indicate the location of land.

The 1976 voyage of the *Hōkūleʻa*, guided from Hawaiʻi to Tahiti by navigator Mau Piailug without the use of modern instrumentation, drew international attention. **11** Its success inspired study of traditional wayfaring and a flurry of additional voyages throughout the Pacific, all attesting to the extraordinary navigational expertise of the Polynesians.

6. A) NO CHANGE
   B) culture's attempt's
   C) cultures' attempt
   D) cultures attempts'

7. A) NO CHANGE
   B) compared with
   C) among
   D) navigation aids among

8. A) NO CHANGE
   B) eludes
   C) has eluded
   D) eluding

9. A) NO CHANGE
   B) navigators' elaborate star paths were developed to guide
   C) navigators developed elaborate star paths to guide
   D) the development of elaborate star paths by navigators guided

10. A) NO CHANGE
    B) has been used to indicate
    C) indicated
    D) that has indicated

11. A) NO CHANGE
    B) It's
    C) Their
    D) There

Answers and Explanations

Verb Agreement Drill

1. B

The subject of the underlined verb is the plural noun "foods," so a plural verb is needed; **(B)** is correct. Choices (A) and (D) are singular verbs, and (C) creates a sentence fragment by eliminating the predicate verb of the sentence.

2. B

The surrounding context uses a verb in the past tense ("was devastated"). The underlined verb describes an action that occurred before the other action in the sentence, so the past perfect "had given," **(B)**, is correct. The simple past tense in (A), the ongoing action of (C), and the future action of (D) do not match the order of events.

3. A

The context ("in the late 1800s to present-day") indicates that art critics debated about Rodin's sculptures in the past and continue to in the present. The verb tense in **(A)** reflects such an action and is correct. Choices (B) and (D) indicate only present, not past, action. Choice (C) indicates action that will continue in the future, which is not suggested in the sentence.

4. C

The subject of the underlined verb is the singular "word," so eliminate the plural in (A). The surrounding context uses a verb phrase in the present tense ("cannot correctly identify"), so eliminate the past tense verb in (D). Choice (B) results in a sentence fragment. The singular, present tense verb in **(C)** is correct.

5. C

The subject of the underlined verb is the singular "online retailer," so eliminate (B) and (D), which use plural verbs. Eliminate (A) because it results in a run-on. Choice **(C)** uses the correct singular verb in context and is correct.

6. B

The surrounding context signals that the underlined verb refers to a "future" action; the verb phrase in **(B)** indicates a future action and is correct. The past tense forms indicated in (A) and (D) and the present

tense in (C) do not match the verb tense required by the context of the sentence.

7. D

The subject of the underlined verb is the singular "competition," so eliminate the plural verb in (A). The context indicates that two events occurred in the past: first, patents were filed, and second, there was an Olympic competition for tandem bicycling. The earlier event correctly uses a verb form ("had been filed") that indicates it occurred before another past action. The underlined verb—the second action—requires only a simple past tense verb, so **(D)** is correct. Choice (B) would indicate the action occurred before another past action. Choice (C) results in a sentence fragment.

8. A

The surrounding context uses verbs in the past tense ("became," "dried"), and the introductory phrase of the sentence identifies all the actions as occurring "In the 1930s." Another past tense verb is required, so **(A)** is correct. Choices (B) and (D) are in the present tense, and (C) indicates action that started in the past and continues into the present.

Pronoun Agreement Drill

1. B

The underlined pronoun is the subject of the verb "finish," so the subjective form is required. The antecedent is a group of people, "athletes," so **(B)** is correct. Choice (A) uses the the objective form, (C) does not refer to people, and (D) results in a nongrammatical sentence.

2. B

The underlined pronoun is ambiguous as written, since it could refer to either the group of students or the pets; eliminate (A) and (D). Choice **(B)** is correct because it is the most concise choice that specifies who or what became "rambunctious."

3. D

The underlined pronoun should be in the subjective form since it is the subject of the verb "worked." Since the pronoun refers to people, the "nurses," the subjective "who" is appropriate; **(D)** is correct. Choice (A) is incorrect because, when used as a pronoun, "which" is not used to refer to people; further, a phrase beginning with "which" would be set off by commas. Choice (B) is in the objective form, and (C) is in the possessive form.

4. A

Both underlined pronouns have the plural "twins" as their antecedent. The first pronoun means "they are," so eliminate (C) and (D). The second pronoun should indicate the twins' possession of "musical preferences," so the plural possessive "their" in **(A)** is correct. Choice (B) uses "there," which shows location.

5. D

The antecedent of the underlined pronoun is the singular "museum," so **(D)** is correct because "its" is the nonperson possessive form. Choice (A) is a plural pronoun, (B) refers to a singular person, and (C) means "they are."

6. A

The underlined pronoun is in possession of "favorite opera," so the possessive form in **(A)** is correct. Choice (B) is in the objective form. Choice (C) is possessive but results in a nongrammatical sentence. Choice (D) is the contraction of "who is."

7. B

The underlined pronoun's antecedent is ambiguous. The nearest antecedent is "conservationists," but the previous sentence indicates that the "invasive insects" were posing a threat. The conservationists likely wanted to minimize the insects'—not their own—impact on wildlife. Choice **(B)** clarifies the meaning and is correct. The other choices are ambiguous in context.

8. D

The subject of the verb "ensures" is the entire idea that precedes it: "That the strawberries have a very short shelf life." No pronoun is needed to separate the subject from the verb, so **(D)** is correct.

Agreement Practice Set

1. C

Difficulty: Medium

Strategic Advice: Use the details of the surrounding context to help determine the correct tense for an underlined verb.

Getting to the Answer: The underlined verb refers to the past action of the "initial populations" when they "first" settled each island. The sentence also indicates that this action occurred prior to another past action: the European navigators later wondering how the traversing had occurred. This chronology is reflected in the verb tense "had traversed," so **(C)** is correct. Choice (A) is past tense, but it is incorrect because it does not indicate that the action occurred before another past action in the sentence. Choice (B) indicates an action that will be completed in the future, which is not correct in context. Choice (D) creates a sentence fragment by removing the predicate verb.

2. D

Difficulty: Easy

Strategic Advice: Use the tense of surrounding verbs to help determine the correct tense for an underlined verb.

Getting to the Answer: The actions in the surrounding sentences are all in the past tense ("wondered," "met," "created"). Nothing in context indicates that a more complex tense than the simple past is needed, so **(D)** is correct. Choices (A) and (C) are incorrect because they create sentence fragments that lack predicate verbs. Choice (B) is incorrect because it is present tense.

3. B

Difficulty: Medium

Strategic Advice: Ensure that underlined pronouns have clear, unambiguous antecedents.

Getting to the Answer: The nearest antecedent of the pronoun "he" is "captain James Cook," though the pronoun could also refer to the "Polynesian navigator Tupaia." Eliminate (A) and (C) because they use pronouns that are ambiguous in context; (C) also does not use a subjective form pronoun, as required by the clause. The remaining choices both refer to the same person as described in the passage; since **(B)** is more concise, it is correct.

4. D

Difficulty: Medium

Strategic Advice: Just as verbs must agree with their subjects and pronouns with their antecedents, related nouns must agree with each other.

Getting to the Answer: The answer choices reveal that there are two issues; evaluate one issue at a time. The noun phrase "conceptual interpretations" is related to the groups "outsiders to Polynesia" and "traditional navigators." Since these groups each have their own "differences" in interpretations of the world, "interpretations" should be plural; eliminate (A) and (B). The word "their/there" should be the possessive pronoun "their" rather than the location word "there," since the "conceptual interpretations" belong to the outsiders and the traditional navigators. Choice **(D)** is correct.

5. D

Difficulty: Hard

Strategic Advice: Make sure that underlined pronouns have unambiguous antecedents with which they are in agreement.

Getting to the Answer: As written, the antecedent of the pronoun "them" is unclear: the writer could be referring to "boats," "islands," "heavens," "canoes," or any combination of these nouns. Eliminate (A). The context and the other answer choices suggest that the navigators were their own "geographic reference points." Since "Polynesian navigators" is plural, eliminate (C). Choice (B) is not a valid pronoun, so it is also incorrect. Choice **(D)** results in a sentence with a clear antecedent-pronoun pair that is in agreement.

6. A

Difficulty: Medium

Strategic Advice: Adjacent nouns with apostrophes signal a possible possessive modifier issue; ensure that any possessive words are correctly punctuated, depending on whether they are plural or singular.

Getting to the Answer: The word "each" indicates that the first word in the underlined portion should be singular. Eliminate (C), which is the possessive of the plural "cultures," and (D). The "attempts" belong to each culture, so the singular possessive "culture's" in (A) and (B) is correct. The "attempts" are not in possession of anything, so **(A)** is correct.

7. C

Difficulty: Hard

Strategic Advice: Words such as "than" or "and" may signal a comparison or a compound; check to ensure such constructions are in parallel form.

Getting to the Answer: The word "than" indicates a comparison between how often Polynesian and European navigators use material navigation aids. The part of the comparison that is not underlined uses the form "less common among X," so the remainder of the comparison should be "than among Y"; **(C)** is correct. Choice (B) results in a comparison that is not in parallel form. Choices (A) and (D) compare unlike things: (A) compares "Polynesian navigators" with the "use of navigation aids" (referenced by the pronoun "that"), and (D) compares "Polynesian navigators" with "navigation aids."

8. A

Difficulty: Medium

Strategic Advice: Locate the subject of any underlined verb to ensure that they are both singular or both plural.

Getting to the Answer: The subject of the underlined verb is "resulting systems"; though other phrases appear between this subject and verb, it is the systems that have eluded explanation. Since "systems" is plural, eliminate (B) and (C). The form of (D) removes the predicate verb from the sentence; it creates a fragment and is thus incorrect. Choice **(A)** is correct because it uses a plural verb to match its subject and surrounding context.

9. C

Difficulty: Hard

Strategic Advice: When answer choices place nouns in different spots within a phrase, check to see whether modifying phrases are adjacent to the noun they are intended to describe.

Getting to the Answer: Since it is the navigators themselves who are "Applying their knowledge," the introductory phrase should describe "navigators." The only choice that correctly places "navigators" immediately after the introductory phrase is **(C)**, so it is correct. Furthermore, **(C)** is preferable because it uses the active rather than the passive voice, making the subject "navigators" the actor of the sentence. Choices (A) and (B) are incorrect because the introductory phrase illogically describes "(navigators') elaborate star paths," which cannot apply knowledge. Choice (D) is incorrect because the introductory phrase describes "the development" of the star paths.

10. B

Difficulty: Hard

Strategic Advice: Make sure that every underlined verb agrees with its subject and matches the tense of the surrounding context.

Getting to the Answer: The subject of the underlined verb is the singular noun "movement." Although other nouns appear between the subject and verb, they are all part of descriptive phrases that describe the "movement"; in other words, it is not the clouds themselves, nor the landmasses or lagoons, that indicate where land is located, but the clouds' *movement* that shows the location of land. Since "movement" is singular, eliminate the plural verb in (A). By adding the word "that," (D) results in a sentence fragment; eliminate (D). Both (B) and (C) match the singular subject, but they use different tenses. The phrase "Among both historical and modern Polynesians" indicates that using cloud movement to locate land started in the past and continues today. The tense of **(B)** conveys this meaning and is correct.

11. A

Difficulty: Medium

Strategic Advice: Match underlined pronouns to their antecedents, and distinguish between the frequently confused word sets *their/there/they're* and *its/it's*.

Getting to the Answer: First, determine whose or what's "success" "inspired" more study and voyages. The previous sentence refers to the "voyage of the *Hōkūleʻa*" and Mau Piailug. Since only the individual Piailug and no groups are mentioned, eliminate the plural pronoun "Their" in (C). Also eliminate "There," (D), which indicates a point or place. The underlined pronoun must refer to the singular antecedent "voyage." The possessive pronoun "Its" indicates that the "success" belongs to the "voyage," so **(A)** is correct. Choice (B) is incorrect because "It's" means "it is."

CHAPTER 10

Conciseness

A concise sentence does not include any unnecessary words. Phrasing that is wordy is considered stylistically incorrect on the SAT and needs to be revised. Each word must contribute to the meaning of the sentence; otherwise, it should be eliminated.

A **redundant** sentence says something twice: *The new policy precipitated a crisis situation.* A crisis is a type of situation, so there is no need to include both "crisis" and "situation." The sentence should be rephrased as, *The new policy precipitated a crisis.* Redundancy is always incorrect on the SAT.

Conciseness Practice Set

DIRECTIONS: Take as much time as you need on these questions. Work carefully and methodically. There will be an opportunity for timed practice in chapter 13.

Questions 1–11 refer to the following passage.

An Old Skill Preserved in a New Land

When Rafael Guastavino emigrated to the United States [1] in 1881, during the late nineteenth century, he may have arrived with few material possessions, but he brought knowledge of a centuries-old technique that would soon become a major contribution to American [2] architecture and design. Born in Valencia, Spain, Guastavino was an architect and engineer who, in his work in Spain, had revived a building technique called the Catalan vault. Catalan vaulting is of obscure origin but likely arose somewhere in the Mediterranean region in the early centuries of the Common Era; it was perfected in Catalonia during the Middle Ages. This ancient system used bricks set in mortar to create large, freestanding vaulted [3] ceilings without any visible supporting structures. Catalan vaulting creates a strong, fireproof, and attractive structure, usually arched or domed, and can be used to build roofs, ceilings, and stairwells.

Guastavino innovated a modern method of building the Catalan vault, which he [4] protected and patented in the United States in 1885. His first major project was completed under the [5] supervision and management of the prestigious Boston architectural firm of McKim, Mead, and White, which had the commission for the construction of the Boston Public Library. Guastavino's soaring vaults over the library's main entrance immediately brought their designer's abilities to the attention of architects all over the country. According to

1. A) NO CHANGE
   B) in 1881,
   C) in 1881, in the nineteenth century,
   D) in 1881, in the late nineteenth century,

2. A) NO CHANGE
   B) architecture.
   C) architectural design.
   D) building design.

3. A) NO CHANGE
   B) ceilings.
   C) ceilings without any visible structures.
   D) ceilings without any supporting structures.

4. A) NO CHANGE
   B) protected by patent
   C) protected with a patent
   D) patented

5. A) NO CHANGE
   B) supervision, management, and direction
   C) supervisory managing
   D) auspices

John Ochsendorf, a professor of architecture at MIT and expert on Guastavino, blueprints for hundreds of buildings would soon have empty spaces where the architects would **6** just write in a few words that indicated "Guastavino here." The architects trusted that Guastavino would provide a sturdy, yet stunningly beautiful, feature that would complement their designs.

In 1889, Raphael Guastavino founded the Guastavino Fireproof Construction Company to manufacture the **7** special interlocking tiles needed for his process. Together with his son, Guastavino was responsible for over 1,000 buildings in the United States, including some of the **8** buildings that truly represent the American spirit, such as New York's Grand Central terminal, the original Pennsylvania Station, Carnegie Hall, Grant's Tomb, and the Great Hall at Ellis Island. In Washington, DC, Guastavino vaults can be found in the Supreme Court building and the National Museum of Natural History on the National Mall.

Because Guastavino was commissioned to work on portions of buildings that were designed and managed by other architects, Ochsendorf calls him "the greatest architect you've never heard of." Ochsendorf believes that **9** it may be impossible to compile a complete inventory of all Guastavino's works. Fittingly, years after his family's arrival on Ellis Island, Guastavino's son Raphael III was called upon to replace the ceiling of the Great Hall. Almost 100 years later, when the facility was renovated in the 1980s, his structure was found to be so well designed and sturdy that only 17 of the almost 29,000 original tiles **10** were in need of replacement—a testimony to the **11** skill and enduring legacy of his father.

6. A) NO CHANGE
   B) simply note
   C) indicate by writing
   D) simply indicate with the words

7. A) NO CHANGE
   B) special
   C) unique
   D) interlocking

8. A) NO CHANGE
   B) most iconic American landmarks,
   C) important American buildings,
   D) famous American buildings,

9. A) NO CHANGE
   B) locating all of Guastavino's works may be impossible.
   C) a complete list of all Guastavino's work may be impossible.
   D) a complete inventory of Guastavino's works may never be established.

10. A) NO CHANGE
    B) replacing
    C) had to be replaced
    D) needing replacement

11. A) NO CHANGE
    B) skill
    C) technical prowess
    D) engineering abilities

Answers and Explanations

Conciseness Practice Set

1.   B

Difficulty: Easy

Strategic Advice: Start by checking the shortest choice; if the sentence is grammatically correct and conveys the same information, it's the correct answer.

Getting to the Answer: Because 1881 is, by definition, the nineteenth century, the choices that include this extra information are incorrect. Choice **(B)** conveys the same information and is the most concise.

2.   A

Difficulty: Hard

Strategic Advice: If a wordier choice provides more relevant information, it is likely correct.

Getting to the Answer: Architecture and design are two distinct disciplines, so removing one of them changes the original meaning of the sentence. Choice **(A)** is correct.

3.   B

Difficulty: Hard

Strategic Advice: Read the entire passage; don't just skip from one question to the next. Frequently, the non-underlined portions of the text provide clues necessary to the correct answer.

Getting to the Answer: "Freestanding," mentioned earlier in the sentence, means "without any visible supporting structures," so the sentence as written contains a redundancy, and **(B)** is correct.

4.   D

Difficulty: Medium

Strategic Advice: If the meaning of a word is repeated, that word is redundant and should be eliminated.

Getting to the Answer: By definition, a patent provides protection, so including both words is redundant. Choice **(D)** is correct.

5.   D

Difficulty: High

Strategic Advice: The SAT values concise writing. If the shortest choice is grammatically correct and retains the original meaning, pick it and move on.

Getting to the Answer: In context, "supervision" and "management" have the same meaning, so they are redundant. Choice **(D)** conveys the same meaning and is the most concise.

6.   B

Difficulty: Medium

Strategic Advice: The shortest choice is not always correct, but if it is grammatically correct and retains the original meaning of the sentence, there is no reason to read the other choices.

Getting to the Answer: The intention of the sentence is to convey that architects would just leave a note in the plans to indicate where Guastavino's work would go. Choice **(B)** is correct.

7.   A

Difficulty: Medium

Strategic Advice: Before automatically choosing the shortest answer choice, be sure no important information is lost.

Getting to the Answer: The words "special" and "interlocking" convey distinct and important aspects of the tile, so they should both be retained. Choice **(A)** is correct.

8.   B

Difficulty: High

Strategic Advice: Look for the choice that expresses the original intention most clearly.

Getting to the Answer: "Buildings that truly represent the American spirit" could be described as American landmarks. Choice **(B)** most concisely expresses this idea. The original sentence is too wordy, and the incorrect choices lose the meaning of why the buildings are "important" or "famous."

9. B

Difficulty: Medium

Strategic Advice: Shorter is better on the SAT. Check the shortest choice first and work up through the longer choices only if you encounter a grammar error, loss of information, or change in meaning.

Getting to the Answer: The original sentence is wordy and uses the weak, indirect structure "it may be." Choice **(B)** is more direct and concise, so it is correct. Choice (C) is redundant; a "complete list," by definition, would contain "all" the works. Choice (D) is unnecessarily wordy.

10. C

Difficulty: Medium

Strategic Advice: As a final check, always put your choice back into the passage and reread the surrounding section.

Getting to the Answer: The meaning of the sentence is that Guastavino's work was so well done that almost none of the original tiles had to be replaced in the 1980s. Choice **(C)** is correct. Choice (A) is too wordy, and the other choices introduce errors in sentence structure.

11. A

Difficulty: Medium

Strategic Advice: The complete meaning of the original sentence must always be preserved.

Getting to the Answer: Because "skill" and "enduring legacy" are two different concepts, neither can be deleted. Choice **(A)** is correct.

CHAPTER 11

Organization

Transitions

Writers use transitions to show relationships such as contrast, cause and effect, continuation, emphasis, and chronology (order of events). Knowing which words indicate which type of transition will help you choose the correct answer on test day.

Contrast Transitions	Cause-and-Effect Transitions	Continuation Transitions	Emphasis Transitions	Chronology Transitions
although but despite even though however nonetheless on the other hand rather than unlike while yet	as a result because consequently since so therefore thus	also furthermore in addition moreover	certainly definitely in fact indeed that is	until before after first (second, etc.) then eventually finally

If a transition word is underlined, you will need to determine the writer's intended meaning and find the transition that best conveys this meaning. Use the surrounding text to pinpoint the appropriate word.

Give the following drill a try. Really think about what type of transition is most appropriate for the meaning in each case. Answers and explanations are at the end of the chapter.

Transitions Drill

1. <u>Due to</u> the hours of direct sunlight, the persistently low temperatures prevented the ice that coated the tree branches from melting.

   A) NO CHANGE
   B) In addition to
   C) Despite
   D) In light of

2. Before the successful invention of the airplane, many considered heavier-than-air flying machines an impossibility. When the Wright brothers announced their first flight, <u>however,</u> their claim was met with widespread skepticism.

   A) NO CHANGE
   B) instead,
   C) by contrast,
   D) therefore,

3. Over time, well-known historical figures can become almost mythical, so that the line between historical reality and fable becomes blurred. <u>Furthermore,</u> the tale of George Washington chopping down a cherry tree is a fabricated story that is widely reported as factual.

   A) NO CHANGE
   B) However,
   C) Finally,
   D) For instance,

4. Onions have long been used by human societies. Archaeological excavation shows that onions were consumed in Bronze Age China, <u>and</u> classical Roman writings mention the onion as an ingredient in food recipes and health remedies.

   A) NO CHANGE
   B) but
   C) so
   D) or

5. During the years 1347 to 1352, a devastating outbreak of bubonic plague swept over Europe. Fatalities were in the millions, and, <u>for instance,</u> the European population was reduced by a third.

   A) NO CHANGE
   B) in spite of this,
   C) as a consequence,
   D) especially,

6. Oak is generally rated as the hardest of the commonly available woods. <u>Therefore,</u> because of its superior resilience, hickory is generally used for axe and pick handles.

   A) NO CHANGE
   B) However,
   C) As a result,
   D) Moreover,

7. Archaeologists who are reluctant to excavate certain study sites will use ground penetrating radar as an alternative to digging. <u>However,</u> this allows them to scan and catalog artifacts that are still buried underground.

   A) NO CHANGE
   B) In addition,
   C) Similarly,
   D) In effect,

8. Bamboo has been used for thousands of years as a building material in Asia. <u>Similarly,</u> it has been used in recent years to produce a soft and durable fabric.

   A) NO CHANGE
   B) Indeed,
   C) For this reason,
   D) Furthermore,

Sentence Placement

Some organization questions will ask you to check and potentially fix the placement of a sentence within a paragraph (or a paragraph within a passage, though this is rare). Others will ask you for the best place to insert a new sentence. Your approach in both cases should be the same: look for specific clues that indicate the best organization. Common clues include the following:

- **Chronology:** If the information is presented in order by the time when it occurred, place the sentence within the correct time frame.

- **Explanation of a term or phrase:** If the passage features a term, such as *nuclear fusion*, the writer will explain what it is (in this case, the joining of two or more nuclei to form a heavier nucleus) before using the term in other contexts.

- **Introduction of a person:** If the passage introduces someone, such as computer scientist and U.S. Navy admiral Grace Hopper, the writer will first refer to the person by first and last name before referring to the person by either first name (Grace) or last name (Hopper) only.

- **Examples:** A general statement is often followed by support in the form of examples.

- **Logic:** Transition words such as *however*, *also*, *furthermore*, and *therefore* may signal the logic of the paragraph. For example, the word *therefore* indicates that a conclusion is being drawn from evidence that should logically come before it.

The practice set that follows contains questions based on transitions and sentence placement. Remember to let the context help you as you give these questions a try.

Organization Practice Set

DIRECTIONS: Take as much time as you need on these questions. Work carefully and methodically. There will be an opportunity for timed practice in chapter 13.

Questions 1–11 refer to the following passage.

The Pros of Becoming "Penniless"

[1]

In an economic climate in which the number of digital transactions is increasing and inflation, as ever, is on the rise, the use of physical currency—actual paper dollars and metal coins—is on the decline. The coins with the lowest values can rarely be used by themselves to make actual purchases: when was the last time you bought something that cost a single penny, nickel, or dime?

[2]

[1] Canada stopped distributing its one-cent coins in 2013. [2] **1** In fact, in light of each penny's 1.6-cent production cost and the total $11 million annual cost for taxpayers, Canadian legislators signed a 2012 bill that ended the coin's manufacture. [3] In the decision's practical application, the government recommended that businesses begin rounding all cash transactions down or up to the nearest five-cent increment. [4] **2** For instance, all non-cash transactions, such as those conducted by check or debit, would still use one-cent increments. [5] Australia, New Zealand, and Mexico have also eliminated one-cent coins in recent decades. **3**

[3]

[1] Proponents of enacting an elimination of the single-cent coin in the United States cite **4** other countries' successful implementation of such a policy, in addition to several other compelling arguments based on costs. [2] Once produced, this multitude of nearly

1. A) NO CHANGE
   B) Therefore,
   C) However,
   D) DELETE the underlined portion and begin the sentence with a capital letter.

2. A) NO CHANGE
   B) Indeed,
   C) Consequently,
   D) Meanwhile,

3. Where is the most logical place in this paragraph to add the following sentence?

   So if your bill for your beverage at a Canadian coffee shop totaled $3.07, you would pay $3.07 if paying with a credit card, but $3.05 if paying with cash.

   A) After sentence 2
   B) After sentence 3
   C) After sentence 4
   D) After sentence 5

4. Which choice provides the most effective transition from the previous paragraph?
   A) NO CHANGE
   B) statistics about the relative number of cash and credit transactions, as well as
   C) the historical precedent of the U.S. Mint's discontinuation of the half-cent coin and
   D) DELETE the underlined portion.

valueless coins must then incur the high cost of secure transport to banks and stores. [3] Perhaps the most obvious reason for eliminating pennies is their production cost. [4] According to the U.S. Mint, each penny cost 2.06 cents to make in 2018. [5] **5** In the same way, since consumers often remove pennies from circulation due to the coins' low value (few bother to pick up pennies from the ground, for example), more pennies must be minted than any other type of coin. **6**

[4]

[1] Assuming cash transactions will be rounded both up and down to the nearest five-cent increment, there should be, on average, no additional costs to consumers or losses for businesses. [2] Advocates also assert that the net impact on costs to consumers and businesses will be neutral. [3] However, economists are not unanimous in this seemingly commonsense assessment. [4] Based on the prevalence of prices ending in 9 and the ability of stores to manipulate prices, one notable economist concluded in a 2000 study that rounding cash purchases would cost American consumers approximately $600 million a year. [5] (**7** Similarly, sales tax, which varies from state to state, might complicate this assessment.) **8**

[5]

Finally, penny-free advocates note that the penny has less purchasing power today than even the half-cent coin did when its production was terminated in the United States in 1857. **9** The U.S. Mint can produce a 25-cent quarter for under 9 cents; **10** surprisingly, with a production cost of approximately 7.5 cents per coin in 2018, the 5-cent nickel should also worry about its currency in American currency.

5. A) NO CHANGE
   B) Further,
   C) Certainly,
   D) In contrast to this reason,

6. To make this paragraph most logical, sentence 2 should be placed

   A) where it is now.
   B) after sentence 3.
   C) after sentence 5.
   D) DELETED from the paragraph.

7. A) NO CHANGE
   B) Notably,
   C) Subsequently,
   D) As a result,

8. To make this paragraph most logical, sentence 1 should be placed

   A) where it is now.
   B) after sentence 2.
   C) after sentence 3.
   D) after sentence 4.

9. Which choice provides the most effective transition between ideas in the paragraph?

   A) NO CHANGE
   B) The half-cent coin underwent five different designs, all featuring Lady Liberty, during its production;
   C) The composition of the American nickel includes both copper and nickel;
   D) Even the nickel is worth relatively less than the half-cent coin of 1857;

10. A) NO CHANGE
    B) notwithstanding
    C) perhaps, with
    D) despite

Question 11 asks about the previous passage as a whole.

11. The writer wants to insert the following sentence.

> If nothing actually costs a mere cent (or, for that matter, a few cents), and if cash transactions are routinely slowed down by the necessity of the cashier tediously counting out pennies to make change, does it make sense for the U.S. Mint to continue circulating the penny?

To make the passage most logical, the sentence should be placed immediately after the last sentence in paragraph

A) 1.

B) 3.

C) 4.

D) 5.

Answers and Explanations

Transitions Drill

1. C

The underlined transition connects the ideas of there being hours of direct sunlight and low temperatures preventing ice from melting. The ideas are in contrast: one would expect sun to melt ice, but low temperatures cause the opposite. Thus, the contrast transition in **(C)** is correct. Choice (A) is a cause-and-effect transition. Choice (B) is a continuation transition. Choice (D) indicates causation or an explanation.

2. D

The underlined transition connects the ideas of many considering flight impossible and the Wright brothers' claim of flight being met with skepticism. Since there is a cause-and-effect relationship between these ideas, **(D)** is correct. The other answer choices are contrast transitions.

3. D

The underlined transition connects the idea of confusing historical fact and fiction and the idea that a fiction story about Washington is reported as fact. Since the Washington story is an example of historical figures being mythologized, **(D)** is correct. Choice (A) is a continuation transition; such a transition is incorrect because the second idea doesn't add an additional idea to the first, but rather provides a direct example of the first. Choice (B) is a contrast transition. Choice (C) is a chronology transition.

4. A

The underlined transition connects the ideas of onions being used in China and being used in Rome. The first sentence introduces the idea of onions' long historical use. Since the details about China and Rome are both examples of onion use, the connector "and," **(A)**, is correct. Choice (B) is a contrast transition. Choice (C) is a cause-and-effect transition. Choice (D) indicates alternatives.

5. C

The underlined transition connects the ideas of millions of fatalities and the population of Europe being reduced by a third. Since there is a cause-and-effect relationship between these ideas, **(C)** is correct. Choice (A) is an example transition. Choice (B) is a contrast transition. Choice (D) is an emphasis transition.

6. B

The underlined transition connects the ideas of oak being rated the hardest wood and hickory being used for handles. Since there is a contrast relationship between these ideas, **(B)** is correct. Choices (A) and (C) are cause-and-effect transitions. Choice (D) is a continuation transition.

7. D

The underlined transition connects the ideas of archaeologists using radar instead of digging and being able to scan and catalog buried artifacts. Since there is a cause-and-effect relationship between these ideas, **(D)** is correct. Choice (A) is a contrast transition. Choices (B) and (C) are continuation transitions.

8. D

The underlined transition connects the ideas of bamboo's long use as a building material and its recent use as a soft, durable fabric. Since both ideas are uses of bamboo, but there is a difference between its use in construction and in fabric, the comparison transition in (A), the emphasis transition in (B), and the cause-and-effect transition in (C) are incorrect. The continuation transition in **(D)** is correct because it connects the ideas of additional uses of bamboo.

Organization Practice Set

1. D
Difficulty: Medium

Strategic Advice: When asked to select a transition word or phrase, first determine how the ideas before and after the transition are related.

Getting to the Answer: The previous sentence states that Canada stopped distributing one-cent coins in 2013, and the sentence with the underline identifies reasons why Canadian legislators decided to end the manufacture of one-cent coins in 2012. Chronologically, the second sentence explains the background of the event mentioned in the first sentence. Using an emphasis transition, as in (A), or a contrast transition, as in (C), is not a logical way to connect these ideas. Choice (B) is a cause-and-effect transition, but it is incorrect because it reverses the cause-and-effect relationship: the end of distribution in 2013 was not the cause, but rather the effect, of the 2012 bill. Deleting the transition, **(D)**, is the correct answer. No transition is necessary: the second sentence simply explains the first.

2. D
Difficulty: Easy

Strategic Advice: If you determine that two ideas in a Transitions question have a contrast, continuation, or cause-and-effect relationship, simply choose the matching transition word or phrase from among the answer choices.

Getting to the Answer: The previous sentence explains how Canadian businesses should handle cash transactions. The sentence with the underline explains how they should handle non-cash transactions. The transition should relate the two different types of transactions. Since "Meanwhile" indicates that two things occur at the same time, **(D)** is correct. Choice (A) is incorrect because the second sentence does not provide an example of cash transactions or rounding. Choice (B) is incorrect because there is no need for an emphasis to be placed on the sentence about non-cash transactions: the paragraph's purpose is to explain how *all* transactions are handled in Canada after the elimination of one-cent coins. Choice (C) is incorrect because non-cash transactions using one-cent increments is not a result of rounding cash transactions.

3. C
Difficulty: Medium

Strategic Advice: When placing a sentence, use both its content and any transitions or key words it contains as clues to determine its placement.

Getting to the Answer: The new sentence begins with the transition word "So," which indicates a cause-and-effect or explanatory relationship. The details in the sentence provide an example, identifying how much someone would pay for a bill in Canada when using a credit card and when using cash. The sentence thus fits logically after the explanations of both cash and non-cash transactions in Canada, so **(C)** is correct. Choice (A) is incorrect because this placement would precede the discussion of both cash and non-cash transactions in Canada. Choice (B) is incorrect because this placement precedes the explanation of non-cash transactions. Choice (D) is incorrect because it does not make sense to describe the specifics of the Canadian system immediately after listing other countries that eliminated one-cent coins in sentence 5.

4. A
Difficulty: Hard

Strategic Advice: Make sure a transition between paragraphs relates to both the main idea of the second paragraph and the main idea or concluding idea of the previous paragraph.

Getting to the Answer: The previous paragraph discussed the discontinuation of the one-cent coin in Canada and concluded with listing other countries that had enacted such a policy. The topic sentence of the second paragraph claims that proponents of eliminating the penny in the United States use "compelling arguments based on costs." Choice **(A)** is correct because it presents the idea that other countries have eliminated the one-cent coin—the concluding idea of the previous paragraph—as a reason cited by proponents of the penny's elimination, "in addition to several other compelling arguments." Although it mentions the detail of cash and non-cash transactions from the previous paragraph, (B) is incorrect because the passage does not explain why such "statistics" would be cited by proponents. Though (C) contains an argument that could be used by penny-elimination proponents, it is incorrect because it does not relate to the previous paragraph. Likewise, (D) would remove any connection to the previous paragraph.

5.   B

Difficulty: Medium

Strategic Advice: Determining the correct transition may require reviewing ideas earlier in the paragraph.

Getting to the Answer: The sentence before the transition simply states the cost of producing a penny; for more context, read back farther. The writer claims in sentence 3 that pennies' production cost may be the most obvious reason to eliminate them. The sentence with the transition then provides the additional detail that the U.S. Mint must produce a lot of pennies. Since this sentence adds to the argument about the cost of pennies, the continuation transition "Further," **(B)**, is correct. Choice (A) is incorrect because the idea that a penny costs 2.06 cents to produce does not equate ("In the same way") with the idea that pennies are often removed from circulation. Nor does it make sense in context to use an emphasis transition ("Certainly") to highlight pennies' removal from circulation after identifying their production cost; (C) is incorrect. Finally, (D) is incorrect because the ideas in the paragraph are not in contrast: high production costs and the necessity of high volume production are both cost-related reasons for eliminating the penny.

6.   C

Difficulty: Hard

Strategic Advice: When the option to delete a sentence appears in the answer choices, make sure that the sentence is closely related to the main idea of the paragraph; if so, use context to determine where it fits logically in the paragraph's flow of ideas.

Getting to the Answer: The topic of the paragraph is cost-based arguments for eliminating the penny. Since sentence 2 provides a cost-based reason (the high cost of penny transport), it should not be deleted; eliminate (D). Sentence 2 begins with the transition "Once produced"; since production is not previously mentioned, eliminate (A). Sentence 4, which identifies the penny's actual production cost in cents, should immediately follow the mention of production costs in sentence 3; eliminate (B). For (C), the idea in sentence 5 that more pennies must be made than any other coin reflects the reference to "this multitude" of coins in sentence 2. Further, sentence 2 logically concludes the paragraph by identifying a cost-based reason—other than production costs—for eliminating the penny; **(C)** is correct.

7.   B

Difficulty: Hard

Strategic Advice: A question that tests transitions may include nonstandard transitions in the answer choices; as always, begin by determining the way in which the ideas are connected and eliminate choices that do not express this connection.

Getting to the Answer: The previous sentence states the conclusion from an economist's study. As the sentence with the transition is in parentheses, it must provide some additional information about either the study or its conclusion. The writer states here that the variable of sales tax "might complicate this assessment," or make the study's conclusion less straightforward. The sentence in parentheses thus provides a qualification about the study's conclusion. A contrast transition could work here, but none appear in the answer choices. Choice (B) provides a logical way to introduce a qualification of a conclusion, so **(B)** is correct. Choice (A) is incorrect because it is a continuation transition, which is opposite of the type of transition needed. Choice (C) is incorrect because "Subsequently" indicates that something occurred after something else, but no chronological events are discussed in this part of the passage. Finally, (D) is incorrect because sales tax posing a complication to the conclusion is not a result of the conclusion, but rather a qualifier of the conclusion.

8.   B

Difficulty: Medium

Strategic Advice: A sentence is unlikely to be the topic or concluding sentence of a paragraph if it does not state the main idea of that paragraph.

Getting to the Answer: As written, sentence 1 is positioned as the topic sentence. Sentence 1 states that rounding should not impact consumers or businesses. However, sentence 2 states that advocates "also" claim "the net impact on costs to consumers and businesses will be neutral." The sentences contain essentially the same claim, so the use of "also" in sentence 2 with this order of sentences is illogical; eliminate (A). Sentence 2 serves as a good topic sentence, since it introduces another argument ("also") of penny-elimination proponents, as begun in the previous paragraph. Placed after sentence 2, sentence 1 would provide an explanation of how "the net impact on costs . . . will be neutral"; **(B)** is correct. Choices (C) and (D) are incorrect because sentence 3 uses the word "However" to shift focus to those who disagree that the impact of rounding costs will be neutral; sentence 2 makes the opposite claim and should thus not be placed after sentence 3 or sentence 4.

9. D

Difficulty: Medium

Strategic Advice: Remember that in Organization questions, all the choices will be grammatically correct, so focus your attention on finding the choice that best connects the passage's ideas.

Getting to the Answer: The previous sentence presents a final argument of "penny-free advocates": the penny's relatively low purchasing power in comparison with the terminated half-cent coin. After the underlined transition, the paragraph indicates that nickels cost more to produce than they are worth and should also be considered for elimination. The transition must connect these ideas. Choice **(D)** is correct because it relates the half-cent coin and the nickel in a way that supports the writer's suggestion that the nickel be eliminated. Choice (A) is incorrect because it introduces a new detail about the quarter and thus does not relate to the ideas before or after the transition. Choice (B) is incorrect because it only relates to the idea before the transition; (C) is incorrect because it only relates to the idea after the transition.

10. C

Difficulty: Hard

Strategic Advice: Some questions about transitions may connect two ideas that both appear after the transition word or phrase.

Getting to the Answer: The underlined transition connects the ideas that the nickel's production costs exceed its value and that the nickel's future is in question. The first idea provides a reason for the second idea, so the contrast transitions "notwithstanding" and "despite," choices (B) and (D), are incorrect. The reader would not be "surprised" by the end of the nickel, as it is worth less than it costs to make; (A) is incorrect. Choice **(C)**, "perhaps," is correct because it indicates the writer's suggestion that, based on the reasoning in the first idea, the action in the second idea should occur.

11. A

Difficulty: Hard

Strategic Advice: Placing a sentence or paragraph within the entire passage requires an understanding of the entire structure of the passage.

Getting to the Answer: The new sentence asks a rhetorical question about whether it makes sense to keep circulating the penny, providing two reasons why the answer may be "no." If placed at the end of the first paragraph, the fact that nothing costs "a mere cent" reflects the idea in the previous sentence that a low-value coin in itself cannot buy anything. This placement also introduces the topic of the penny, which is discussed in the rest of the passage. Choice **(A)** is correct.

Placing the new sentence at the end of the third paragraph may appear logical, since the paragraph discusses reasons to eliminate pennies. However, the paragraph focuses on reasons related to costs, while the new sentence contains reasons based on purchasing power and efficiency; (B) is incorrect. Choice (C) is incorrect because the second half of the fourth paragraph discusses the view that rounding prices after eliminating the penny would be costly to American consumers: this is a reason against rather than in favor of the penny's elimination. And while a rhetorical question could be an appropriate way to end an essay, (D) is incorrect because the current last sentence of the essay shifts focus to the nickel, so adding a final sentence about the penny would result in a jump in topics.

CHAPTER 12

Development

Questions testing the development of a passage will ask about things like word choice and the relevance of a detail to the author's argument. These questions test your understanding of the logic of the passage rather than grammar rules.

Word Choice

Some questions test your knowledge of the correct word to use in context. You must identify which word(s) best convey the writer's intended meaning and best fit the tone of the passage.

To answer word choice questions correctly, read the sentence containing the underlined word but substitute a blank for the word in question. Make your own prediction about what word should go there before looking at the answer choices. Then look for a choice that matches the meaning of your prediction. If one or more of the words among the answer choices are unfamiliar, the process of elimination can still help you get to the correct answer.

Use the following drill to get a sense for what these questions are like. Really think about the context and remember to rely on your own predictions—don't get bogged down in the choices. Use the answers and explanations at the end of the chapter to check your work.

Word Choice Drill

1. The tourist's <u>firsthand</u> knowledge of the local language made it difficult for her to communicate with the city's population.

   A) NO CHANGE
   B) sufficient
   C) expansive
   D) meager

2. The company had invested little time or money in the venture since it was in a <u>mature</u> stage of development; thus, the manager decided to discontinue the project when the corporate office mandated budget cuts.

   A) NO CHANGE
   B) preliminary
   C) blossoming
   D) robust

3. The tremendous popularity and undeniable skill of martial arts star Bruce Lee <u>entranced</u> many thousands of people to learn martial arts.

   A) NO CHANGE
   B) inspired
   C) aspired
   D) elated

4. One of the richest underwater environments on Earth, the Amazon River <u>teems</u> with an immense variety of fish species.

   A) NO CHANGE
   B) rebounds
   C) overruns
   D) bristles

5. Most novice painters prefer to use latex-based paints, since the benign fumes, fast drying times, and chemical-free cleanup of latex-based paints make them more <u>congenial</u> than oil-based paints.

   A) NO CHANGE
   B) user-friendly
   C) influential
   D) laid-back

6. While the average citizen often struggles to comprehend the complexities of the legal system, judges and lawyers are expected to understand its <u>hierarchies</u>.

   A) NO CHANGE
   B) discretion.
   C) intricacies.
   D) distractions.

7. When Neil Armstrong set foot on the moon in 1969, the event was the <u>summit</u> of years of previous work in America's space program.

   A) NO CHANGE
   B) promotion
   C) vertex
   D) culmination

8. Some students consider courses in statistics to be tedious, but a good understanding of statistical principles <u>incites</u> more accurate thinking.

   A) NO CHANGE
   B) provokes
   C) originates
   D) engenders

Relevance

Some questions will ask you to choose the most relevant information to include at a specific point in a passage. In questions like this, all of the answer choices are grammatically and stylistically correct. Given this fact, your task is to determine which option provides information that is most pertinent to the passage. The correct choice will relate directly to the surrounding text and will provide one or more of the following:

- An example
- Support for a point
- A transition to a new idea

Note that when the question has a question stem, you are not being tested on conciseness, even when asked about deleting information. *When you see a question stem, focus on relevance rather than conciseness.*

Revising Text

These questions ask about deleting an underlined portion or adding new text. They have answer choices in a binary "yes/no" or "kept/deleted" format. Consider what information the selection provides and whether that information (1) matches the writer's focus and (2) helps express the purpose of the sentence or paragraph. Consider what the passage might gain or lose if the proposed revision were made. Read the passage both ways—with and without the proposed change—to see which sounds more cohesive. Be sure to read the sentences before and after the proposed revision to best assess the change in context.

Introductions and Conclusions

Some questions ask you to improve the beginning or ending of a paragraph or passage. Therefore, it is good to familiarize yourself with the components of a sound introduction and conclusion.

- An introduction should:
  - Explain the topic and purpose of a paragraph/passage
  - Include information discussed later in the paragraph/passage
  - When applicable, provide an appropriate transition for the previous paragraph
- A conclusion should:
  - Summarize the topic and purpose of a paragraph/passage
  - Include information discussed earlier in the paragraph/passage
  - When applicable, provide an appropriate transition for the next paragraph

Development questions take longer than grammar-based questions, so don't worry if the practice set that follows takes you a bit longer than some of the earlier ones in this book.

Development Practice Set

DIRECTIONS: Take as much time as you need on these questions. Work carefully and methodically. There will be an opportunity for timed practice in chapter 13.

Questions 1–11 refer to the following passage.

Earth to Mars

[1] Constructing living spaces that are functional yet comfortable for multi-year space missions, as would be required to travel to Mars, may be nearly as vital to crew safety as protection from any physical dangers. Astronauts may not be able to perform effectively, especially in emergency situations, if concurrently battling debilitating depression, fatigue, or anxiety, any of which can be psychosomatic symptoms of living in a stressful or isolating environment. [2] Discontinuity in a tiny space with just a few fellow humans for years at a time would try the patience of anyone, even extensively trained astronauts who were selected [3] through the multi-step application process established by NASA.

Astronauts' experiences on the International Space Station (ISS), which houses crews from different countries' space agencies on 3- to 12-month missions while traveling in low-Earth orbit, are [4] diverse. Crew members have commonly reported issues such as irritability and cognitive impairment caused by factors that would also be present on multi-year missions: high

1. Which choice provides the most appropriate introduction to the passage?

   A) NO CHANGE
   B) Management of the psychological and interpersonal impacts of
   C) Designing crew living quarters to protect against the intense radiation exposure during
   D) Providing counseling to help astronauts communicate effectively on

2. A) NO CHANGE
   B) Imprisonment
   C) Indignation
   D) Confinement

3. The writer wants to complete the sentence with a detail that identifies a quality in astronauts that NASA initially considers when determining whether to hire them. Which choice best accomplishes this goal?

   A) NO CHANGE
   B) for their ability to keep calm under extensive pressure.
   C) years ago and have since developed positive relationships with their work colleagues.
   D) before such long-term missions were scientifically feasible.

4. Which choice most effectively sets up the information that follows?

   A) NO CHANGE
   B) elusive.
   C) instructive.
   D) shocking.

levels of CO_2, language barriers, and the **[5]** incessant noise of the fans and machinery necessary to sustain life in space. **[6]** American astronaut Scott Kelly so acutely missed the feeling of water on his body that he jumped into a swimming pool as soon as he returned home from his one-year mission on the ISS.

[7] The technology required for multi-year space travel is far more sophisticated than that currently necessary to operate the ISS. For example, astronauts in low-Earth orbit can participate in real-time video calls with loved ones on Earth. In contrast, there will be a 22-minute delay each way on Earth-Mars communications. Further, many ISS astronauts note that viewing Earth from orbit is a comforting daily part

5. Which choice best maintains the tone established in the passage?

A) NO CHANGE

B) electrifying

C) mind-numbing

D) malicious

6. At this point, the writer is considering adding the following sentence.

> All astronauts report yearning for features of life on Earth that cannot be replicated in low or zero gravity.

Should the writer make this addition here?

A) Yes, because it provides a logical transition into the specific example that follows.

B) Yes, because it introduces an alternative position to the one discussed in the paragraph thus far.

C) No, because it shifts focus away from the main focus of the paragraph.

D) No, because it presents a new claim that the writer fails to support with evidence.

7. Which choice is the best introduction to the paragraph?

A) NO CHANGE

B) The potential for direct contact between ISS astronauts and their family and friends is facilitated by a network of multiple satellites.

C) Astronauts on the ISS have access to few of the luxuries that will be available to astronauts on multi-year missions.

D) Strategies that have proven effective in boosting individuals' morale on the ISS missions will be impossible to employ during long-distance travel.

of life in space. [8] However, the ISS astronaut schedules, typically filled with research and science tasks, don't allow for lengthy Earth-gazing. Researchers are already [9] employing the term *Earth-out-of-view phenomenon* to describe the isolation that may result from missions during which Earth appears as a mere dot in the sky. With limited encouragement available from outside sources on multi-year missions, crew members will need to provide each other especially effective and prolonged support.

As space agencies attempt to anticipate the mental strains of multi-year space travel—and select and train astronauts accordingly—one valuable source of data is a 500-day simulated space mission conducted in Russia. [10] The simulation occurred at the Institute for Biomedical Problems in Moscow. Perhaps the most significant finding was that participants had both the best outlook and performance when allowed to work with a high level of autonomy. Overall, preparation objectives that focus on cooperation, coping mechanisms, and self-reliance will prove vital for long-term space missions that succeed not only in meeting their scientific goals but also in [11] creating astronaut crews that can function independent of support from Earth.

8. Which choice best supports the statement made in the previous sentence?

   A) NO CHANGE

   B) Regularly utilizing special equipment that enables vigorous exercise in low gravity also helps ISS astronauts maintain a positive outlook.

   C) Earth-gazing has provided some astronauts with a profound, almost spiritual, sense of connection to all humankind.

   D) Since the ISS orbits the Earth every 90 minutes, astronauts on board can view most locations on the planet multiple times in an Earth-day.

9. A) NO CHANGE

   B) promoting

   C) throwing around

   D) communicating

10. The writer is considering deleting the underlined sentence. Should the sentence be kept or deleted?

   A) Kept, because it adds information that is necessary for understanding the results of the simulation.

   B) Kept, because it sets up the summary of the simulation results that follows.

   C) Deleted, because it provides details that are not relevant to the writer's purpose for mentioning the simulation.

   D) Deleted, because it fails to supply sufficient background information about when the simulation occurred.

11. Which choice most clearly ends the passage with a summary of the writer's primary focus?

   A) NO CHANGE

   B) being the first to step foot on another planet.

   C) proactively finding solutions to eliminate all potential sources of stress in space.

   D) preserving the well-being of their astronauts.

Answers and Explanations

Word Choice Drill

1. D

If communication was difficult, predict that the tourist's knowledge of the language was *bad* or *limited*. Choice **(D)** is correct because "meager" indicates that his knowledge was lacking. The other choices are incorrect because they reflect a knowledge of the language that would make it easier, not more difficult, to communicate. "Firsthand," (A), means "based on experience"; "sufficient," (B), means "adequate"; and "expansive," (C), means "wide-ranging."

2. B

The transition word "since" indicates a cause-and-effect relationship between the project's stage of development and its lack of investment; predict that a project in *early* development would have had little time or money invested in it. "Preliminary" refers to "preparatory actions," so **(B)** is correct. The other choices are opposite of the required meaning; a project whose development is "mature" ("fully developed"), "blossoming" ("growing productively"), or "robust" ("vigorous") would have experienced a high level of investment.

3. B

The underlined word identifies the connection between the popularity and skill of Bruce Lee and people learning martial arts. Predict a word such as *motivated* to describe this cause-and-effect relationship; **(B)** is correct. While people may have been "entranced" ("filled with wonder") or "elated" ("made very happy") by Lee, one is not "entranced" or "elated" to learn martial arts; (A) and (D) are incorrect. "Aspired" means "aimed for," which is not an action that Lee's popularity and skill could do to people, so (C) is incorrect.

4. A

The clues "richest" and "immense variety" indicate that the river is *rich* in fish species, so **(A)**, "teems," which means "be full of," is correct. The clues do not indicate that the river "rebounds," or "bounces back," with fish. Nor does it indicate there are too many fish; the river is not "overrun" with them. Neither is the river "bristling"—"covered in" or "reacting angrily to"—the many fish species.

5. B

The underlined word describes a quality of latex-based paints that makes them the preferred choice of "novice," or "inexperienced," painters. Since someone inexperienced would likely prefer using a material that is *easy to use*, **(B)** is correct. None of the other choices are appropriate ways to describe an inanimate object such as paint. "Congenial," (A), means "pleasant and like-minded"; "influential," (C), means "impactful"; and "laid-back," (D), means "relaxed." Although the painter or the painting experience may be "congenial" or "laid-back," the paint itself would not be.

6. C

The clue "complexities" provides a prediction for the underlined word, which identifies a characteristic of the legal system that professionals are expected to understand. Choice **(C)**, "intricacies," is a synonym for "complexities" and is correct. "Hierarchies," (A), are "ranked systems," which may or may not be complex. Neither "discretion"—which can refer to "avoiding offense" or "being able to make decisions"—nor "distractions" reflect the "complex" nature of the legal system.

7. D

"Years of previous work" describes the nature of the underlined word, which characterizes the moon-walking event, so a prediction like *result* is appropriate. Choice **(D)**, "culmination," which means "the result of long work," is correct. "Summit" and "vertex," (A) and (C), both mean "the highest point." Nothing in the sentence indicates that Armstrong's moon walk was the highest result of the previous work of the space program, so (A) and (C) are incorrect. Choice (B), "promotion," is incorrect because the moon walk was the result, not the "encouragement" or "elevation," of previous work.

8. D

The underlined word indicates the relationship between a good understanding of statistical principles and more accurate thinking. Since better understanding would result in more accurate thinking, a prediction such as *leads to* is appropriate. Choice **(D)** is correct because "engenders" means "causes." Both (A) and (B) have a connotation of causing negative behaviors or feelings, while the sentence does not reflect a negative result. Choice (C) reverses the relationship between ideas: accurate ideas originate in understanding statistical principles.

Development Practice Set

1. B

Difficulty: Medium

Strategic Advice: Questions that ask about introductions or conclusions for the entire passage are usually best saved until the end of the set. Focus especially on the ideas in the first and last paragraphs to summarize the main idea of the essay.

Getting to the Answer: The writer claims that the detail in the underlined phrase is just as vital to crew safety as protection from "physical dangers." Eliminate (C), which addresses a physical danger. The first paragraph mentions issues such as "depression, fatigue, or anxiety"; living in an environment that is "stressful or isolating"; and being in a "tiny space" with just a few other people. These are all potential mental and social issues of multi-year space missions, affirmed by the mention of "mental strains" in the final paragraph. Choice **(B)** is correct because it introduces both types of challenges. Choice (A) is incorrect because it addresses the specific issue of comfortable living spaces rather than the broad concerns of mental and social issues as addressed by the essay. Choice (D) mentions only social, not mental, difficulties.

2. D

Difficulty: Medium

Strategic Advice: Use clues in the sentence to determine the precise meaning required on Word Choice questions.

Getting to the Answer: The underlined word reflects a situation in which astronauts live in a small space with a few people for years, which the writer claims would test anyone's patience. The word should thus reflect the difficulties of spending a lengthy time in tight living quarters; **(D)** is correct because "Confinement" addresses the stress of not being able to leave the small space. Choice (A) is incorrect because "Discontinuity" refers to an inconsistent situation; the sentence describes astronauts in an unchanging environment. Choice (B) is too extreme, as the astronauts were not forcibly imprisoned in the space capsule. Choice (C) is also too extreme. "Indignation" refers to "anger result-

ing from perceived unfairness"; the sentence refers to astronauts' patience being tested, not their anger.

3. B

Difficulty: Easy

Strategic Advice: Evaluate each answer choice to determine whether it meets the criteria set forth in the question stem.

Getting to the Answer: The underlined phrase must identify a quality that NASA might consider when deciding whether to hire an astronaut in the first place. Choice (A) is incorrect because it fails to mention a specific quality required of astronauts, only summarizing the application process as involving multiple steps. Keep (B) in consideration; keeping calm under pressure is a specific ability for which astronauts could be selected. Choice (C) is incorrect because it identifies a quality—the development of good work relationships—that could not have been a factor in astronauts being *initially* hired. Choice (D) does not reference astronaut qualities at all. Choice **(B)** is correct.

4. C

Difficulty: Medium

Strategic Advice: Summarize the details of the rest of the paragraph to determine which word best introduces them.

Getting to the Answer: The paragraph describes astronauts' experiences on the ISS. The sentence after the underline identifies various issues reported by ISS astronauts, and the last sentence relates the specific example of Scott Kelly's pining for water. Since the writer specifies that the causes of these difficulties would "also be present on multi-year missions," predict that these experiences of ISS astronauts on shorter missions must *provide insight* about longer missions; **(C)**, "instructive," is correct. Choice (A) is incorrect because the paragraph does not emphasize how astronauts' experiences were different, or "diverse," but rather what they "commonly" report. Choice (B) is incorrect because the paragraph lists numerous examples of astronauts' experiences; they are not "elusive," or "difficult to grasp." Nothing in the paragraph implies that the astronauts' experiences were "shocking," so (D) is incorrect.

5. A

Difficulty: Medium

Strategic Advice: When asked about the writer's tone, consider whether the essay has a generally positive, negative, or neutral viewpoint and a formal or informal style.

Getting to the Answer: The writer advocates for consideration of the mental and social issues that may affect astronauts on multi-year missions. While the writer builds a case that these concerns are valid, she maintains a relatively neutral and formal tone throughout. Referring to the noise as "electrifying" (which means "arousing excitement") or "malicious" (which means "intending to do harm") does not match the neutral tone, so (B) and (D) are incorrect. Choice (C) is too informal. "Incessant" matches the neutral, formal tone of the passage and accurately relates the nature of the noise in space, so **(A)** is correct.

6. A

Difficulty: Hard

Strategic Advice: Make sure that there is a logical connection between all ideas in a paragraph: here, there should be a smooth transition between the overall discussion of ISS experiences and the example of one specific astronaut.

Getting to the Answer: The sentence after the possible insertion point describes how astronaut Kelly missed water and jumped into a pool. This specific instance must be an example of whatever information precedes it. The Kelly experience is *not* an example of the details in the sentence before the insertion point: missing water is not an example of "irritability"; "cognitive impairment"; or an issue caused by CO_2, language, or noise. Eliminate (C) and (D), since there must be an additional sentence that sets up the Kelly example. Choice **(A)** correctly identifies the reason for adding the new sentence: missing water is an example of "yearning for features of life on Earth."

7. D

Difficulty: Medium

Strategic Advice: Read and summarize the entire paragraph before choosing an introduction.

Getting to the Answer: The paragraph describes two ways in which long space missions will differ from prior missions: delayed communication and a sense of

isolation due to the distance from Earth. The last sentence concludes the paragraph with the idea that astronauts will need to support each other because outside encouragement will be limited. Choice (D) relates the two examples to the concluding statement by introducing the idea that previous morale-boosting strategies will not be possible on multi-year missions; thus, **(D)** is correct. Choice (A) incorrectly focuses on technology rather than crew encouragement. Choice (B) provides background information for the first example rather than addressing the main idea of the entire paragraph. Choice (C) is incorrect because it distorts the details in the paragraph: ISS astronauts have *more* luxuries due to their proximity to Earth than will astronauts on multi-year missions.

8. C

Difficulty: Medium

Strategic Advice: Identify the claim made in the previous statement, and then eliminate any answer choices that do not support that claim.

Getting to the Answer: The correct answer will provide evidence that supports the idea that many ISS astronauts think viewing Earth is "comforting." While (A) may be true, it provides a qualification, rather than support, for this idea, so (A) is incorrect. Choice (B) provides an additional example of something that encourages astronauts; it is incorrect because it does not support the claim about Earth-viewing. Choice **(C)** is correct because it identifies a reason (a "sense of connection to all humankind") why astronauts would find Earth-gazing comforting. Choice (D) is incorrect because, although it relates to Earth-viewing, it addresses only the logistics rather than the comforting nature of the practice.

9. A

Difficulty: Medium

Strategic Advice: Use context clues to determine exactly what the writer intends the underlined word to convey.

Getting to the Answer: The underlined word refers to what researchers are doing to the term "Earth-out-of-view phenomenon," even though astronauts have not experienced it yet. Since this action is "already" being done, it makes sense that researchers are already *using* the word; "employing" can mean "using," so **(A)** is correct. The context never indicates that the researchers are actively advocating for the use of the term over other alternatives, so (B), "promoting," is incorrect.

Choice (C), "throwing around," does not match the essay's formal tone. "Communicating," (D), means to "exchange information"; though researchers might use the term *as* they are communicating, they are not "communicating" the term itself.

10. C

Difficulty: Hard

Strategic Advice: Paraphrase the main idea of the paragraph, determine whether the sentence should be kept or deleted based on that main idea, and select the answer choice that provides the correct reasoning.

Getting to the Answer: The paragraph concerns anticipating the "mental strains of multi-year space travel" and identifies a simulation in Russia as providing relevant data. While the following sentence describes a finding related to achieving participants' "best outlook and performance," the underlined sentence does not include relevant details about the simulation's relation to the mental strains of space travel. The sentence should be deleted, so eliminate (A) and (B). Precisely when the simulation occurred is irrelevant to its findings about mental strain, so (D) is incorrect. Choice (C) identifies the sentence as irrelevant to the writer's purpose of using the simulation findings to discuss mental strain, so **(C)** is correct.

11. D

Difficulty: Hard

Strategic Advice: Use the entire essay, particularly the ideas in the introduction and conclusion, to summarize the writer's primary focus.

Getting to the Answer: The writer used observations from the ISS and a simulation to discuss the mental and social issues that could be challenges to astronauts on multi-year space missions. The final sentence of the essay affirms these potential issues, claiming that preparation must focus on "cooperation, coping mechanisms, and self-reliance." The underlined portion should reflect not the "scientific goals" of the mission but the goals related to mental and social health. Choice **(D)** summarizes the nature of these goals and is correct. (A) is incorrect because the end of the third paragraph indicates that encouragement from outsiders will be "limited," not nonexistent. Choice (B) is incorrect because it identifies a scientific goal of long-term missions. Choice (C) is incorrect because the writer never implies that *all* stress of space travel can be prevented through preparation; rather, the writer advocates the development of "coping mechanisms."

CHAPTER 13

Writing and Language Practice Sets

Writing and Language Practice Set 1

> **DIRECTIONS:** For testlike practice, give yourself 9 minutes to complete this question set. Be sure to study the explanations, even for questions you got right.

Questions 1–11 refer to the following passage.

Euclid's Elements

Euclid was an ancient Greek mathematician [1] whom [2] lived in the fourth century BCE, and worked in Alexandria, Egypt. His most famous work, the *Elements*, drew together and clarified many results from previous generations of Greek mathematicians. The *Elements* is primarily known as a geometry text; however, it also contains sections on number theory and proportions. [3]

1. A) NO CHANGE
   B) who
   C) whose
   D) who's

2. A) NO CHANGE
   B) lived in the fourth century BCE and worked
   C) lived, in the fourth century BCE, and worked
   D) lived in the fourth century BCE; working

3. The writer wants to link the first paragraph with the ideas that follow. Which choice best accomplishes this goal?

   A) Many modern students are less familiar with number theory than students of previous generations were, which sometimes hinders their grasp of more abstract materials.

   B) Euclid's famous parallel postulate remained the subject of much consternation for centuries and eventually spawned the field of non-Euclidean geometry.

   C) Apollonius of Perga, another famous Greek geometer who lived after Euclid, described the conic sections that are still taught in high school mathematics classes.

   D) Euclid's *Elements* was not only the seminal work of its time but also remained the standard of mathematical rigor for well over 2,000 years.

In addition to summarizing the results of his predecessors, Euclid introduces a number of innovations. Perhaps his greatest contribution to mathematics **4** is his presentation in the *Elements* of an axiomatic deductive system. He begins his work by listing a small set of **5** axioms: statements intended to be self-evident and assumed without proof, and then begins drawing conclusions from them. At first, the results seem minor and perhaps uninteresting, but over the course of Euclid's presentation, they build upon each other to become a marvelous intellectual **6** accomplishment. This deductive style of reasoning is what separates mathematics from every other intellectual endeavor.

It is hard to overestimate Euclid's influence on Western culture. The *Elements* was studied by countless students in the university system as part of the medieval **7** quadrivium, and, until the mid-20th century, it was considered required reading for all educated people. **8** Indeed, luminaries such as Isaac Newton, Johannes Kepler, Galileo Galilei, Baruch Spinoza, Bertrand Russell, and Albert Einstein all drew inspiration from the text. Even non-mathematicians have looked to Euclid for comfort and inspiration. Abraham Lincoln famously studied the *Elements* late at night by candlelight, purportedly saying to himself, "You never can make a lawyer if you do not understand what *demonstrate* means."

To modern readers, some of Euclid's methods may seem peculiar. **9** For example, while ancient Greek mathematicians did have a system of numbers, it was not particularly well-suited for doing complex

4. A) NO CHANGE
   B) are
   C) were
   D) was

5. A) NO CHANGE
   B) axioms; statements intended to be self-evident and assumed without proof,
   C) axioms, statements intended to be self-evident and assumed without proof,
   D) axioms, statements intended to be self-evident and assumed without proof;

6. Which choice is most consistent in style and content with the imagery in the paragraph?

   A) NO CHANGE
   B) edifice.
   C) pile.
   D) belief.

7. A) NO CHANGE
   B) medieval quadrivium; and, until the mid-20th century, it was considered required reading
   C) medieval quadrivium, and, until the mid-20th century; it was considered required reading
   D) medieval quadrivium, and; until the mid-20th century, it was considered required reading

8. A) NO CHANGE
   B) Alternatively,
   C) Finally,
   D) Meanwhile,

9. A) NO CHANGE
   B) The ancient Greek mathematicians, for example, not particularly well-suited for doing complex calculations, did have a system of numbers.
   C) The ancient Greek system of numbers was not particular well-suited for mathematicians to do complex calculations, for example.
   D) The ancient Greek numbers, for example, did have a system, but one that was not particularly well-suited for doing complex calculations.

calculations. **10** Additionally, algebra as we know it today had not yet been invented. Therefore, Euclid had to derive geometrically results that most modern students would be more comfortable thinking about arithmetically or algebraically. This may cause some of his proofs to seem awkward to modern readers. However, any would-be critic of Euclid must always bear in mind that the *Elements* has served as a foundational text for mathematicians for over 23 centuries. **11** Mathematician and historian W. W. Rouse Ball declared that the fact that the *Elements* was "the usual textbook on the subject raises a strong presumption that it is not unsuitable for that purpose."

10. The writer is considering deleting the underlined sentence. Should the sentence be kept or deleted?

A) Kept, because it provides details needed to understand Euclid's proofs.

B) Kept, because it provides additional reasoning to support the statement that follows.

C) Deleted, because it contradicts what has been previously stated in the passage.

D) Deleted, because it blurs the focus of the paragraph by introducing loosely related information.

11. The writer wants to write a conclusion that addresses some of the criticism that has been leveled at Euclid. Which choice best accomplishes this goal?

A) NO CHANGE

B) Bertrand Russell, a philosopher who studied the application of logic to mathematics, once said of Euclid, "His definitions do not always define, his axioms are not always indemonstrable, his demonstrations require many axioms of which he is quite unconscious."

C) Albert Einstein expressed his enthusiasm for Euclid in the following terms, "If Euclid failed to kindle your youthful enthusiasm, then you were not born to be a scientific thinker."

D) Issac Newton, whose own *Philosophiae Naturalis Principia Mathematica* drew heavily from the *Elements*, wrote, "It's the glory of geometry that from so few principles it can accomplish so much."

Writing and Language Practice Set 2

DIRECTIONS: For testlike practice, give yourself 9 minutes to complete this question set. Be sure to study the explanations, even for questions you got right.

Questions 1–11 refer to the following passage.

Conlon Nancarrow

Classical music aficionados are likely familiar with the names of Bach, Mozart, Beethoven, and Schubert. However, many are unaware of an American visionary born in the early part of the twentieth **1** century: Conlon Nancarrow. Nancarrow's life and career are in many ways the **2** archetype of those of a typical **3** composer, and his music is equally unconventional.

[1] Conlon Nancarrow was born on October 27, 1912, in Texarkana, Arkansas. [2] To avoid persecution from the U.S. government due to his political views, in 1940 he moved to Mexico and became a citizen of that country in 1956. [3] Growing up, he played trumpet in a jazz **4** band and later traveling to Ohio and Boston to study music. [4] In Boston, he joined the Communist Party, a decision that would have far-reaching consequences for the rest of his life. **5**

6 Poorly isolated from both the American and Mexican musical establishments and without easy access to other musicians, Nancarrow began experimenting with new ways to make music. His solution to his seclusion and poverty was to concentrate his creative efforts on the player piano. Although the device was already considered an anachronism in his day, he was intrigued by its ability to keep flawless time and to play exceedingly complex rhythms at speeds far beyond anything a human could hope to achieve.

1. A) NO CHANGE
   B) century;
   C) century, whose name was
   D) century, who was named

2. A) NO CHANGE
   B) antithesis
   C) antidote
   D) epitome

3. A) NO CHANGE
   B) composers,
   C) composers',
   D) composer's,

4. A) NO CHANGE
   B) band and later traveled
   C) band, and later traveled
   D) band; and later traveled

5. To make this paragraph most logical, sentence 2 should be placed

   A) where it is now.
   B) before sentence 1.
   C) after sentence 3.
   D) after sentence 4.

6. A) NO CHANGE
   B) Isolated and poor from both the American and Mexican musical establishments, and without easy access to other musicians,
   C) Poor, isolating from both the American and Mexican musical establishments, and without easy access to other musicians,
   D) Poor, isolated from both the American and Mexican musical establishments, and without easy access to other musicians,

7 Nancarrow's compositions have been called the most rhythmically complex ever created. Jazz influences from his youth sometimes crop up, but the musical form that interested him most was the canon. This ancient art form features an initial melodic line and one or more "followers" that imitate this melody. ("Row, Row, Row Your Boat" is a simple and popular example.) Oftentimes, these musical lines are played in certain ratios of each other. **8** In contrast, the follower may play twice as quickly as the leader. Johann Sebastian Bach most often used 1:1 ratios, and certain Renaissance composers experimented with more complex configurations like 1:2:3. In contrast, Nancarrow's canons may be in proportions of $\frac{1}{\sqrt{\pi}} : \sqrt{\frac{2}{3}}$ or $\frac{1}{3\sqrt{\pi}} : \sqrt[3]{\frac{13}{16}}$. **9**

Nancarrow lived most of his life outside the public eye, only **10** becoming known in his 70s widely. Listening to this musical hermit is at once a **11** bewildering, spiritual, and deeply intellectual experience.

7. Which choice provides the most effective transition between paragraphs?

 A) Additionally, the player piano was also able to play far more notes at once than a human could.

 B) Consequently, in many ways, Nancarrow is the father of electronic music.

 C) Moreover, the player piano is also capable of much more subtle dynamics than a human is.

 D) Thus, Nancarrow both circumvented his precarious financial position and pushed the boundaries of 20th-century music.

8. A) NO CHANGE

 B) Meanwhile,

 C) For example,

 D) Altogether,

9. At this point, the author wants to add a statement that provides further support for the claim that Nancarrow's music is complex. Which of the following best accomplishes this goal?

 A) Sometimes two melodies begin in unison, but over the course of the piece one gradually begins to speed up or slow down, moving the two lines "out of phase."

 B) Mathematicians call numbers like $\sqrt{\frac{2}{3}}$ "irrational numbers."

 C) Interestingly, most of Nancarrow's work features very little change in dynamics.

 D) Fellow composer Grigoryi Ligeti proclaimed, "His music is so utterly original, enjoyable, perfectly constructed, but at the same time emotional. . . . For me it's the best music of any living composer today."

10. A) NO CHANGE

 B) becoming known in his widely 70s.

 C) becoming widely known in his 70s.

 D) widely becoming known in his 70s.

11. Which choice best maintains the tone established in the passage?

 A) NO CHANGE

 B) disturbing,

 C) crazy,

 D) groundbreaking,

Writing and Language Practice Set 3

DIRECTIONS: For testlike practice, give yourself 9 minutes to complete this question set. Be sure to study the explanations, even for questions you got right.

Questions 1–11 refer to the following passage.

Problem-Solving Crows

Stereotypical views of animal intelligence tend to restrict sophisticated reasoning abilities to mammals: dolphins, gorillas, and chimpanzees probably spring to mind. However, there is another animal whose problem-solving ability far surpasses [1] them—the humble crow.

[1] Crows belong to the corvid family, whose other members include jays, ravens, jackdaws, and magpies. [2] The entire family is known for [2] their large brain capacity and incredible adaptability. [3] [3] Nevertheless, crows in Akita, Japan, have learned how to eat nuts, a food that was previously inaccessible to them, by dropping them in the street and waiting for cars to run over the nuts. [4] Once the cars broke the shells, the [4] crows next challenge was to figure out how to eat the nuts without being run over. [5] In light of this new information, the crows modified their approach and [5] began dropping the nuts in crosswalks and waiting until the light changed to come down and feed. [6] In time, the crows learned that traffic stops at pedestrian crosswalks. [6]

In the wild, crows have been observed using sticks as tools to extract insects from trees. Interestingly, many crows have also been seen to tinker with the sticks' original shape to create hooks. Although many individuals have hit upon this enhancement

1. A) NO CHANGE
   B) theirs
   C) it
   D) its

2. A) NO CHANGE
   B) there
   C) its
   D) it's

3. A) NO CHANGE
   B) For example,
   C) In contrast,
   D) Additionally,

4. A) NO CHANGE
   B) crow
   C) crow's
   D) crows'

5. A) NO CHANGE
   B) dropped
   C) dropping
   D) began to drop

6. To make this paragraph most logical, sentence 6 should be placed

   A) where it is now.
   B) after sentence 4.
   C) after sentence 2.
   D) before sentence 4.

independently, crows also **7** do seem to have the ability to share knowledge and learn from their elders.

Wild crows can even recognize human faces. Scientists in Seattle performed an experiment in which they **8** donned two types of **9** masks, being a "threatening" one and a "neutral" one. Those wearing the "threatening" mask captured and banded wild crows on the University of Washington campus, while those with the "neutral" mask ignored the birds. Several months later, the scientists put on their masks again and strolled through campus. **10** The scientists wearing the threatening masks were scolded by the crows, ignoring those wearing the neutral masks. **11** Perhaps most spectacularly of all, the younger crows that had not been previously captured knew which humans to avoid, so the older crows must have communicated this information to them in some way.

Although they have often been regarded as pests, crows' superior ability to learn on their own and from each other suggests that they may in fact be the most intelligent nonhuman animals on earth, warranting close observation and study. Humans may yet be surprised by what can be learned from them.

7. A) NO CHANGE
    B) seems
    C) seeming
    D) seemed

8. A) NO CHANGE
    B) doffed
    C) divested
    D) derelict

9. A) NO CHANGE
    B) masks: a
    C) masks; a
    D) masks. A

10. A) NO CHANGE
    B) The crows scolded the scientists wearing the threatening masks and ignored those wearing the neutral masks.
    C) Scolding the threatening masks, the crows ignored the scientists wearing the neutral masks.
    D) The crows, scolding the scientists wearing the threatening masks, ignored those wearing the neutral masks.

11. The writer is considering deleting the underlined sentence. Should the writer do this?

    A) Yes, because it repeats information that has been provided in an earlier paragraph.
    B) Yes, because it fails to support the main idea of the passage as introduced in the first paragraph.
    C) No, because it provides a transition to the next paragraph.
    D) No, because it blurs the paragraph's focus with a loosely related detail.

Answers and Explanations

Writing and Language Practice Set 1

1. B

Difficulty: Low

Strategic Advice: Recall that "who" is a subjective pronoun, while "whom" is objective.

Getting to the Answer: Examine how the pronoun is being used in context. Here, it functions as the subject of the relative clause. Thus, **(B)** is correct.

Choice (A) is incorrect because "whom" is the objective form. "Whose" is possessive, so (C) is incorrect. Finally, "who's" in (D) is short for "who is," which does not make sense in context.

2. B

Difficulty: High

Strategic Advice: When a comma is underlined, suspect a sentence structure issue.

Getting to the Answer: Look carefully at how the comma is being used. Here, two verb phrases are being joined, so no comma is needed. Choice **(B)** is correct.

Choice (A) is incorrect because a comma is not used before a FANBOYS conjunction joining two verb phrases. Choice (C) is incorrect because the phrase "in the fourth century BCE" is not parenthetical and need not be offset from the rest of the sentence with commas. Finally, a semicolon joins two complete sentences, not a complete sentence and a fragment, so (D) is incorrect.

3. D

Difficulty: Medium

Strategic Advice: When you are asked to transition between two paragraphs, summarize the first paragraph and read a little bit into the second paragraph for more context.

Getting to the Answer: The first paragraph describes Euclid's *Elements*, ending with a discussion of how he drew together work from previous generations. The next paragraph discusses Euclid's innovations. Choice **(D)** provides the best link between these two ideas.

Choices (A), (B), and (C) are irrelevant; modern students, the Parallel Postulate, and Apollonius of Perga are not discussed in the next paragraph.

4. A

Difficulty: Medium

Strategic Advice: The noun closest to a verb may not be its subject.

Getting to the Answer: Do not trust your ear; instead, go back and find the subject of the verb. Here, the subject is "greatest contribution." Since this is a singular noun, a singular verb is needed. Eliminate (B) and (C). Since the rest of the paragraph is in the present tense, eliminate the past tense verb in (D). Choice **(A)** is correct.

5. C

Difficulty: Medium

Strategic Advice: Commas are used to offset parenthetical information from the rest of the sentence. Semicolons join two independent clauses. Colons introduce something.

Getting to the Answer: Carefully examine the phrase surrounded by punctuation marks, *statements intended to be self-evident and assumed without proof*. Since this phrase is not grammatically essential to the rest of the sentence, it must be offset with two commas, two parentheses, or two dashes. Choice **(C)** is correct. Choices (A), (B), and (D) are incorrect because they do not enclose the phrase with a pair of commas.

6. B

Difficulty: High

Strategic Advice: Context is critical in Word Choice questions. Go back and read a little bit before and after the underline and look for clues.

Getting to the Answer: The previous sentence describes Euclid's method of starting with small, perhaps uninteresting results, and then gradually building them up to create something more complex. Predict something like *building* or *structure*. Choice **(B)**, "edifice," means "a large and imposing building," so it is correct.

Choice (A) does not capture the idea of Euclid's propositions building on one another, so it is incorrect. Choice (C), "pile," does not match the scholarly tone of the rest of the passage. Choice (D) does not capture the cumulative nature of Euclid's work.

7. A

Difficulty: High

Strategic Advice: When one or more punctuation marks are underlined, make sure to avoid creating run-ons or fragments.

Getting to the Answer: Examine each answer choice. Choice **(A)** correctly uses a comma and the FANBOYS conjunction "and" to join two independent clauses. Additionally, it offsets the parenthetical phrase "until the mid-20th century" with commas.

Choice (B) is incorrect because it uses a semicolon and a FANBOYS conjunction to join two independent clauses. While a comma and a FANBOYS conjunction is a valid choice, a semicolon and a FANBOYS conjunction is not. Choices (C) and (D) are incorrect because in both cases the clause before the semicolon cannot stand on its own. Semicolons must join two independent clauses.

8. A

Difficulty: Medium

Strategic Advice: When a transition word is underlined, read a little bit before and after the underline to determine what type of transition is appropriate.

Getting to the Answer: The sentence before the underline describes how the *Elements* was studied by countless university students and was considered an essential part of any educated person's curriculum. The sentence with the underline lists famous mathematicians and scientists who were influenced by Euclid's work. Choice **(A)** is correct because it emphasizes how these two ideas are connected.

Choice (B) is incorrect because "alternatively" is a contrast word. Choice (C), "finally," implies a chronological sequence, which is not present here. Choice (D), "meanwhile," indicates that two things are happening simultaneously, which also does not match the surrounding context.

9. A

Difficulty: Medium

Strategic Advice: When you are asked to rewrite a sentence, pay careful attention to punctuation and the logical flow of ideas.

Getting to the Answer: Examine each answer choice. Choice (A) puts the transition phrase "for example" at the very beginning of the sentence and correctly

punctuates the clauses that follow. There are no obvious errors, so keep it for now.

Choice (B) can be eliminated because the phrase "not particularly well-suited for doing complex calculations" is modifying "the ancient Greek mathematicians." This phrase should actually modify "system of numbers." Choice (C) is incorrect because it uses the adjective "particular" instead of the adverb "particularly." Additionally, the transition phrase "for example" is awkwardly placed. Finally, (D) distorts the intended meaning; it is incorrect to say that the numbers had a system. Choice **(A)** is correct.

10. B

Difficulty: High

Strategic Advice: First, determine whether the statement should be kept or deleted. Then examine the reasoning for each choice.

Getting to the Answer: Read around the underlined section for additional context. The previous sentence describes a weakness of the Greek number system. The underlined segment gives another reason why Euclid's proofs may sometimes seem unusual to modern readers. Therefore, the underlined section should be kept. Choices (C) and (D) are incorrect. Now examine the reasoning behind (A) and (B). Choice (A) is incorrect because the passage does not actually discuss any of Euclid's proofs. Choice **(B)** is correct because the lack of modern algebra supports the statement that follows, which says that Euclid's proofs can sometimes be hard to understand.

11. A

Difficulty: Medium

Strategic Advice: A good conclusion should tie together the whole passage and restate its main idea.

Getting to the Answer: Pay careful attention to the question's directions. You are looking for a conclusion that refutes Euclid's critics. Eliminate (B) immediately, since it provides more criticism. While (C) and (D) both praise Euclid, neither provides a rebuttal against his critics. Choice **(A)** is correct.

Writing and Language Practice Set 2

1. A

Difficulty: Easy

Strategic Advice: In addition to being grammatically correct, the correct answer must also be concise.

Getting to the Answer: The sentence in question introduces the name of a visionary American composer. Since colons are used to provide introductions and explanations, **(A)** is correct.

Choice (B) is incorrect because semicolons join two complete sentences, and "Conlon Nancarrow" is not a complete sentence. Choices (C) and (D) are both grammatically correct but are too wordy.

2. B

Difficulty: Medium

Strategic Advice: Context is critical in Word Choice questions. Go back and read a little bit before and after the underlined word.

Getting to the Answer: The paragraph states that many classical music fans are unaware of Conlon Nancarrow. The paragraph ends by saying that his music is "equally unconventional." Since "unconventional" means "out of the ordinary," predict that his life would be the "opposite" of a typical composer's. Choice **(B)** is correct.

Choice (A), "archetype," means "typical example." This is the opposite of what you are looking for. Choice (C), "antidote," means "medicine," which doesn't make sense in context. Choice (D), "epitome," means "the greatest." Reading this word back into the sentence would suggest that Nancarrow was "the greatest" at being a typical composer, which is the opposite of what the passage states.

3. D

Difficulty: High

Strategic Advice: Do not trust your ear! Instead, analyze the sentence's structure to determine which form to use.

Getting to the Answer: The sentence begins with the possessive phrase "Nancarrow's life and career." To make the comparison in the sentence logical, the thing being compared must be a possessive phrase as well. Eliminate (A) and (B). Since Nancarrow is a singular noun, the singular possessive form is required. Choice **(D)**, rather than (C), is correct.

4. B

Difficulty: High

Strategic Advice: The two verbs in a verb phrase must be correctly punctuated and in parallel form.

Getting to the Answer: Since the first verb in the verb phrase is "played," the second verb must also be in the past tense; eliminate (A). A comma and a FANBOYS conjunction can join two complete sentences, but not two verb phrases; eliminate (C). A semicolon joins two complete sentences, not two verb phrases; eliminate (D). Choice **(B)** is correct.

5. D

Difficulty: Medium

Strategic Advice: In Organization questions, your goal is to group similar ideas together.

Getting to the Answer: Sentence 2 describes how Nancarrow moved to Mexico to escape persecution due to his political views. It does not make sense where it is now, since the first sentence makes no mention of his political views; eliminate (A). For the same reason, it also does not make sense to move it to the very beginning of the paragraph; eliminate (B). Since sentence 4 describes how Nancarrow joined the Communist Party, sentence 2 should be placed directly after it. Choice **(D)** is correct.

6. D

Difficulty: Hard

Strategic Advice: Examine the sentence as it is written and determine its intended meaning. Then choose the answer that most clearly reflects this meaning.

Getting to the Answer: As written, the adverb "poorly" is modifying the adjective "isolated." This makes it seem that Nancarrow was not well isolated from the American and Mexican musical establishments, when in fact he was. Eliminate (A). Choice (B) uses the strange construction "poor from both the American and Mexican musical establishments," so it can be eliminated as well. Choice (C) uses the incorrect form "isolating" instead of "isolated." It also results in a nonparallel list. Choice **(D)** correctly separates the list of three modifying phrases with commas and preserves the logical integrity of the ideas.

7. D

Difficulty: Hard

Strategic Advice: To determine the best transition, read a little bit into the next paragraph for additional context.

Getting to the Answer: The current paragraph describes how the player piano provided a solution to many of Nancarrow's problems. The next paragraph details some of the rhythmic innovations in Nancarrow's music. Eliminate (A), since the number of notes played has no direct connection to rhythm. Choice (B) can also be eliminated, since the next paragraph does not discuss electronic music. Finally, eliminate (C), since dynamics are not mentioned in the next paragraph. Choice **(D)** is correct because it functions as the paragraph's concluding statement.

8. C

Difficulty: Easy

Strategic Advice: Look carefully at the surrounding context to determine what type of transition is appropriate.

Getting to the Answer: The sentence before the underline states that musical lines in a canon are often played in certain ratios of each other. The sentence with the underline describes how a follower can sometimes play twice as quickly as a leader. This is not a contrast relationship, so eliminate (A) and (B). The word "Altogether" summarizes previous ideas. Since the sentence with the underline is not summarizing but giving an example of what was discussed in the previous sentence, **(C)** is correct.

9. A

Difficulty: Medium

Strategic Advice: Pay careful attention to what the question is asking. You are looking for a statement that reinforces the claim that Nancarrow's music is complex.

Getting to the Answer: Consider each answer choice systematically. Choice (A) describes how Nancarrow sometimes moves different melody lines "out of phase." This looks promising, so keep it for now. Choice (B) has no bearing on Nancarrow's music, so eliminate it. Choice (C) describes an aspect of Nancarrow's music that is *not* complex, so it can also be eliminated. Choice (D) praises Nancarrow, but it does not specifically say how his music is complex. Choice **(A)** is correct.

10. C

Difficulty: Medium

Strategic Advice: Modifiers must be placed directly next to what they are intended to modify.

Getting to the Answer: Examine the answer choices. The only difference between them is the placement of the word "widely." Since "widely" is intended to modify "known," it must be placed directly next to that word. Choice **(C)** is correct. Choices (A), (B), and (D) all fail to place "widely" directly next to "known."

11. A

Difficulty: Medium

Strategic Advice: The author's tone is respectful and appreciative. Look for a word with these characteristics.

Getting to the Answer: The word "bewildering" means "baffling" or "hard to understand." The previous paragraph describes the complexities of Nancarrow's music, so this seems like a reasonable description. Keep it for now.

Choice (B), "disturbing," does not match the positive tone of the passage. Choice (C) does not match the respectful tone of the passage. Choice (D) may be tempting, but Nancarrow himself, not listening to his music, is "groundbreaking." Choice **(A)** is correct.

Writing and Language Practice Set 3

1. B

Difficulty: High

Strategic Advice: Comparisons must be logically structured.

Getting to the Answer: Examine the sentence and see what is being compared. The sentence compares "problem-solving ability" to the underlined word. It is not logical to compare "problem-solving ability" (an intellectual ability) to crows (an animal), so eliminate (A). Since the crows, plural, possess the problem-solving ability, the singular pronouns in (C) and (D) can be eliminated as well. Choice **(B)** is correct.

2. C

Difficulty: Medium

Strategic Advice: Pronouns must agree with their antecedents.

Getting to the Answer: Determine what the underlined pronoun is intended to refer to. It refers back to "family," which is a singular noun. Therefore, the singular possessive form in **(C)** is correct.

Choice (A) is a plural possessive, so it is incorrect. Choice (B) is not a possessive pronoun at all. Finally, (D) is a contraction of "it is."

3. B

Difficulty: Low

Strategic Advice: Transition words join two ideas together.

Getting to the Answer: Always read a little bit before and after a transition word for additional context. The previous sentence describes how corvids are known for their intelligence and adaptability. The sentence with the underline describes how crows learned how to eat nuts by making cars run over them. Eliminate (A) and (C), since these are not contrasting ideas. Choice (D) can also be eliminated, since "Additionally" is used to introduce an extra factor that must be considered. Since the next sentence provides an example of corvid intelligence, not an extra factor, **(B)** is correct.

4. D

Difficulty: Medium

Strategic Advice: A singular possessive ends with 's. A plural possessive ends with s'.

Getting to the Answer: Look at the structure of the sentence. The crows, plural, are possessing the challenge, so the plural possessive form in **(D)** is correct.

Choices (A) and (B) are not possessive forms. Choice (C) is the singular possessive form.

5. A

Difficulty: Medium

Strategic Advice: Verbs in a compound must be in parallel form.

Getting to the Answer: This sentence has two main verbs, "modified" and "began." Additionally, the verb "began" takes two complements, "dropping" and

"waiting." As written, the sentence correctly uses these two forms. Choice **(A)** is correct.

Choice (B) creates the nonparallel structure "dropped the nuts in the crosswalk and waiting." Choice (C) results in "modified their approach and dropping," which is also not parallel. Finally, (D) yields "began to drop the nuts in the crosswalk and waiting," another nonparallel structure.

6. B

Difficulty: High

Strategic Advice: In Organization questions, your goal is to group similar ideas together.

Getting to the Answer: Pronouns can be helpful in Organization questions. Sentence 5 contains the phrase "in light of this new information." What new information? Placing sentence 6 after sentence 4 makes this reference more intelligible. Choice **(B)** is correct. Placing it where it is now, after sentence 2, or before sentence 4 mangles the chronological sequence of events in the paragraph.

7. A

Difficulty: Medium

Strategic Advice: Verbs must agree with their subject and match the context of the rest of the paragraph in tense.

Getting to the Answer: Most of the verbs in the paragraph are in the past tense. At first glance, this might lead you to think that (D) is correct. However, this distorts the intended meaning of the sentence, since it makes it seem like the crows used to have the ability to share knowledge in the past but are now no longer able to. Choice (C) can also be eliminated, since it creates a sentence fragment. Finally, (B) results in incorrect subject-verb agreement, so it is also incorrect. The emphatic present tense in **(A)** is correct.

8. A

Difficulty: Medium

Strategic Advice: If you are unsure of the meaning of a word, see if it looks or sounds similar to a word that you already know.

Getting to the Answer: The sentence with the underline describes how the scientists put on masks as part of their experiment. Look carefully at the answer choices.

Choices (A) and (B) seem very similar; it's almost like a *d* was added to the words "on" and "off." In fact, that is exactly what they mean! "Don" means "to put on a piece of clothing" and "doff" means "to take off a piece of clothing." Thus, **(A)** is correct. Choices (C) and (D), although they both begin with the letter *d*, do not pertain to putting on or taking off clothing.

9. B

Difficulty: Medium

Strategic Advice: Whenever a punctuation mark is underlined, check for run-ons and sentence fragments.

Getting to the Answer: Examine the structure of the underlined segment. This sentence is introducing two different types of masks. Since colons are used to introduce things, **(B)** is correct.

Choice (A) may be tempting, but the addition of "being" creates an ungrammatical structure. Choice (C) is incorrect because a semicolon is used to join two independent clauses, and the phrase after the semicolon cannot stand on its own. Choice (D) is incorrect for the same reason; the phrase after the period is not a complete sentence.

10. B

Difficulty: High

Strategic Advice: Parallel ideas must have parallel sentence structure.

Getting to the Answer: As written, the phrase "were scolded" is not parallel with "ignoring." Eliminate (A). Choice **(B)** coordinates "scolded" and "ignored," so it is correct. Choice (C) changes the intended meaning of the sentence. Choice (D) incorrectly coordinates "scolding" with "ignored."

11. C

Difficulty: High

Strategic Advice: First determine whether the sentence should be kept or deleted. Then examine the reasoning for each answer choice.

Getting to the Answer: Consider what would happen if the sentence were deleted. The paragraph would end with a discussion of how the crows scolded threatening people while ignoring neutral people. This would be directly followed by the concluding paragraph, which discusses the intelligence of crows and references their ability to "learn from each other." This lack of any transition is jarring, so eliminate (A) and (B). Choice (D) is incorrect because a discussion of crow communication is certainly relevant to the topic at hand. Choice **(C)** is correct: the phrase "most spectacularly of all" sets up the idea at the start of the final paragraph that crows are the most intelligent nonhuman animals, and crows' "ability to learn from each other" refers to the the transmission of information about threatening humans.

PART THREE

Practice Test

CHAPTER 14

Reading and Writing & Language Practice Test

How to Score Your Practice Test

To get your raw score, add the number of Reading questions you answered correctly to the number of Writing and Language questions you answered correctly. Then convert your raw score to a scaled score using the following table.

Evidence-Based Reading and Writing			
Total Raw Score	Scaled Score	Total Raw Score	Scaled Score
0	200	49	490
1	200	50	500
2	210	51	500
3	220	52	510
4	240	53	510
5	260	54	520
6	270	55	520
7	270	56	530
8	290	57	530
9	290	58	540
10	300	59	540
11	300	60	550
12	310	61	550
13	320	62	560
14	320	63	560
15	330	64	570
16	330	65	570
17	340	66	580
18	340	67	580
19	350	68	590
20	350	69	590
21	360	70	600
22	360	71	600
23	370	72	610
24	370	73	610
25	370	74	610
26	380	75	620
27	380	76	620

Evidence-Based Reading and Writing			
Total Raw Score	**Scaled Score**	**Total Raw Score**	**Scaled Score**
28	380	77	630
29	380	78	630
30	390	79	640
31	390	80	640
32	400	81	660
33	400	82	660
34	410	83	670
35	410	84	680
36	420	85	690
37	430	86	700
38	430	87	700
39	440	88	710
40	440	89	710
41	450	90	730
42	450	91	740
43	460	92	750
44	460	93	760
45	470	94	780
46	480	95	790
47	480	96	800
48	490		

SAT Practice Test Answer Sheet

Remove (or photocopy) this answer sheet and use it to complete the test. See the answer key following the test when finished.

Start with number 1 for each section. If a section has fewer questions than answer spaces, leave the extra spaces blank.

SECTION 1

1. Ⓐ Ⓑ Ⓒ Ⓓ
2. Ⓐ Ⓑ Ⓒ Ⓓ
3. Ⓐ Ⓑ Ⓒ Ⓓ
4. Ⓐ Ⓑ Ⓒ Ⓓ
5. Ⓐ Ⓑ Ⓒ Ⓓ
6. Ⓐ Ⓑ Ⓒ Ⓓ
7. Ⓐ Ⓑ Ⓒ Ⓓ
8. Ⓐ Ⓑ Ⓒ Ⓓ
9. Ⓐ Ⓑ Ⓒ Ⓓ
10. Ⓐ Ⓑ Ⓒ Ⓓ
11. Ⓐ Ⓑ Ⓒ Ⓓ
12. Ⓐ Ⓑ Ⓒ Ⓓ
13. Ⓐ Ⓑ Ⓒ Ⓓ

14. Ⓐ Ⓑ Ⓒ Ⓓ
15. Ⓐ Ⓑ Ⓒ Ⓓ
16. Ⓐ Ⓑ Ⓒ Ⓓ
17. Ⓐ Ⓑ Ⓒ Ⓓ
18. Ⓐ Ⓑ Ⓒ Ⓓ
19. Ⓐ Ⓑ Ⓒ Ⓓ
20. Ⓐ Ⓑ Ⓒ Ⓓ
21. Ⓐ Ⓑ Ⓒ Ⓓ
22. Ⓐ Ⓑ Ⓒ Ⓓ
23. Ⓐ Ⓑ Ⓒ Ⓓ
24. Ⓐ Ⓑ Ⓒ Ⓓ
25. Ⓐ Ⓑ Ⓒ Ⓓ
26. Ⓐ Ⓑ Ⓒ Ⓓ

27. Ⓐ Ⓑ Ⓒ Ⓓ
28. Ⓐ Ⓑ Ⓒ Ⓓ
29. Ⓐ Ⓑ Ⓒ Ⓓ
30. Ⓐ Ⓑ Ⓒ Ⓓ
31. Ⓐ Ⓑ Ⓒ Ⓓ
32. Ⓐ Ⓑ Ⓒ Ⓓ
33. Ⓐ Ⓑ Ⓒ Ⓓ
34. Ⓐ Ⓑ Ⓒ Ⓓ
35. Ⓐ Ⓑ Ⓒ Ⓓ
36. Ⓐ Ⓑ Ⓒ Ⓓ
37. Ⓐ Ⓑ Ⓒ Ⓓ
38. Ⓐ Ⓑ Ⓒ Ⓓ
39. Ⓐ Ⓑ Ⓒ Ⓓ

40. Ⓐ Ⓑ Ⓒ Ⓓ
41. Ⓐ Ⓑ Ⓒ Ⓓ
42. Ⓐ Ⓑ Ⓒ Ⓓ
43. Ⓐ Ⓑ Ⓒ Ⓓ
44. Ⓐ Ⓑ Ⓒ Ⓓ
45. Ⓐ Ⓑ Ⓒ Ⓓ
46. Ⓐ Ⓑ Ⓒ Ⓓ
47. Ⓐ Ⓑ Ⓒ Ⓓ
48. Ⓐ Ⓑ Ⓒ Ⓓ
49. Ⓐ Ⓑ Ⓒ Ⓓ
50. Ⓐ Ⓑ Ⓒ Ⓓ
51. Ⓐ Ⓑ Ⓒ Ⓓ
52. Ⓐ Ⓑ Ⓒ Ⓓ

☐ # correct in Section 1

☐ # incorrect in Section 1

SECTION 2

1. Ⓐ Ⓑ Ⓒ Ⓓ
2. Ⓐ Ⓑ Ⓒ Ⓓ
3. Ⓐ Ⓑ Ⓒ Ⓓ
4. Ⓐ Ⓑ Ⓒ Ⓓ
5. Ⓐ Ⓑ Ⓒ Ⓓ
6. Ⓐ Ⓑ Ⓒ Ⓓ
7. Ⓐ Ⓑ Ⓒ Ⓓ
8. Ⓐ Ⓑ Ⓒ Ⓓ
9. Ⓐ Ⓑ Ⓒ Ⓓ
10. Ⓐ Ⓑ Ⓒ Ⓓ
11. Ⓐ Ⓑ Ⓒ Ⓓ

12. Ⓐ Ⓑ Ⓒ Ⓓ
13. Ⓐ Ⓑ Ⓒ Ⓓ
14. Ⓐ Ⓑ Ⓒ Ⓓ
15. Ⓐ Ⓑ Ⓒ Ⓓ
16. Ⓐ Ⓑ Ⓒ Ⓓ
17. Ⓐ Ⓑ Ⓒ Ⓓ
18. Ⓐ Ⓑ Ⓒ Ⓓ
19. Ⓐ Ⓑ Ⓒ Ⓓ
20. Ⓐ Ⓑ Ⓒ Ⓓ
21. Ⓐ Ⓑ Ⓒ Ⓓ
22. Ⓐ Ⓑ Ⓒ Ⓓ

23. Ⓐ Ⓑ Ⓒ Ⓓ
24. Ⓐ Ⓑ Ⓒ Ⓓ
25. Ⓐ Ⓑ Ⓒ Ⓓ
26. Ⓐ Ⓑ Ⓒ Ⓓ
27. Ⓐ Ⓑ Ⓒ Ⓓ
28. Ⓐ Ⓑ Ⓒ Ⓓ
29. Ⓐ Ⓑ Ⓒ Ⓓ
30. Ⓐ Ⓑ Ⓒ Ⓓ
31. Ⓐ Ⓑ Ⓒ Ⓓ
32. Ⓐ Ⓑ Ⓒ Ⓓ
33. Ⓐ Ⓑ Ⓒ Ⓓ

34. Ⓐ Ⓑ Ⓒ Ⓓ
35. Ⓐ Ⓑ Ⓒ Ⓓ
36. Ⓐ Ⓑ Ⓒ Ⓓ
37. Ⓐ Ⓑ Ⓒ Ⓓ
38. Ⓐ Ⓑ Ⓒ Ⓓ
39. Ⓐ Ⓑ Ⓒ Ⓓ
40. Ⓐ Ⓑ Ⓒ Ⓓ
41. Ⓐ Ⓑ Ⓒ Ⓓ
42. Ⓐ Ⓑ Ⓒ Ⓓ
43. Ⓐ Ⓑ Ⓒ Ⓓ
44. Ⓐ Ⓑ Ⓒ Ⓓ

☐ # correct in Section 2

☐ # incorrect in Section 2

Practice Test

Reading Test

> **DIRECTIONS:** Read each passage or pair of passages, then answer the questions that follow. Choose your answers based on what the passage(s) and any accompanying graphics state or imply.

Questions 1–10 are based on the following passage.

The following passage is adapted from Leo Tolstoy's 1873 novel, *Anna Karenina* (translated from the original Russian by Constance Garnett). Prior to this excerpt, one of the major characters, Levin, has realized that he is in love with his longtime friend Kitty Shtcherbatsky.

At four o'clock, conscious of his throbbing heart, Levin stepped out of a hired sledge at the Zoological Gardens, and turned along the path to the frozen mounds and the skating ground,
5 knowing that he would certainly find her there, as he had seen the Shtcherbatskys' carriage at the entrance.

It was a bright, frosty day. Rows of carriages, sledges, drivers, and policemen were standing in
10 the approach. Crowds of well-dressed people, with hats bright in the sun, swarmed about the entrance and along the well-swept little paths between the little houses adorned with carving in the Russian style. The old curly birches of the
15 gardens, all their twigs laden with snow, looked as though freshly decked in sacred vestments.

He walked along the path towards the skating-ground, and kept saying to himself—"You mustn't be excited, you must be calm. What's the matter
20 with you? What do you want? Be quiet, stupid," he conjured his heart. And the more he tried to compose himself, the more breathless he found himself. An acquaintance met him and called him by his name, but Levin did not even
25 recognize him. He went towards the mounds, whence came the clank of the chains of sledges as they slipped down or were dragged up, the rumble of the sliding sledges, and the sounds of merry voices. He walked on a few steps, and the
30 skating-ground lay open before his eyes, and at once, amidst all the skaters, he knew her.

He knew she was there by the rapture and the terror that seized on his heart. She was standing talking to a lady at the opposite end of the ground.

35 There was apparently nothing striking either in her dress or her attitude. But for Levin she was as easy to find in that crowd as a rose among nettles. Everything was made bright by her. She was the smile that shed light on all
40 round her. "Is it possible I can go over there on the ice, go up to her?" he thought. The place where she stood seemed to him a holy shrine, unapproachable, and there was one moment when he was almost retreating, so overwhelmed was he
45 with terror. He had to make an effort to master himself, and to remind himself that people of all sorts were moving about her, and that he too might come there to skate. He walked down, for a long while avoiding looking at her as at the sun,
50 but seeing her, as one does the sun, without looking.

On that day of the week and at that time of day people of one set, all acquainted with one another, used to meet on the ice. There were
55 crack skaters there, showing off their skill, and learners clinging to chairs with timid, awkward movements, boys, and elderly people skating with hygienic motives. They seemed to Levin an elect band of blissful beings because they were here,
60 near her. All the skaters, it seemed, with perfect self-possession, skated towards her, skated by her, even spoke to her, and were happy, quite apart from her, enjoying the capital ice and the fine weather.

65 Nikolay Shtcherbatsky, Kitty's cousin, in a short jacket and tight trousers, was sitting on a garden seat with his skates on. Seeing Levin, he shouted to him:

"Ah, the first skater in Russia! Been here long?
70 First-rate ice—do put your skates on."

1. According to the passage, how did Levin first know that Kitty was at the Zoological Gardens?

   A) Kitty's carriage was parked near the entrance.

   B) Nikolay said he had been skating with Kitty earlier.

   C) He saw her talking with another woman near the pond.

   D) Kitty invited him to meet her there at a certain time.

2. As used in line 11, "swarmed" most nearly means

   A) invaded.

   B) gathered.

   C) flew.

   D) obstructed.

3. The passage most strongly suggests that which of the following is true of Levin?

   A) He worries about his appearance.

   B) He wants Kitty to be more enthusiastic.

   C) He is a very passionate person.

   D) He is wary of his surroundings.

4. Which choice provides the best evidence for the answer to the previous question?

   A) Lines 8–14 ("It was a bright, frosty day . . . in the Russian style")

   B) Lines 23–29 ("An acquaintance met him . . . merry voices")

   C) Lines 41–48 ("The place where . . . there to skate")

   D) Lines 52–58 ("On that day . . . hygienic motives")

5. What theme does the passage communicate through the experiences of Levin?

   A) Love is a powerful emotion.

   B) People long to have company.

   C) Life should be filled with joy.

   D) People are meant to work hard.

6. The passage most strongly suggests that which of the following is true of how Levin appears to others?

   A) People think that Levin looks agitated because of the way he is acting.

   B) People think that Levin is sick because he seems to be feverish.

   C) People think that Levin seems normal because he is doing nothing unusual.

   D) People think that Levin is in trouble because he is not protecting himself emotionally.

7. Which choice provides the best evidence for the answer to the previous question?

   A) Lines 1–7 ("At four o'clock . . . at the entrance")

   B) Lines 10–14 ("Crowds . . . the Russian style")

   C) Lines 25–31 ("He went . . . he knew her")

   D) Lines 65–70 ("Nikolay Shtcherbatsky . . . your skates on")

8. As used in line 21, "conjured" most nearly means

   A) begged.

   B) created.

   C) summoned.

   D) tricked.

9. The author's use of the word "throbbing" in line 1 implies that Levin

   A) has cut himself badly.

   B) has a sudden pain in his chest.

   C) is about to collapse.

   D) is in an agitated state.

10. Based on the tone of this passage, what emotion does the author wish the reader to feel about Levin?

    A) Empathy

    B) Cynicism

    C) Hostility

    D) Disgust

Questions 11–20 are based on the following passage.

This passage is adapted from a speech delivered by President Franklin Roosevelt on January 6, 1941, to the United States Congress. In the passage, Roosevelt reveals his intention to preserve and spread American ideals around the world.

The Nation takes great satisfaction and much strength from the things which have been done to make its people conscious of their individual stake in the preservation of democratic life in
5 America. Those things have toughened the fibre of our people, have renewed their faith and strengthened their devotion to the institutions we make ready to protect.

Certainly this is no time for any of us to stop
10 thinking about the social and economic problems which are the root cause of the social revolution which is today a supreme factor in the world.

For there is nothing mysterious about the foundations of a healthy and strong democracy.
15 The basic things expected by our people of their political and economic systems are simple. They are:
• Equality of opportunity for youth and for others.
20 • Jobs for those who can work.
• Security for those who need it.
• The ending of special privilege for the few.
• The preservation of civil liberties for all.
• The enjoyment of the fruits of scientific
25 progress in a wider and constantly rising standard of living.

These are the simple, basic things that must never be lost sight of in the turmoil and unbelievable complexity of our modern world.
30 The inner and abiding strength of our economic and political systems is dependent upon the degree to which they fulfill these expectations.

Many subjects connected with our social economy call for immediate improvement.
35 As examples:
• We should bring more citizens under the coverage of old-age pensions and unemployment insurance.
• We should widen the opportunities for
40 adequate medical care.

• We should plan a better system by which persons deserving or needing gainful employment may obtain it.

I have called for personal sacrifice. I am
45 assured of the willingness of almost all Americans to respond to that call.

A part of the sacrifice means the payment of more money in taxes. In my Budget Message I shall recommend that a greater portion of this
50 great defense program be paid for from taxation than we are paying today. No person should try, or be allowed, to get rich out of this program; and the principle of tax payments in accordance with ability to pay should be constantly before
55 our eyes to guide our legislation.

If the Congress maintains these principles, the voters, putting patriotism ahead of pocketbooks, will give you their applause.

In the future days, which we seek to make
60 secure, we look forward to a world founded upon four essential human freedoms.

The first is freedom of speech and expression—everywhere in the world.

The second is freedom of every person to
65 worship God in his own way—everywhere in the world.

The third is freedom from want—which, translated into world terms, means economic understandings which will secure to every nation
70 a healthy peacetime life for its inhabitants— everywhere in the world.

The fourth is freedom from fear—which, translated into world terms, means a world-wide reduction of armaments to such a point and in
75 such a thorough fashion that no nation will be in a position to commit an act of physical aggression against any neighbor—anywhere in the world.

That is no vision of a distant millennium. It is a definite basis for a kind of world attainable in
80 our own time and generation. That kind of world is the very antithesis of the so-called new order of tyranny which the dictators seek to create with the crash of a bomb.

To that new order we oppose the greater
85 conception—the moral order. A good society is

able to face schemes of world domination and foreign revolutions alike without fear.

Since the beginning of our American history, we have been engaged in change—in a perpetual
90 peaceful revolution—a revolution which goes on steadily, quietly adjusting itself to changing conditions—without the concentration camp or the quick-lime in the ditch. The world order which we seek is the cooperation of free
95 countries, working together in a friendly, civilized society.

This nation has placed its destiny in the hands and heads and hearts of its millions of free men and women; and its faith in freedom under the
100 guidance of God. Freedom means the supremacy of human rights everywhere. Our support goes to those who struggle to gain those rights or keep them. Our strength is our unity of purpose. To that high concept there can be no end save
105 victory.

11. The primary purpose of President Roosevelt's speech is to

   A) highlight the individuality inherent in patriotism.

   B) define the basic needs of the country.

   C) request money to support worthy causes.

   D) promote support for essential human rights.

12. Which choice provides the best evidence for the answer to the previous question?

   A) Lines 15–16 ("The basic things . . . are simple")

   B) Lines 33–34 ("Many subjects . . . improvement")

   C) Lines 56–58 ("If the Congress . . . applause")

   D) Lines 59–61 ("In the future days . . . freedoms")

13. As used in line 44, "sacrifice" most nearly means

   A) religious offerings to a deity.

   B) service in the military.

   C) losses of limbs in battle.

   D) surrender of interests to a greater good.

14. The passage most strongly suggests a relationship between which of the following?

   A) Protection of human rights abroad and military service

   B) Spread of freedom abroad and defense of democracy at home

   C) Defeat of tyrants abroad and establishment of democratic government at home

   D) Investment in global democracies abroad and strengthening of patriotism at home

15. Which choice provides the best evidence for the answer to the previous question?

   A) Lines 27–32 ("These are . . . expectations")

   B) Lines 56–58 ("If the Congress . . . applause")

   C) Lines 78–83 ("That is no . . . of a bomb")

   D) Lines 100–103 ("Freedom means . . . unity of purpose")

16. In line 57, "pocketbooks" most nearly refers to

   A) local, state, and national taxes.

   B) war debt accumulated by the nation.

   C) citizens' individual monetary interests.

   D) Americans' personal investment in the defense industry.

17. In lines 78–80 ("That is no . . . generation"), President Roosevelt is most likely responding to what counterclaim to his own argument?

   A) The spread of global democracy is idealistic and unrealistic.

   B) The defeat of tyrannical dictators in Europe is implausible.

   C) The commitment of the American people to the war effort is limited.

   D) The resources of the United States are insufficient to wage war abroad.

18. Which choice offers evidence that the spread of global democracy is achievable?

   A) Lines 51–52 ("No person . . . this program")

   B) Lines 60–61 ("we look forward . . . human freedoms")

   C) Lines 88–89 ("Since the beginning . . . in change")

   D) Line 103 ("Our strength . . . purpose")

19. In lines 67–71 ("The third is . . . world"), President Roosevelt sets a precedent by which he would most likely support which of the following policies?

   A) Military defense of political borders

   B) Investment in overseas business ventures

   C) Aid to nations struggling due to conflict and other causes

   D) Reduction of domestic services to spur job growth

20. The function of the phrase "the so-called new order of tyranny" in lines 81–82 is to

   A) connect the global conflict for human rights to citizens on a personal level.

   B) demonstrate the power of the global opposition to the United States.

   C) present an alternative vision of the world without democracy.

   D) provide examples of the political and social revolutions underway.

Questions 21–31 are based on the following passage and supplementary material.

The United States Constitution has been amended 27 times since its ratification. Rights such as freedom of speech, religion, and press, for example, are granted by the First Amendment. This passage focuses on the Nineteenth Amendment, which gave women the right to vote.

The American political landscape is constantly shifting on a myriad of issues, but the voting process itself has changed over the years as well. Electronic ballot casting, for example, provides the

5 public with instantaneous results, and statisticians are more accurate than ever at forecasting the winners of elections. Voting has always been viewed as an intrinsic American right and was one of the major reasons for the nation's secession

10 from Britain's monarchical rule. Unfortunately, although all "men" were constitutionally deemed equal, equality of the sexes was not extended to the voting booth until 1920.

The American women's suffrage movement

15 began in 1848, when Elizabeth Cady Stanton and Lucretia Mott organized the Seneca Falls Convention. The meeting, initially an attempt to have an open dialogue about women's rights, drew a crowd of nearly three hundred women

20 and several dozen men. Topics ranged from a woman's role in society to law, but the issue of voting remained a contentious one. A freed slave named Frederick Douglass spoke eloquently about the importance of women in

25 politics and swayed the opinion of those in attendance. At the end of the convention, one hundred people signed the Seneca Falls Declaration, which demanded "immediate admission to all the rights and privileges

30 which belong to [women] as citizens of the United States."

Stanton and Mott's first victory came thirty years later when a constitutional amendment allowing women to vote was proposed to

35 Congress in 1878. Unfortunately, election practices were already a controversial issue, as unfair laws that diminished the African American vote had been passed during Reconstruction. Questionable literacy tests and a "vote tax" levied against the

40　poor kept minority turnout to a minimum. And
　　while several states allowed women to vote,
　　federal consensus was hardly as equitable. The
　　rest of the world, however, was taking note—and
　　women were ready to act.

45　　　In 1893, New Zealand allowed women the
　　right to vote, although women could not run for
　　office in New Zealand. Other countries began
　　reviewing and ratifying their own laws as well.
　　The United Kingdom took small steps by
50　allowing married women to vote in local elections
　　in 1894. By 1902, all women in Australia could
　　vote in elections, both local and parliamentary.

　　　The suffrage movement in America slowly
　　built momentum throughout the early twentieth
55　century and exploded during World War I.
　　President Woodrow Wilson called the fight
　　abroad a war for democracy, which many
　　suffragettes viewed as hypocritical. Democracy,
　　after all, was hardly worth fighting for when half
60　of a nation's population was disqualified based on
　　gender. Public acts of civil disobedience, rallies,
　　and marches galvanized pro-women advocates
　　while undermining defenders of the status quo.
　　Posters read "Kaiser Wilson" and called into
65　question the authenticity of a free country with
　　unjust laws. The cry for equality was impossible
　　to ignore and, in 1919, with the support of
　　President Wilson, Congress passed the
　　Nineteenth Amendment to the Constitution. It
70　was ratified one year later by three-quarters of
　　the states, effectively changing the Constitution.
　　Only one signatory from the original Seneca Falls
　　Declaration lived long enough to cast her first
　　ballot in a federal election.

75　　　America's election laws were far from equal for
　　all, as tactics to dissuade or prohibit African
　　Americans from effectively voting were still
　　routinely employed. However, the suffrage
　　movement laid the groundwork for future
80　generations. Laws, like people's minds, could
　　change over time. The civil rights movement in
　　the mid-to late-twentieth century brought an end
　　to segregation and so-called Jim Crow laws that
　　stifled African American advancement. The
85　Voting Rights Act of 1965 signaled the end of

discriminatory voting laws; what emerged was a
free nation guided by elections in which neither
skin color nor gender mattered, but only the will
of all citizens.

Women's Suffrage in the United States

1848	Seneca Falls Convention.
1878	19th Amendment submitted; not ratified.
1911	Several states now grant women suffrage.
1914	Start of World War I.
1917	Picketing at the White House.
1918	Amendment passes in the House but fails in the Senate.
1919	Both the House and Senate pass the amendment.
1920	19th Amendment ratified.

21. The stance the author takes in the passage is best described as that of

A) an advocate of women's suffrage proposing a constitutional amendment.

B) a legislator reviewing the arguments for and against women's suffrage.

C) a scholar evaluating the evolution and impact of the women's suffrage movement.

D) a historian summarizing the motivations of women's suffrage leaders.

22. Lines 75–76 ("America's election laws . . . equal for all") most clearly support which claim?

A) The founders of the Constitution did not provide for free and fair elections.

B) The United States still had work to do to secure equal voting rights for some people.

C) Most women in the United States did not want suffrage and equal rights.

D) The women's suffrage movement perpetuated discriminatory voting laws.

23. Which choice provides the best evidence for the answer to the previous question?

    A) Lines 14–15 ("The American . . . in 1848")

    B) Lines 45–46 ("In 1893 . . . to vote")

    C) Lines 68–69 ("Congress . . . the Constitution")

    D) Lines 84–86 ("The Voting Rights Act . . . voting laws")

24. As used in line 62, "galvanized" most nearly means

    A) displaced.

    B) divided.

    C) excited.

    D) organized.

25. The function of lines 80–81 ("Laws, like . . . could change") is to

    A) connect the success of legislative reform with shifts in public sentiment.

    B) dissuade reformers from focusing on grass-roots activity rather than political campaigns.

    C) evaluate the effectiveness of judicial rulings based on popular response to public polls.

    D) reject the need for legal actions and court proceedings to attain social change.

26. The passage most strongly suggests that

    A) the American government adapts to the changing needs and ideas of society.

    B) the best-organized reform movements are most likely to achieve their goals.

    C) the nation is more vulnerable to change during the confusion of wartime.

    D) the civil rights movement would not have happened without women suffragists.

27. Which choice provides the best evidence for the answer to the previous question?

    A) Lines 4–7 ("Electronic ballot casting . . . of elections")

    B) Lines 7–10 ("Voting has . . . monarchical rule")

    C) Lines 17–20 ("The meeting . . . dozen men")

    D) Lines 81–84 ("The civil rights . . . advancement")

28. The graphic most clearly illustrates which idea?

    A) The Nineteenth Amendment happened as a result of World War I.

    B) The states slowed reform of national voting rights laws.

    C) Women's suffrage resulted from a slow evolution of events.

    D) Acts of civil disobedience won support for suffrage in Congress.

29. In line 65, the word "authenticity" most nearly means

    A) reliability.

    B) realism.

    C) legitimacy.

    D) truth.

30. The passage suggests that President Wilson contributed to the success of the women's suffrage movement by

    A) circulating government propaganda in support of women's suffrage.

    B) framing the fight in World War I as a fight for democracy and freedom.

    C) engaging in a foreign war to distract the nation from political debate.

    D) working with legislators to write the Nineteenth Amendment.

31. The graphic helps support which statement referred to in the passage?

    A) Early women suffragists did not live to vote in national elections.

    B) The Nineteenth Amendment passed within a few years of its introduction.

    C) A majority of state representatives opposed women's suffrage in 1918.

    D) Many state governments approved suffrage before the federal government did.

Questions 32–42 are based on the following passages and supplementary material.

Passage 1 is about how scientists use radioisotopes to date artifacts and remains. Passage 2 discusses the varying problems with radioactive contaminants.

Passage 1

Archaeologists often rely on measuring the amounts of different atoms present in an item from a site to determine its age. The identity of an atom depends on how many protons it has in
5 its nucleus; for example, all carbon atoms have 6 protons. Each atom of an element, however, can have a different number of neutrons, so there can be several versions, or isotopes, of each element. Scientists name the isotopes by the total number
10 of protons plus neutrons. For example, a carbon atom with 6 neutrons is carbon-12 while a carbon atom with 7 neutrons is carbon-13.

Some combinations of protons and neutrons are not stable and will change over time. For
15 example, carbon-14, which has 6 protons and 8 neutrons, will slowly change into nitrogen-14, with 7 protons and 7 neutrons. Scientists can directly measure the amount of carbon-12 and carbon-14 in a sample or they can use radiation
20 measurements to calculate these amounts. Each atom of carbon-14 that changes to nitrogen-14 emits radiation. Scientists can measure the rate of emission and use that to calculate the total amount of carbon-14 present in a sample.

25 Carbon-14 atoms are formed in the atmosphere at the same rate at which they decay. Therefore, the ratio of carbon-12 to carbon-14 atoms in the atmosphere is constant. Living plants and animals have the same ratio of carbon-12 to
30 carbon-14 in their tissues because they are constantly taking in carbon in the form of food or carbon dioxide. After the plant or animal dies, however, it stops taking in carbon and so the amount of carbon-14 atoms in its tissues starts to
35 decrease at a predictable rate.

By measuring the ratio of carbon-12 to carbon-14 in a bone, for example, a scientist can determine how long the animal the bone came from has been dead. To determine an object's age
40 this way is called "carbon-14 dating." Carbon-14

dating can be performed on any material made by a living organism, such as wood or paper from trees or bones and skin from animals. Materials with ages up to about 50,000 years old
45 can be dated. By finding the age of several objects found at different depths at an archeological dig, the archeologists can then make a timeline for the layers of the site. Objects in the same layer will be about the same age. By using carbon
50 dating for a few objects in a layer, archeologists know the age of other objects in that layer, even if the layer itself cannot be carbon dated.

Passage 2

Radioactive materials contain unstable atoms that decay, releasing energy in the form of
55 radiation. The radiation can be harmful to living tissue because it can penetrate into cells and damage their DNA. If an explosion or a leak at a nuclear power plant releases large amounts of radioactive materials, the surrounding area could
60 be hazardous until the amount of radioactive material drops back to normal levels. The amount of danger from the radiation and the amount of time until the areas are safe again depends on how fast the materials emit radiation.

65 Scientists use the "half-life" of a material to indicate how quickly it decays. The half-life of a material is the amount of time it takes for half of a sample of that material to decay. A material with a short half-life decays more quickly than a
70 material with a long half-life. For example, iodine-131 and cesium-137 can both be released as a result of an accident at a nuclear power plant. Iodine-131 decays rapidly, with a half-life of 8 days. Cesium-137, however, decays more slowly,
75 with a half-life of 30 years.

If an accident releases iodine-131, therefore, it is a short-term concern. The amount of radiation emitted will be high but will drop rapidly. After two months, less than one percent of the original
80 iodine-131 will remain. An accidental release of cesium-137, however, is a long-term concern. The amount of radiation emitted at first will be low but will drop slowly. It will take about 200 years for the amount of cesium-137 remaining to drop
85 below one percent. The total amount of radiation

Practice Test

emitted in both cases will be the same, for the same amount of initial material. The difference lies in whether the radiation is all released rapidly at high levels in a short time, or is released slowly
90 at low levels, over a long time span.

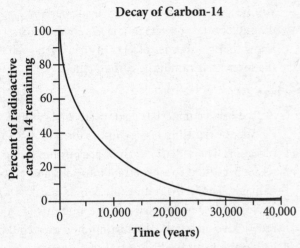

Decay of Carbon-14

This data is from the *Journal of Research of the National Bureau of Standards*, Vol. 64, No. 4, April 1951, pp. 328–333.

32. Based on the information in Passage 1, which of the following could be dated using carbon-14 dating?

   A) An iron pot found in a cave

   B) A rock at the bottom of a quarry

   C) An arrowhead made from bone

   D) The remains of a house made from stone

33. Which choice provides the best evidence for the answer to the previous question?

   A) Lines 10–12 ("For example . . . carbon-13")

   B) Lines 28–32 ("Living plants . . . dioxide")

   C) Lines 32–35 ("After the plant . . . rate")

   D) Lines 40–43 ("Carbon-14 dating . . . animals")

34. As used in line 26, "decay" most nearly means

   A) yield.

   B) deteriorate.

   C) discharge.

   D) circulated.

35. Which statement best describes the relationship between carbon-12 and carbon-14 in living tissue?

   A) There is more carbon-14 than carbon-12.

   B) There is more carbon-12 than carbon-14.

   C) The ratio of carbon-12 to carbon-14 is constant.

   D) The ratio of carbon-12 to carbon-14 fluctuates greatly.

36. Which choice provides the best evidence for the answer to the previous question?

   A) Lines 13–14 ("Some combinations . . . time")

   B) Lines 25–26 ("Carbon-14 atoms . . . decay")

   C) Lines 28–32 ("Living plants . . . carbon dioxide")

   D) Lines 32–35 ("After the plant . . . rate")

37. In Passage 2, the author refers to an accident that results in the release of iodine-131 as a "short-term concern" (line 77) because the initial amount of radiation released is

   A) low but will drop slowly.

   B) high but will drop quickly.

   C) low and will drop quickly.

   D) high and will drop slowly.

38. According to Passage 2, living tissue exposed to radioactive material can

   A) be destroyed by high levels of heat caused by the radiation.

   B) become radioactive itself and damage surrounding tissue.

   C) suffer injury when the cells' components are damaged.

   D) be killed by extra protons released by the radioactive material.

39. As used in line 79, "original" most nearly means

   A) earliest.

   B) unique.

   C) unusual.

   D) critical.

40. According to Passage 2, scientists use the half-life of radioactive material to determine the

    A) amount of danger posed by radiation immediately following a nuclear accident.

    B) likelihood of a nuclear accident involving the release of radioactive material at any given location.

    C) amount of radiation contained in a sample of iodine-131 or cesium-137 used in nuclear reactions.

    D) length of time that must pass until an area is safe after the release of radioactive material.

41. Which generalization about the study of physics is supported by both passages?

    A) The study of atomic and nuclear physics can have many applications in a variety of fields.

    B) The study of physics has helped revolutionize how archaeologists study artifacts.

    C) Scientists use physics to keep people and wildlife safe following a nuclear accident.

    D) Scientists use different concepts to date ancient items and assess danger from nuclear accidents.

42. Based on the graph and the information in the passages, which statement is accurate?

    A) Carbon-14 has a half-life of about 5,400 years.

    B) The half-life of carbon-14 is similar to that of cesium-137.

    C) The half-life of iodine-131 is greater than that of cesium-137.

    D) All radioactive materials have a half-life of 30 to 5,400 years.

Questions 43–52 are based on the following passage and supplementary material.

The following passage is adapted from an essay about the field of biomimicry, which focuses on the design of materials and systems that are based on biological structures.

In 1948, Swiss chemist George de Mestral was impressed with the clinging power of burrs snagged in his dog's fur and on his pant legs after he returned from a hike. While examining the
5 burrs under a microscope, he observed many hundreds of small fibers that grabbed like hooks. He experimented with replicas of the burrs and eventually invented Velcro®, a synthetic clinging fabric that was first marketed as "the zipperless
10 zipper." In the 1960s, NASA used de Mestral's invention on space suits, and now, of course, we see it everywhere.

You might say that de Mestral was the father of biomimicry, an increasingly essential field that
15 studies nature, looking for efficiencies in materials and systems, and asks the question "How can our homes, our electronics, and our cities work better?" As one biomimetics company puts it: "Nature is the largest laboratory that ever
20 existed and ever will."

Architecture is one field that is constantly exploring new ways to incorporate biomimicry. Architects have studied everything from beehives to beaver dams to learn how to best use materials,
25 geometry, and physics in buildings. Termite mounds, for example, very efficiently regulate temperature, humidity, and airflow, so architects in Zimbabwe are working to apply what they've learned from termite mounds to human-made
30 structures.

Says Michael Pawlyn, author of *Biomimicry in Architecture*, "If you look beyond the nice shapes in nature and understand the principles behind them, you can find some adaptations that can
35 lead to new, innovative solutions that are radically more resource-efficient. It's the direction we need to take in the coming decades."

Designers in various professional fields are drawing on biomimicry; for example, in optics,
40 scientists have examined the surface of insect

eyes in hopes of reducing glare on handheld
device screens. Engineers in the field of robotics
worked to replicate the property found in a
gecko's feet that allows adhesion to smooth
45 surfaces.

Sometimes what scientists learn from nature
isn't more advanced, but simpler. The abalone
shrimp, for example, makes its shell out of
calcium carbonate, the same material as soft
50 chalk. It's not a rare or complex substance, but
the unique arrangement of the material in the
abalone's shell makes it extremely tough. The
walls of the shell contain microscopic pieces of
calcium carbonate stacked like bricks, which are
55 bound together using proteins just as concrete
mortar is used. The result is a shell three
thousand times harder than chalk and as tough
as Kevlar® (the material used in bullet-proof
vests).

60 Often it is necessary to look at the nanoscale
structures of a living material's exceptional
properties in order to re-create it synthetically.
Andrew Parker, an evolutionary biologist, looked
at the skin of the thorny devil (a type of lizard)
65 under a scanning electron microscope, in search
of the features that let the animal channel water
from its back to its mouth.

Examples like this from the animal world
abound. Scientists have learned that colorful birds
70 don't always have pigment in their wings but are
sometimes completely brown; it's the layers of
keratin in their wings that produce color.
Different colors, which have varying wavelengths,
reflect differently through keratin. The discovery
75 of this phenomenon can be put to use in creating
paints and cosmetics that won't fade or chip. At
the same time, paint for outdoor surfaces can be
made tougher by copying the structures found in
antler bone. Hearing aids are being designed to
80 capture sound as well as the ears of the *Ormia* fly
do. And why can't we have a self-healing material
like our own skin? Researchers at the Beckman
Institute at the University of Illinois are creating
just that; they call it an "autonomic materials
85 system." A raptor's feathers, a whale's fluke, a
mosquito's proboscis—all have functional features
we can learn from.

The driving force behind these innovations,
aside from improved performance, is often
90 improved energy efficiency. In a world where
nonrenewable energy resources are dwindling
and carbon emissions threaten the planet's health,
efficiency has never been more important. Pawlyn
agrees: "For me, biomimicry is one of the best
95 sources of innovation to get to a world of zero
waste because those are the rules under which
biological life has had to exist."

Biomimicry is a radical field and one whose
practitioners need to be radically optimistic, as
100 Pawlyn is when he says, "We could use natural
products such as cellulose, or even harvest carbon
from the atmosphere to create bio-rock."

*Tiny florets in a sunflower's center are arranged in an
interlocking spiral, which inspired engineers in the
design of this solar power plant. Mirrors positioned
at the same angle as the florets bounce light toward
the power plant's central tower.*

Adapted from David Ferris, "Innovate: Solar Designs
from Nature." © 2014 by Sierra Club.

43. The central focus of the passage is

A) the field of biomimicry, which is the study of
materials and systems found in nature and
replicated in ways that benefit people.

B) the work of George de Mestral, the Swiss
chemist who invented Velcro® after observing
burrs under a microscope.

C) the ways in which architects use termite
mounds as models for human-made structures
in Zimbabwe.

D) how scientists are seeking ways to improve
energy efficiency as nonrenewable energy
sources decline.

44. Which choice provides the best evidence for the answer to the previous question?

    A) Lines 1–6 ("In 1948 . . . hooks")

    B) Lines 13–20 ("You might say . . . ever will'")

    C) Lines 25–30 ("Termite mounds . . . structures")

    D) Lines 88–93 ("The driving . . . more important")

45. The author includes a quote in paragraph 4 in order to

    A) explain why architects are looking to biomimicry for solutions in architecture.

    B) provide an argument for more scientists to study biomimicry.

    C) give an explanation as to why someone might choose a career in architecture.

    D) provide a counterargument to the author's central claim.

46. Based on the information in paragraph 6, how does the shell of an abalone shrimp compare with soft chalk?

    A) The essential building blocks are arranged in a similar manner, but the material that makes up the shell of an abalone shrimp is harder.

    B) Both are made from the same essential building blocks, but the shell of the abalone shrimp is much harder because of the manner in which the materials are arranged.

    C) The essential building blocks of both are the same, but the abalone shrimp shell is harder because the soft chalk lacks a protein binding the materials together.

    D) They are made from different essential building blocks, but they have a similar hardness because the materials are arranged in a similar manner.

47. In paragraph 9, what is the function of the quote from Pawlyn about efficiency?

    A) To convince readers that Pawlyn is an expert in his field

    B) To prove that great strides are being made in creating products that do not generate waste

    C) To demonstrate the limits of what biomimicry can achieve

    D) To support the statement that energy efficiency "has never been more important"

48. In line 33, "principles" most nearly means

    A) sources.

    B) attitudes.

    C) standards.

    D) concepts.

49. Of the following, the most reasonable inference from the passage is that

    A) more scientists will utilize solutions developed through biomimicry in the future.

    B) the field of biomimicry will eventually decline as more nonrenewable resources are discovered.

    C) scientists will leave the fields they are currently working in and begin research in biomimicry.

    D) doctors will create a self-healing skin called an "autonomic materials system" using methods based in biomimicry.

50. Which choice provides the best evidence for the answer to the previous question?

    A) Lines 38–42 ("Designers . . . screens")

    B) Lines 60–62 ("Often it is . . . synthetically")

    C) Lines 68–72 ("Examples like . . . color")

    D) Lines 98–102 ("Biomimicry . . . bio-rock")

51. As used in line 98, "radical" most nearly means

    A) pervasive.

    B) drastic.

    C) essential.

    D) revolutionary.

52. The graphic and caption that accompany this passage help illustrate how biomimicry can be used to

    A) make a solar plant more attractive.

    B) increase waste generated by energy sources.

    C) improve the efficiency of existing technologies.

    D) replicate a pattern common in nature.

IF YOU FINISH BEFORE TIME IS CALLED, YOU MAY CHECK YOUR WORK ON THIS SECTION ONLY. DO NOT TURN TO ANY OTHER SECTION IN THE TEST.   STOP

Practice Test

142 K

Writing and Language Test

This section corresponds to Section 2 of your answer sheet.

> **DIRECTIONS**: Each passage in this section is followed by several questions. Some questions will reference an underlined portion in the passage; others will ask you to consider a part of a passage or the passage as a whole. For each question, choose the answer that reflects the best use of grammar, punctuation, and style. If a passage or question is accompanied by a graphic, take the graphic into account in choosing your response(s). Some questions will have "NO CHANGE" as a possible response. Choose that answer if you think the best choice is to leave the sentence as written.

Questions 1–11 are based on the following passage.

The Age of the Librarian

When Kristen Harris **1** is in college, she worked in her university's library and was constantly told, "You really should be studying to be a librarian; this is **2** your home" however Harris was pursuing a bachelor's degree in elementary education at the time. Little did she realize that becoming a school librarian was indeed **3** elective. During the 21st century, the age of information, what could be more necessary than an individual trained to gather, process, and disseminate information? So, after teaching children in the classroom, Harris went back to school to earn her Master of Library Science degree.

Today, Harris is preparing a story time for a group of young students. As it has done with everything else, the technology revolution has elevated the school library to "Library 2.0." Harris's tablet-integrated story time begins when she projects images for *The Very Cranky Bear* onto a projector screen. As a child, Harris got excited whenever a puppet appeared during story time, but now she uses an interactive app (application software) to enhance her own story time and **4** integrate this next generation of children.

1. A) NO CHANGE
   B) has been
   C) was
   D) had been

2. A) NO CHANGE
   B) your home," however Harris
   C) your home.."; However Harris
   D) your home." However, Harris

3. A) NO CHANGE
   B) imminent.
   C) threatening.
   D) optional.

4. A) NO CHANGE
   B) enervate
   C) energize
   D) elucidate

As she introduces the children to the problem of cheering up a cranky [5] bear, Harris sees Miguel scouring the library shelves for another book by a popular author. [6] Miguel had said asking Harris for a book two weeks earlier "If you have any funny stories, I like those." "It will always be satisfying," reflects Harris, "to find books for students and have them return to say, 'I really liked that one. Are there any more by that author?'"

[7] Harris maintains active profiles on multiple social media networks to connect with her students more effectively. Harris would call herself a media mentor as much as a librarian because she regularly visits her favorite websites for reviews of apps and other digital tools to suggest to students and parents. Librarians have always been an important resource for families in a community, but this importance has grown exponentially because of the advent of technology. Librarians are offering guidance about new media to address the changing information needs in our communities. Furthermore, libraries are becoming increasingly technology driven, for example, [8] enabling access to collections of other libraries, offering remote access to

5. A) NO CHANGE
   B) bear; Harris sees Miguel
   C) bear: Harris sees Miguel
   D) bear Harris sees Miguel

6. A) NO CHANGE
   B) Miguel had said, "If you have any funny stories, I like those," asking Harris for a book two weeks earlier.
   C) Asking Harris for a book two weeks earlier, Miguel had said, "If you have any funny stories, I like those."
   D) Miguel asked Harris for a book two weeks earlier had said, "If you have any funny stories, I like those."

7. Which sentence would most effectively establish the main idea of the paragraph?

   A) NO CHANGE
   B) In addition to finding books for students, Harris is expected to meet their digital needs.
   C) Librarians still perform many traditional tasks such as putting great literature in the hands of their students.
   D) In the future, many school libraries are unlikely to have books on the shelves because students prefer electronic media.

8. A) NO CHANGE
   B) by enabling access to collections of other libraries, offering remote access to databases, or by housing video production studios.
   C) they enable access to collections of other libraries, offering remote access to databases, or they house video production studios.
   D) enabling access to collections of other libraries, offering remote access to databases, or housing video production studios.

databases, or they house video production studios. [9] Harris sponsors a weekly "Fun Read" book discussion club that is well attended by many of the students at her school. So, in Harris's opinion, librarians must be masters of the digital world.

Harris finishes her story time and heads across the library. A young student stops her and asks, "Ms. Harris, what's new in the library?" [10] She chuckles and thinks about the many collections, services, and programs their school library offers. "Have you seen the Trendy 10 list? You read the books on the list and blog [11] your ideas about them. I'll set you up with a password and username so you can blog," says Harris. In this library full of information, she's the gatekeeper.

9. Which sentence provides evidence that best supports the main idea of the paragraph?

    A) NO CHANGE

    B) Librarians continue to help students and teachers locate the perfect book in the library's collection.

    C) Teachers frequently ask Harris to recommend educational apps to support early literacy for their students.

    D) Many parents are concerned with online safety and digital citizenship due to the proliferation of social media.

10. A) NO CHANGE

    B) He chuckles

    C) Harris chuckles

    D) They chuckle

11. A) NO CHANGE

    B) they're

    C) you're

    D) their

Questions 12–22 are based on the following passage.

Unforeseen Consequences: The Dark Side of the Industrial Revolution

There is no doubt that the Industrial Revolution guided America through the nascent stages of independence **12** and into being a robust economic powerhouse. Inventions like the cotton gin revolutionized the textile industry, and the steam engine ushered in the advent of expeditious cross-country distribution.

The Industrial Revolution marked a shift from an agrarian to an industry-centered society. People eschewed farming in favor of **13** more lucrative enterprises in urban areas which put a strain on existing local resources. Necessary goods such as **14** food crops, vegetables, and meat products also had to be shipped in order to meet the dietary needs of a consolidated population. And because there were fewer people farming, food had to travel farther and in higher quantities to meet demand. Issues like carbon dioxide emissions, therefore, arose not only as by-products of industrial production but also from the delivery of these products. Moreover, booming metropolises needed additional lumber, metal, and coal shipped from rural areas to sustain population and industrial growth.

15 [1] The negative effects of such expansion on humans were immediately apparent; improper water sanitation led to cholera outbreaks in big cities. [2] Miners suffered from black lung after spending hours harvesting coal in dark caverns. [3] Combusted fossil

12. A) NO CHANGE
    B) and into the role of a robust economic powerhouse.
    C) and turned into a robust economic powerhouse.
    D) and then became a robust economic powerhouse.

13. A) NO CHANGE
    B) more lucrative enterprises in urban areas, which put a strain on
    C) more lucrative enterprises in urban areas; which put a strain on
    D) more lucrative enterprises in urban areas. Which put a strain on

14. A) NO CHANGE
    B) food
    C) food crops
    D) vegetables and meat products

15. To effectively transition from paragraph 2, which sentence should begin paragraph 3?
    A) Sentence 1
    B) Sentence 2
    C) Sentence 3
    D) Sentence 4

fuels [16] <u>released unprecedented amounts of human-made carbon dioxide into the air</u>, resulting in respiratory ailments. [4] The fact remains that smog, now an internationally recognized buzzword, simply did not exist before the factories that produced it.

The critical impact on the environment must also [17] <u>be taken into account. Proper regulations</u> were either not in place or not enforced. Industrial waste was often disposed of in the nearest river or buried in landfills, where it [18] <u>polluted</u> groundwater essential for wildlife to thrive. Deforestation across the United States served the dual purpose of providing inhabitable land and wood, but it also caused animals to migrate or die out completely.

Although the Industrial Revolution heralded an age of consumer ease and excess, it also invited a cyclical process of destruction and reduced resources. [19] <u>Greenhouse gases were released into the atmosphere.</u> Numerous health problems caused by [20] <u>depressing</u> working conditions prevented rural emigrants from thriving. And the environment that had cradled

16. Which graphic would best support the underlined claim?

A) A line graph plotting an increase in atmospheric carbon dioxide over time

B) A pie chart comparing the present percentages of carbon dioxide and other atmospheric gases

C) A timeline tracking carbon dioxide emissions testing dates

D) A bar graph showing levels of atmospheric carbon dioxide in different locations

17. Which choice most effectively combines the sentences at the underlined portion?

A) be taken into account, and proper regulations

B) be taken into account since without proper regulations

C) be taken into account because proper regulations

D) be taken into account; however, proper regulations

18. A) NO CHANGE

B) disturbed

C) drained

D) enhanced

19. Which choice should be added to the end of the underlined sentence to better support the claim in the preceding sentence?

A) NO CHANGE

B) while carbon dioxide–consuming trees were cut down to make way for new living spaces.

C) and caused an increase in global temperatures as well as a rise in coastal sea levels.

D) faster than they could be absorbed by the atmosphere's shrinking ozone layer.

20. A) NO CHANGE

B) urban

C) substandard

D) developing

humankind since its inception was slowly being

[21] <u>degraded. All</u> in the name of progress. [22]

21. A)   NO CHANGE

   B)   degraded; all

   C)   degraded! All

   D)   degraded—all

22. Which choice most effectively states the central idea of the essay?

   A)   The Industrial Revolution created a new consumer society that replaced the existing farming society.

   B)   Politicians and historians today disagree about the true consequences of the Industrial Revolution.

   C)   Although some analysts suggest that industrialization had many problems, its immense benefits outweigh these concerns.

   D)   Unfortunately, progress came at the expense of environmental and ecological preservation and may well have ruined the future that once looked so bright.

Questions 23–33 are based on the following passage.

Remembering Freud

Psychology has grown momentously over the past century, largely due to the influence of Sigmund Freud, a pioneer of the field. This Austrian-born neurologist founded the practice of psychoanalysis and [23] began scientific study of the unconscious mind. [24] Since his career which ended in the mid-twentieth century, Freud has remained a common cultural and scientific reference point. [25] Even the abiding popularity of terms such as "id," "ego," and talking about a "Freudian slip" serves to indicate how this psychologist lingers powerfully in Western memory.

As neuroscience has progressed, many early practices and theories, including some of Freud's, have been dismissed as outdated, unscientific, or even harmful. Much of Freud's theory, clinical practice, and even lifestyle are now discredited. But when considered in his historical context, alongside the astounding progress catalyzed by his work, Freud's contribution was significant indeed.

[26] Because he is now widely referred to as the Father of Psychoanalysis, Freud was among the first to develop the now-commonplace psychological method of inviting patients to speak freely. For Freud, this was both study and treatment. It helped doctors to understand patients, but more importantly it helped patients to understand themselves. Freud employed the classic (now largely outdated) psychiatric style in which the patient lies face-up on a clinical bed, allegedly enabling

23. A) NO CHANGE
    B) continued
    C) spearheaded
    D) led to

24. A) NO CHANGE
    B) Since his career, which ended in the mid-twentieth century, Freud has remained
    C) Since his career ending in the mid-twentieth century; Freud has remained
    D) Since his career (ending in the mid-twentieth century) Freud has remained

25. A) NO CHANGE
    B) Even the abiding popularity of terms such as the "id," "ego," and a "Freudian slip"
    C) Even the abiding popularity of terms such as talking about an "id," "ego," and "Freudian slip"
    D) Even the abiding popularity of terms such as "id," "ego," and "Freudian slip"

26. A) NO CHANGE
    B) Widely remembered as the Father of Psychoanalysis, Freud was among the first to develop the now-commonplace psychological method of inviting patients to speak freely.
    C) Freud was among the first to develop the now-commonplace psychological method of inviting patients to speak freely, which is why he is now widely remembered as the Father of Psychoanalysis.
    D) Although he is widely remembered as the Father of Psychoanalysis, Freud was among the first to develop the now-commonplace psychological method of inviting patients to speak freely.

Practice Test

access to deep [27] parts of the mind. These are better known as the unconscious or subconscious, and they fascinated Freud.

[28] He believed that uncovering repressed memories, was necessary for recovery. For Freud, understanding the activity of the innermost mind was essential. [29] In dealing with the conditions of patients, like neurosis or other psychological trauma, he suspected that there was a great deal going on beneath the "surface" of the psyche. He thought it was possible to reunite external, or conscious, thought with the internal, or unconscious. [30] At the same time that Freud practiced, many people were interested in spiritualism. Moreover, the method of inviting patients to speak and process their thoughts aloud remains central to today's psychological practice.

Freud altered the course of twentieth-century medicine by initiating what would become a grand, global conversation about the [31] still vastly mysterious human mind before Freud, medicine had barely scratched the surface in understanding mental health. Patients were met with very few answers, let alone

27. A) NO CHANGE
    B) recesses
    C) places
    D) components

28. A) NO CHANGE
    B) He believed that uncovering repressed memories, being necessary for recovery.
    C) He believed that uncovering repressed memories was necessary for recovery.
    D) He believed that uncovering, repressed memories was necessary for recovery.

29. A) NO CHANGE
    B) In dealing with patients' conditions, like neurosis or other psychological trauma, he suspected that
    C) In dealing with patients like neurosis or other psychological trauma conditions he suspected that
    D) He suspected that, in dealing with patients' conditions like neurosis or other psychological trauma,

30. Which sentence provides the best support for the ideas presented in this section?

    A) NO CHANGE
    B) Freud lived and worked mostly in London although he had originally trained in Austria.
    C) While some of Freud's more unusual practices have been criticized or abandoned, his interest in the unconscious altered the trajectory of the field.
    D) Psychologists today employ many theories, not just those developed by Freud.

31. A) NO CHANGE
    B) still vastly mysterious human mind. Before Freud, medicine
    C) still vastly mysterious human mind, before Freud, medicine
    D) still vastly mysterious human mind before Freud. Medicine

recovery protocols. **32** Through trial and error—scientific method in action—Freud's finding of a method that seemed to work. Since then, decades of ever-sharpening science have used his work as a launching pad. Therefore, as long as occasions arise to celebrate the progress of **33** the field, Sigmund Freud will be remembered for groundbreaking work that enabled countless advances.

32. A) NO CHANGE
    B) Through trial and error—scientific method in action—Freud's finding a method that seems to work.
    C) Through trial and error—scientific method in action—Freud finds a method that seemed to work.
    D) Through trial and error—scientific method in action—Freud found a method that seemed to work.

33. A) NO CHANGE
    B) the field; Sigmund Freud will be remembered for groundbreaking work that
    C) the field Sigmund Freud will be remembered for groundbreaking work that
    D) the field Sigmund Freud will be remembered for groundbreaking work, and that

Questions 34–44 are based on the following passage and supplementary material.

Success in Montreal

The Montreal Protocol on Substances That Deplete the Ozone Layer is an international treaty that was created to ensure that steps would be taken to reverse damage to Earth's ozone layer and [34] preventing future damage. [35] It was signed in 1987. This document created restrictions on chemicals that were known to be dangerous to the protective barrier that the ozone layer offers Earth. Without the ozone layer, the sun's dangerous UV rays would alter our climate so drastically, life on land and in water would cease to exist.

A hole in Earth's ozone layer was discovered over Antarctica [36] as long as two years prior to the signing of the treaty. The discovery brought the human impact on the environment to the forefront of [37] international conversation, the massive hole was evidence that a global response was necessary and that large-scale action was needed. The Montreal Protocol became effective January 1, 1989, and nearly 100 gases deemed dangerous to the ozone layer have been phased out. As a result, [38] the average size of the ozone hole decreased significantly during the 1990s.

34. A) NO CHANGE
    B) to prevent
    C) prevented
    D) was preventing

35. Which choice most effectively combines the sentences in the underlined portion?

    A) Signed in 1987, this document
    B) Because it was signed in 1987, this document
    C) It was signed in 1987, and this document
    D) It was signed in 1987 so this document

36. A) NO CHANGE
    B) long ago, two years prior.
    C) two years prior.
    D) years prior.

37. A) NO CHANGE
    B) international conversation, yet the massive hole
    C) international conversation. The massive hole
    D) international conversation, so the massive hole

38. Which choice completes the sentence with accurate data based on the graphic?

    A) NO CHANGE
    B) the average size of the ozone hole leveled off beginning in the 1990s.
    C) the average size of the ozone hole decreased beginning in the 2000s.
    D) the average size of the ozone hole increased beginning in the 1980s.

Now that a substantial amount of time has passed since the treaty was put into place, the effects can begin to be [39] looked at. As a part of the treaty, the Montreal Protocol's Scientific Assessment Panel was created to gauge [40] their effect on the hole in the ozone layer. The Panel has since reported the results every four years. The Panel predicts that the ozone layer will return to its former state of health by 2075. [41]

[1] While the treaty is already an obvious success, work continues to ensure that human strides in technology and industry do not reverse the healing process. [2] The Montreal Protocol's Multilateral Fund was established to help developing countries transition away from the consumption and production of harmful chemicals. [3] So far, over $3 billion has been invested by the Fund. [4] The developing countries are referred to as "Article 5 countries." [42]

[1] The Montreal Protocol is a living document. [2] A current amendment proposition has been put forth by the United States, Mexico, and Canada jointly. [3] It aims to cut down on harmful gases that were put into use as an alternative to the gases specified in the original Montreal

39. A) NO CHANGE
    B) controlled.
    C) measured.
    D) governed.

40. A) NO CHANGE
    B) its
    C) it's
    D) there

41. Which choice could be added to paragraph 3 to most effectively convey its central idea?

    A) It is the Panel's current estimation that the ozone layer is beginning to heal, but the rate of progress is slow.

    B) The Panel meets once a year to assess the increase or decrease of each gas that has been identified as dangerous.

    C) Of much concern to the Panel was the effect of ultraviolet radiation on the ozone layer.

    D) The Panel has recently updated procedures for the nomination and selection of its membership.

42. Which sentence in paragraph 4 provides the least amount of support for the central idea of the paragraph?

    A) Sentence 1
    B) Sentence 2
    C) Sentence 3
    D) Sentence 4

Protocol treaty. [4] It has been amended four times since its inception. [5] Combating the erosion of our ozone layer will take time and flexibility, but the research is clear: if humans stay conscious of what we emit into the atmosphere, we can not only stall the damage we have done in the past, but we can <u>43 change</u> it. 44

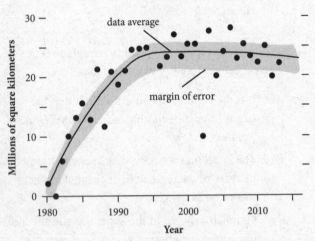

Size of Ozone Hole

Adapted from Ozone Hole Watch, NASA Goddard Space Flight Center.

43. A) NO CHANGE
    B) switch
    C) invert
    D) reverse

44. For the sake of cohesion of this paragraph, sentence 4 should be placed

    A) where it is now.
    B) before sentence 1.
    C) after sentence 1.
    D) after sentence 2.

IF YOU FINISH BEFORE TIME IS CALLED, YOU MAY CHECK YOUR WORK ON THIS SECTION ONLY. DO NOT TURN TO ANY OTHER SECTION IN THE TEST.

STOP

Answer Key

Reading Test

1. A	14. B	27. D	40. D
2. B	15. D	28. C	41. A
3. C	16. C	29. C	42. A
4. C	17. A	30. B	43. A
5. A	18. D	31. D	44. B
6. C	19. C	32. C	45. A
7. D	20. C	33. D	46. B
8. A	21. C	34. B	47. D
9. D	22. B	35. C	48. D
10. A	23. D	36. C	49. A
11. D	24. C	37. B	50. C
12. D	25. A	38. C	51. D
13. D	26. A	39. A	52. C

Writing and Language Test

1. C	12. B	23. C	34. B
2. D	13. B	24. B	35. A
3. B	14. B	25. D	36. C
4. C	15. A	26. B	37. C
5. A	16. A	27. B	38. B
6. C	17. C	28. C	39. C
7. B	18. A	29. B	40. B
8. D	19. B	30. C	41. A
9. C	20. C	31. B	42. D
10. C	21. D	32. D	43. D
11. A	22. D	33. A	44. C

Answers and Explanations

Reading Test

Suggested passage map notes:

P1: Levin goes to skating rink to find Kitty

P2: Description of day, people

P3: Walks to skating area; nervous, sees K skating

P4: Knows her right away, still nervous

P5: Lots of happy people skating

P6: Cousin greets him

1. A

Difficulty: Easy

Category: Detail

Getting to the Answer: Make sure to read the passage closely so events are clearly understood. The first paragraph explicitly states how Levin knew that Kitty was there: he saw her family's carriage. Choice **(A)** matches the information stated in the passage.

2. B

Difficulty: Medium

Category: Vocab-in-Context

Getting to the Answer: Use context clues to help you distinguish the shades of meaning each word has. Two of the answer choices have a somewhat negative connotation. The author is not describing the scene in a negative way. In this passage, the word "swarmed" means "gathered." Therefore, **(B)** is the correct answer. The other words' connotations do not fit with the context of the sentence.

3. C

Difficulty: Hard

Category: Inference

Getting to the Answer: Look for clues in the text that suggest what Levin is like. Emotionally charged phrases, such as "the rapture and the terror that seized on his heart" (lines 32–33), help reveal Levin's personality. Choice **(C)** reflects the depiction of Levin as a passionate person.

4. C

Difficulty: Hard

Category: Command of Evidence

Getting to the Answer: Eliminate answer choices that don't include a description of Levin. Because the excerpt focuses on Levin's feelings toward Kitty, evidence of the kind of person he is will probably reflect this. Choice **(C)** provides the best evidence.

5. A

Difficulty: Medium

Category: Global

Getting to the Answer: The central theme of a passage is the insight about life that the author is trying to get across to the reader. Eliminate any themes that are not revealed by the experiences of Levin. Though you may personally agree with more than one of the themes presented, **(A)** is the only answer choice that is supported by details in the passage. Levin's feelings and actions support this theme.

6. C

Difficulty: Medium

Category: Inference

Getting to the Answer: Examine the passage to see what other characters do in response to Levin. The other skaters go about their business. Most take little notice of Levin. Therefore, **(C)** is the correct answer.

7. D

Difficulty: Medium

Category: Command of Evidence

Getting to the Answer: Reread each quote in the context of the passage. This will help you decide the correct answer. Of all the answer choices, Nikolay's way of greeting Levin is the strongest evidence that people think Levin seems normal. Choice **(D)** is the correct answer.

8. A

Difficulty: Medium

Category: Vocab-in-Context

Getting to the Answer: The context of the passage can help reveal the meaning of the word. Insert each choice in the sentence to see which one makes the most sense. Levin speaks directly to his heart, asking it to behave. Choice **(A)**, "begged," comes closest to meaning the same thing as "conjured" in this context.

9. D

Difficulty: Medium

Category: Function

Getting to the Answer: Think about the entire scene described in the passage, and decide why the author chose to describe Levin's heart as "throbbing." Choice **(D)** is the correct answer. The author chose this word to capture Levin's agitated state.

10. A

Difficulty: Hard

Category: Inference

Getting to the Answer: Eliminate answer choices that are clearly not representative of the author's feelings or attitude about Levin. The author presents Levin's situation as one that is painful. The passage's tone suggests that Levin is worthy of the reader's empathy. Choice **(A)** fits this tone.

Suggested passage map notes:

P1: U.S. devoted to democracy

P2: Must think about soc. & eco. problems which → soc. revol.

P3: List of basics of dem.

P4: Must maintain basics

P5: List of what should be improved

P6: Americans will personally sacrifice for them

P7: Explain tax changes

P8: People will be okay with them

P9: Four essential human freedoms

P10: Freedom of speech and expression

P11: Freedom of religion

P12: Freedom from want

P13: Freedom from fear

P14: Are attainable now; against new order of tyranny

P15: Moral order

P16: Change can made done peacefully

P17: U.S. supports human rights everywhere and will win

11. D

Difficulty: Hard

Category: Global

Getting to the Answer: The introduction to the passage states that President Roosevelt intends to preserve and spread democracy. Choice **(D)** makes clear that the president wants to promote human rights, which can be achieved by spreading "American ideals around the world."

12. D

Difficulty: Hard

Category: Command of Evidence

Getting to the Answer: Be careful of choices that do not provide direct evidence to support the president's purpose. The correct answer will relate specifically to the stated purpose, or intent, of the passage. President Roosevelt makes clear that his intention is to provide support for global efforts to end tyranny and spread democracy and to garner the support of the American people for these goals. In the previous question, his stated purpose is to "make its people conscious of their individual stake in the preservation of democratic life in America" (lines 3–5). Only **(D)** provides direct evidence for the previous question.

13. D

Difficulty: Easy

Category: Vocab-in-Context

Getting to the Answer: All answer choices are alternate meanings of the word "sacrifice." The correct answer will relate directly to the context of the passage. Despite the fact that Roosevelt gave the speech on the eve of America's involvement in World War II, neither (B) nor (C) is the meaning he's after. Choice **(D)**, "surrender of interests to a greater good," is the correct answer.

14. B

Difficulty: Hard

Category: Inference

Getting to the Answer: Keep in mind that you're looking for a relationship that is suggested, not stated. To reach the correct answer, you must infer, or make a logical guess, based on information in the passage. The correct answer will provide support for the stated purpose of the passage while demonstrating a logical relationship. Choice **(B)** provides support for the stated goal of winning support among U.S. citizens for the spread of democracy abroad. It does so by suggesting that the security of U.S. democracy depends on the advancement of human rights and freedoms globally.

15. D

Difficulty: Medium

Category: Command of Evidence

Getting to the Answer: Avoid answers that provide evidence for incorrect answers to the previous question. The correct answer will use language reflective of the correct answer above to demonstrate a relationship. Principles and ideas such as democracy, freedom, and protection of human rights are used interchangeably throughout Roosevelt's speech. The lines in **(D)** draw the connection between freedom at home and freedom everywhere.

16. C

Difficulty: Easy

Category: Vocab-in-Context

Getting to the Answer: Substitute each answer choice for the word in question, and decide which one fits the context provided in the passage. In the context of the passage, **(C)** works best. It draws a distinction between individual citizens' monetary interests, or their pocketbooks, and the cause of patriotism, or the greater good.

17. A

Difficulty: Medium

Category: Inference

Getting to the Answer: Keep in mind that the correct answer will relate directly to the meaning of the elements in the identified lines. President Roosevelt is arguing against those who would oppose the overarching goal of

his speech, namely to garner support for the spread of democracy overseas. Choice **(A)** fits best; Roosevelt asserts that his goals are realistic and attainable, not just idealistic visions as his opponents might claim.

18. D

Difficulty: Medium

Category: Command of Evidence

Getting to the Answer: Be wary of answers like (A) and (B) that seem to offer specific advice or state specific goals relevant to the purpose of the passage without suggesting how those goals might be achieved. The correct answer will offer a tool, a condition, or another asset for achieving the passage's claim—in this case, the spread of democracy. The previous question identifies that President Roosevelt considers the spread of global democracy achievable. This question asks you to identify how the president envisions achieving that purpose. Choice **(D)** matches the intent. In this line, President Roosevelt identifies "our unity of purpose" as an asset that will help achieve his goal.

19. C

Difficulty: Hard

Category: Inference

Getting to the Answer: Be careful of answers that cite other policies that the president might support that are not related to the lines quoted. The correct answer will relate directly to the specific lines in question. In this speech, Roosevelt identifies four freedoms that he views the United States as obligated to defend. The freedom from want signifies a commitment to helping struggling populations at home and abroad. Choice **(C)** fits. The president urges economic understandings among nations to help those in need.

20. C

Difficulty: Medium

Category: Function

Getting to the Answer: Be careful of answers like (A) that offer other viable uses of rhetoric within the larger passage. The correct answer will relate specifically to the text cited in the question. Roosevelt suggests that the preservation of American freedoms cannot exist without the preservation of human rights on a global scale. To cement this connection, he contrasts democratic movements with tyrannical movements occurring in the world. Choice **(C)** is the correct answer. President Roosevelt references "the so-called new order of tyranny" in order to show what might happen should the United States and the American people not support other nations in their fight against such tyranny.

Suggested passage map notes:

P1: Changes in Am. voting process

P2: Women's voting history; Seneca Falls declaration

P3: 1878—amendment proposed, federal gov't not ready

P4: Women voting in New Zealand, Australia, United Kingdom

P5: WWI → female activism; 19th Amendment passed in 1919, ratified 1920

P6: Elections still not equal b/c Af. Americans often disenfranchised; 1965 Voting Rights Act → voting equality for all

21. C

Difficulty: Medium

Category: Inference

Getting to the Answer: Keep in mind that the "stance" of an author refers to his or her perspective or attitude toward the topic. The passage is written by a scholar or a historian who is looking back on the events that led to the adoption of the Nineteenth Amendment. It is not written by a primary source, such as a legislator or an advocate in the midst of the movement's events. For this reason, **(C)** is the correct answer. The author of the passage is clearly a scholar evaluating not just the motivation of women's suffrage leaders but the key events and impact of the movement as a whole.

22. B

Difficulty: Hard

Category: Inference

Getting to the Answer: Avoid answers like (A) that refer to related issues not relevant to the passage's purpose and answers like (D) that go too far. The correct answer will identify a claim that is supported by the quotation. In the quote, the author notes that election laws following passage of the Nineteenth Amendment did not secure equal voting rights for all. From this statement, it

becomes clear that other groups of people still needed support for their voting rights. Answer **(B)** is correct.

23. D

Difficulty: Medium

Category: Command of Evidence

Getting to the Answer: Reread the line quoted in the previous question, and notice that it occurs in the passage after ratification of the Nineteenth Amendment. Therefore, the evidence you're looking for will refer to an event that came later. The author suggests that the Nineteenth Amendment did not win equal voting rights for all citizens but that it did serve as an important step on the way to free and fair elections. Choice **(D)** demonstrates that a later event expanded voting rights further to citizens regardless not only of gender but also of race.

24. C

Difficulty: Easy

Category: Vocab-in-Context

Getting to the Answer: Consider the events that are being described in the paragraph in which the word appears. This will help you choose the best answer. It's clear in this paragraph that the women's suffrage movement was gaining momentum at this time. Events and tactics excited those who supported the movement and attracted more supporters. Therefore, **(C)** reflects the correct meaning of "galvanized."

25. A

Difficulty: Hard

Category: Function

Getting to the Answer: Carefully review the paragraph in which the line appears before choosing the best answer. Choice **(A)** demonstrates the connection between successfully changing one element (people's minds) in order to change the other (laws).

26. A

Difficulty: Hard

Category: Inference

Getting to the Answer: Be wary of answers like (D) that go too far in asserting unsubstantiated causal relationships. The correct answer will reference an idea or a relationship that is supported by the content of the passage. Choice **(A)** expresses the idea implicit in the passage that the American government responds, sometimes slowly, to the changing needs and sentiments of the American people.

27. D

Difficulty: Hard

Category: Command of Evidence

Getting to the Answer: Watch for answers like (A) and (C) that cite specific changes or examples but do not provide direct support. The correct answer to the previous question states the idea implicit in the passage that the government responds and adapts to changes in U.S. society. This suggests a gradual change. Choice **(D)** demonstrates the idea that both society and the government have changed over time as the civil rights movement of the late twentieth century overcame social and legal inequalities inherited from earlier in the nation's history.

28. C

Difficulty: Medium

Category: Inference

Getting to the Answer: Be careful of answers that aren't backed by sufficient evidence in the graphic. The graphic shows proof that women's suffrage unfolded through a series of events over a long period of time. Choice **(C)** is the correct answer.

29. C

Difficulty: Medium

Category: Vocab-in-Context

Getting to the Answer: Read the sentence in which the word appears. The correct answer should be interchangeable with the word. The passage states in lines 64–66 that "Posters . . . called into question the authenticity of a free country with unjust laws." Choice **(C)** is the correct answer as "legitimacy" refers to something that is in accordance with established principles.

30. B

Difficulty: Medium

Category: Inference

Getting to the Answer: Be cautious about answers that present accurate facts but that do not directly relate to the content of the question. Choice **(B)** is the correct answer. Wilson's framing of the conflict abroad as a fight for democracy and freedom helped women suffragists draw attention to the fact that the U.S. government was fighting for justice abroad while denying justice at home.

31. D

Difficulty: Medium

Category: Inference

Getting to the Answer: A question like this is asking you to compare information provided in the graphic with information provided in the passage text. Consider each answer choice as you make your comparison. Choice **(D)** is the correct answer. Both the graphic and the passage indicate that women's suffrage gained early victories in several states quite a few years before becoming law at the federal level through passage of the Nineteenth Amendment.

Suggested passage map notes:

Passage 1

P1: Central idea: use atoms to date things; isotopes def. & exs.

P2: Isotopes unstable; measure C-14

P3: C-14 decay = predictable

P4: C-14 dating; materials; timeline based on layers

Passage 2

P1: Def. radioactive; why dangerous; danger = radiation rate

P2: Half-life def. = decay rate; exs.

P3: Long half-life = long problem

32. C

Difficulty: Hard

Category: Inference

Getting to the Answer: Use your passage map to locate the paragraph that explains carbon-14 dating. This paragraph will contain the description of what materials can be dated using this method. In paragraph 4, the author states that carbon-14 dating can be used on materials made by a living organism. An arrowhead made from a bone is constructed of such material, choice **(C)**.

33. D

Difficulty: Hard

Category: Command of Evidence

Getting to the Answer: Locate each of the answer choices in the passage. The correct answer should provide direct support for the answer to the previous question: the bone arrowhead can be dated using carbon-14 dating. In paragraph 4, the author describes the process for carbon-14 dating. Choice **(D)** is correct because this sentence provides a direct description of the materials that can be dated using carbon-14 dating.

34. B

Difficulty: Medium

Category: Vocab-in-Context

Getting to the Answer: Pretend that the word "decay" is a blank. Reread around the cited word to predict a word that could substitute for "decay" in context. The previous paragraph discusses how scientists measure the rate of emission to calculate the amount of carbon-14 in a sample. "Emission" means release; therefore, the amount of carbon-14 is becoming smaller if the atoms are releasing it. In this sentence, therefore, predict "decay" means to *decrease*, which matches "deteriorate," choice **(B)**.

35. C

Difficulty: Easy

Category: Detail

Getting to the Answer: Look at your notes for paragraph 3. Summarize the ratio of carbon-12 to carbon-14 in living tissue in your own words. Look for

the answer choice that most closely matches your prediction. In paragraph 3, the author explains that the ratio of carbon-12 to carbon-14 for living things is the same as the ratio in the atmosphere: constant. Choice **(C)** is correct.

36. C

Difficulty: Medium

Category: Command of Evidence

Getting to the Answer: Review what part of the passage you used to predict an answer for the previous question: the ratio is constant for living things. Of the answer choices, only lines 28–32 explain the ratio of carbon-12 to carbon-14 in living things. Choice **(C)** is correct.

37. B

Difficulty: Medium

Category: Detail

Getting to the Answer: Read around the cited lines. The author directly states why a release of iodine-131 is not cause for long-term concern. In paragraph 3, the author explains that the initial release of radiation from an accident involving iodine-131 will be high, but the level of radiation will drop quickly (lines 73–74). Choice **(B)** is correct.

38. C

Difficulty: Medium

Category: Detail

Getting to the Answer: Use your passage map to find the information about why exposure to radiation is dangerous.

Getting to the Answer: In paragraph 1, lines 55–57, the author explains that radiation is harmful to living tissue because it can cause damage to the cells' DNA, which matches choice **(C)**.

39. A

Difficulty: Easy

Category: Vocab-in-Context

Getting to the Answer: Pretend that the word "original" is a blank. Reread around the cited word to predict a word that could substitute for "original" in context. The previous paragraph explains how scientists use "half-life" to determine how quickly material decays. If the material is decaying, then predict "original" refers to the *first* material. Choice **(A)** matches your prediction.

40. D

Difficulty: Medium

Category: Detail

Getting to the Answer: Review your notes for Passage 2. Try to put into your own words how scientists use half-life calculations of radioactive materials. Look for the answer that most closely matches your idea. In paragraph 1, the author explains that the level of danger posed by radiation released during a nuclear accident depends on how quickly radiation is released (lines 61–64). In paragraph 2, the author discusses how the half-life of radioactive material is used to determine how long a material will emit radiation. Paragraph 3 then explains how different half-lives translate into short-term or long-term radiation concerns. Choice **(D)** is correct because it most clearly paraphrases the information in the passage about how scientists use half-life calculations.

41. A

Difficulty: Hard

Category: Inference

Getting to the Answer: The central idea will be supported by all of the evidence presented in both passages. Review the central idea you identified for each passage in your passage maps. Passage 1 discusses the application of atomic and nuclear physics in archaeology, while Passage 2 details how scientists apply atomic and nuclear physics to studies of radioactivity in nuclear power plant accidents. Choice **(A)** is correct.

42. A

Difficulty: Hard

Category: Inference

Getting to the Answer: Analyze the graph to see that it describes the decay of carbon-14 over time. Think about how this data relates to the texts. The graph portrays the decay of carbon-14 as described in Passage 1. The definition of "half-life" is given in Passage 2. The half-life of a material is the amount of time it takes for half of that material to decay. The graph shows that about 50% of carbon-14 remains after 5,400 years. Choice **(A)** is correct.

Suggested passage map notes:

P1: George de Mestral—invented velcro

P2: Biomimicry—study nature to improve people's homes, cities, etc.

P3: Used in architecture

P4: Michael Pawlyn—adapt principles behind natural shapes → innovative solutions

P5: Used in optics and robotics

P6: Some natural stuff not advanced, but simple: abalone shell

P7: Nanoscale features; Andrew Parker—skin of thorny devil

P8: Can learn from animal features

P9: Improve energy efficiency

P10: Radical, optimistic field

43. A

Difficulty: Medium

Category: Global

Getting to the Answer: Look for the answer choice that describes an idea supported throughout the passage rather than a specific detail. The passage cites several examples of biomimicry, the study of how materials and systems found in nature can be replicated to benefit humans. Therefore, **(A)** is the best summary of the central idea of the passage.

44. B

Difficulty: Medium

Category: Command of Evidence

Getting to the Answer: Think back to why you chose your answer to the previous question. This will help you pick the correct quote as evidence. Choice **(B)** is the correct answer because it provides evidence for the central idea that the author presents about the field of biomimicry.

45. A

Difficulty: Hard

Category: Function

Getting to the Answer: Think about the primary purpose of the quote. Eliminate any answer choices that don't support this purpose. The quote, which is from a book on architecture, explains why architects turn to biomimicry for solutions in their work. Choice **(A)** is the correct answer.

46. B

Difficulty: Medium

Category: Inference

Getting to the Answer: Reread the paragraph that the question is asking about. Look for specific details about the abalone shrimp shell and soft chalk. The passage clearly states that the abalone shrimp shell is harder than soft chalk because of the way the basic material composing each is arranged, so **(B)** is the correct answer.

47. D

Difficulty: Medium

Category: Function

Getting to the Answer: In order to understand why an author includes a quote from another person, examine the surrounding sentences. This often makes clear the author's reason for including the quotation. The author includes the quote from Pawlyn to support and strengthen his or her own view that energy efficiency "has never been more important." Therefore, **(D)** is the correct answer.

48. D

Difficulty: Easy

Category: Vocab-in-Context

Getting to the Answer: Replace the word in question with each of the answer choices. This will help you eliminate the ones that don't make sense in the context. Choice **(D)**, "concepts," is the only answer choice that makes sense in this context because it reflects the foundational reasons behind the structures.

49. A

Difficulty: Medium

Category: Inference

Getting to the Answer: Keep in mind that you're being asked to make an inference, a logical guess based on information in the passage. Therefore, the correct answer is not stated in the passage. The variety of examples of biomimicry mentioned in the passage make

it reasonable to infer that more scientists will utilize solutions developed through biomimicry in the future. Choice **(A)** is the correct answer.

50. C

Difficulty: Medium

Category: Command of Evidence

Getting to the Answer: Reread each quotation in the context of the passage. Consider which one is the best evidence to support the inference made in the previous question. The examples cited in **(C)** provide strong evidence for the inference that more scientists will probably make use of biomimicry in years to come.

51. D

Difficulty: Medium

Category: Vocab-in-Context

Getting to the Answer: Eliminate answer choices that are synonyms for the word in question but do not work in the context of the sentence. Because biomimicry is such an innovative approach, it makes sense that the meaning of "radical" in this context is closest to **(D)**, "revolutionary."

52. C

Difficulty: Hard

Category: Inference

Getting to the Answer: Remember that a graphic might not refer to something explicitly stated in the passage. Instead, it often provides a visual example of how an important concept discussed in the passage works. The graphic and its caption help illustrate an example of biomimicry not mentioned in the passage: that of a solar power plant designed to mimic the arrangement of petals in a sunflower. This directs more energy toward the power plant's central tower and improves the efficiency of the power plant. Choice **(C)** is the correct answer.

Writing and Language Test

1. C

Difficulty: Easy

Category: Agreement: Verbs

Getting to the Answer: Examine the verb tense in the rest of the sentence. This will help you find the correct answer. As written, the sentence switches verb tense mid-sentence. Other verbs in the sentence, "worked" and "was," indicate that the events happened in the past. Choice **(C)** is the correct choice because it correctly uses the past tense of the target verb.

2. D

Difficulty: Medium

Category: Sentence Structure: The Basics

Getting to the Answer: Pay attention to the quotation marks. Reading through the sentence and the answer choices shows that two issues might need correcting. The sentence inside the quotation marks is a complete sentence. The correct answer needs to punctuate that sentence before closing the quote. Additionally, "however" is being used as a connector or transition word and needs to be followed by a comma after beginning the new sentence. Choice **(D)** appropriately uses a period prior to the end quotes and correctly inserts a comma after the transition word "However."

3. B

Difficulty: Medium

Category: Development: Precision

Getting to the Answer: Watch out for choices that distort the tone of the passage. The passage suggests that people expected or anticipated that Harris would become a librarian. Evidence for this idea is found in the statement that she was "constantly told" that she "should be studying to be a librarian." Harris was certainly aware that people anticipated this course of study for her, but the presence of the phrase "Little did she realize" tells you that she didn't expect to become one. The correct choice is **(B)**, "imminent," meaning that becoming a librarian was about to occur despite her own expectations.

4. C

Difficulty: Hard

Category: Development: Precision

Getting to the Answer: Read the sentence carefully for context clues. Also, think about the tone of what is being described. This will help you choose the best answer. Given the phrasing of the sentence, the answer must be close in meaning to "excited," which is used earlier in the sentence. Therefore, **(C)** is the correct answer.

5. A

Difficulty: Medium

Category: Sentence Structure: The Basics

Getting to the Answer: Determine whether a clause is dependent or independent to decide between a comma and a semicolon. Choice **(A)** is the correct answer. The sentence is correctly punctuated as written because it uses a comma at the end of the introductory dependent clause.

6. C

Difficulty: Medium

Category: Agreement: Modifiers

Getting to the Answer: Read the sentence carefully. The sentence sounds clunky and awkward. Look for an answer choice that makes the sentence clear and easy to understand. Notice that the word "asking" is part of a participial phrase that modifies "Miguel." A participial phrase should be placed as close as possible to the noun it modifies. When a participial phrase begins a sentence, it should be set off with a comma. Choice **(C)** is correct. The placement of commas and modifiers makes the content easy to understand, and the sentence is free of grammatical or punctuation errors.

7. B

Difficulty: Medium

Category: Development: Introductions and Conclusions

Getting to the Answer: Read the entire paragraph carefully and predict the main idea. Then look for a close match with your prediction. The paragraph discusses how the role of librarian has changed due to an increased use of technology. Choice **(B)** is the correct answer as it explicitly addresses the changing role of the librarian.

8. D

Difficulty: Medium

Category: Agreement: Verbs

Getting to the Answer: Read the sentence and note the series of examples. A series should have parallel structure. The sentence is not correct as written. The items in the series switch forms from participial phrases beginning with "enabling" and "offering" to "they house." All of the items need to fit the same pattern or form. Choice **(D)** is correct because it appropriately begins each item in the series with a participle.

9. C

Difficulty: Hard

Category: Development: Introductions and Conclusions

Getting to the Answer: Don't be fooled by answer choices that are true statements but do not directly support the main idea of the paragraph. The paragraph concerns how the role of the librarian has changed due to an increased use of technology. The correct answer needs to support the idea that librarians work with technology in new ways. Choice **(C)** works best. It offers a specific example of how teachers look to the librarian to be a "media mentor" and illustrates this new role for school librarians.

10. C

Difficulty: Easy

Category: Agreement: Pronouns

Getting to the Answer: Read the sentence prior to the pronoun and determine whom the pronoun is referencing. Pronouns should not be ambiguous and they must match the verb in number. The sentence is ambiguous as written. "She" would presumably refer back to the "young student," but it seems unlikely that the student would be laughing and thinking about the collections in the library after asking the librarian a question. Choice **(C)** is the best choice. It clearly indicates the subject of the sentence (Harris) and avoids ambiguity.

11. A

Difficulty: Medium

Category: Agreement: Pronouns

Getting to the Answer: Figure out whom the pronoun refers to and make sure it matches the antecedent in

number. Watch out for confusing contractions and possessives. The pronoun in the sentence needs to indicate who will have the ideas. Harris is talking to a single student, so the sentence will need a singular possessive pronoun. Choice **(A)** is correct. As it is, the sentence correctly uses a singular possessive pronoun.

12. B

Difficulty: Medium

Category: Agreement: Parallelism

Getting to the Answer: Be careful of answers that sound correct when they stand alone but do not conform to the structure of the sentence as a whole. The existing text is incorrect as it does not maintain parallel structure. Choice **(B)** is the correct answer as it maintains the parallel structure of preposition ("into") + noun ("the role").

13. B

Difficulty: Easy

Category: Sentence Structure: The Basics

Getting to the Answer: Eliminate answers that confuse the usage of commas and semicolons. Choice **(B)** is correct. Without the comma, the following clause modifies "urban areas" when it should modify the entire preceding clause.

14. B

Difficulty: Medium

Category: Organization: Conciseness

Getting to the Answer: Avoid choices that are redundant and imprecise. The correct answer will use the clearest, most concise terminology to communicate the idea. Choice **(B)** is correct. It is the most concise—and clearest—word choice because all of the items listed in the original sentence are simply types of food. The other choices use more words than necessary to convey meaning.

15. A

Difficulty: Medium

Category: Organization: Transitions

Getting to the Answer: The first sentence should function as a transition between ideas in the previous paragraph and ideas in the current paragraph. Choice **(A)**

makes sense. This choice connects ideas from the previous paragraph with the content of paragraph 3. The sentences that follow provide details to support that introductory idea.

16. A

Difficulty: Hard

Category: Graphs

Getting to the Answer: Eliminate answers like (B) that fail to support the cited sentence directly. The underlined sentence references "unprecedented amounts of human-made carbon dioxide into the air." This suggests an increase in the amount of carbon dioxide in the atmosphere over time. Therefore, **(A)** is the correct answer.

17. C

Difficulty: Medium

Category: Development: Transitions

Getting to the Answer: Choose the answer that presents the correct relationship between ideas. Choice **(C)** is correct. It shows the causal relationship without adding verbiage.

18. A

Difficulty: Easy

Category: Development: Precision

Getting to the Answer: Plug in the answer choices and select the one that reflects a specific meaning relevant to the sentence. The paragraph focuses on the negative effects of industrialization and waste production. Therefore, **(A)** is the correct answer.

19. B

Difficulty: Hard

Category: Development: Relevance

Getting to the Answer: Be careful of choices that relate to the underlined portion of the text without showing clearly how the underlined portion supports the full implications of the preceding sentence. The paragraph explains that industrialization resulted in the destruction of resources. The correct answer, **(B)**, serves as clear evidence of the "process of destruction and reduced resources."

20. C

Difficulty: Medium

Category: Development: Precision

Getting to the Answer: Be careful of answers that make sense but do not fully support the meaning of the content. The correct answer will not only flow logically but will also reflect the precise purpose and meaning of the larger sentence and paragraph. Choice **(C)** is the correct answer. "Substandard" communicates clearly that the working conditions were the cause of the health problems.

21. D

Difficulty: Medium

Category: Sentence Structure: The Basics

Getting to the Answer: Eliminate choices that result in sentence fragments or fragmented clauses. The correct answer will maintain appropriate syntax without misusing punctuation. Choice **(D)** is correct. It sets off the dependent clause without using incorrect punctuation to signal a hard break before an independent clause or second complete sentence.

22. D

Difficulty: Hard

Category: Development: Introductions and Conclusions

Getting to the Answer: Avoid answers that draw on similar ideas but combine those ideas in a way that communicates a proposition not supported by the essay as a whole. The correct answer will make sense within the larger context of the essay. The central idea of the entire essay is that industrialization and progress came at a cost that made the promise of a bright future difficult to fulfill. Choice **(D)** is the correct answer.

23. C

Difficulty: Hard

Category: Development: Precision

Getting to the Answer: Consider the fact that there may be a choice that helps make the meaning of the sentence very precise. Choice **(C)** most accurately indicates that Freud led a whole movement.

24. B

Difficulty: Medium

Category: Sentence Structure: Commas, Dashes, and Colons

Getting to the Answer: Plug in each answer choice and select the one that seems most correct. Choice **(B)** makes it clear to the reader that there is extra information modifying the word "career."

25. D

Difficulty: Medium

Category: Agreement: Parallelism

Getting to the Answer: Remember that in a list, all things listed should be presented with the same grammatical structure. "Id," "ego," and "Freudian slip" are all nouns. Choice **(D)** is the correct answer because it uses a parallel structure for all three nouns.

26. B

Difficulty: Hard

Category: Development: Introductions and Conclusions

Getting to the Answer: Notice that the underlined sentence is the first sentence in the paragraph. Think about which choice would make the best topic sentence, given the content of the rest of the paragraph. Choice **(B)** correctly makes the free-speaking technique the focus of the paragraph's topic sentence, while suggesting that the technique was radical enough to earn Freud his title.

27. B

Difficulty: Medium

Category: Development: Precision

Getting to the Answer: Eliminate any choices that don't seem as precise as others. Choice **(B)** is correct. The word "recesses" is more precise; it connotes smaller parts of the brain and a sense of being hidden.

28. C

Difficulty: Easy

Category: Sentence Structure: The Basics

Getting to the Answer: Think about how the sentence sounds when read aloud. This often helps you get a good sense of whether or not a comma is needed. Choice **(C)** would fit here. The sentence eliminates the unneeded comma.

29. B

Difficulty: Hard

Category: Agreement: Modifiers

Getting to the Answer: Remember that a modifier should be adjacent to the noun it is modifying and set off by punctuation. Choice **(B)** is correct. The modifier "like neurosis or other psychological trauma" should come directly after "conditions."

30. C

Difficulty: Hard

Category: Development: Relevance

Getting to the Answer: Consider how this sentence relates to the one before it and the one that follows it. Does it offer strong support of the connecting ideas? This section discussed the development and lasting influence of Freud's ideas. The best supporting sentence will provide details connecting these concepts. Choice **(C)** is correct. It emphasizes that Freud developed new ideas that have had a lasting influence on psychological practices.

31. B

Difficulty: Medium

Category: Structure: The Basics

Getting to the Answer: Notice that you are dealing with a run-on sentence. Identify the point in the run-on where it appears two sentences have been fused together. Choice **(B)** is correct. This choice splits the run-on sentence into two separate, grammatically correct sentences.

32. D

Difficulty: Easy

Category: Agreement: Verbs

Getting to the Answer: Eliminate answer choices that are not complete sentences or do not maintain the correct verb tense. Choice **(D)** correctly changes the phrase "Freud's finding of a method" to "Freud found a method," making the sentence complete. It also corrects the verb tense.

33. A

Difficulty: Hard

Category: Sentence Structure: Commas, Dashes, and Colons

Getting to the Answer: Recall that when a dependent clause precedes an independent clause, it should be set off with a comma. Choice **(A)** is the best choice. Although lengthy, the dependent clause in the sentence ("as long as occasions arise . . .") is correctly combined with its independent clause ("Sigmund Freud will be remembered . . .") by use of a comma.

34. B

Difficulty: Easy

Category: Agreement: Verbs

Getting to the Answer: Always check whether two or more verbs that serve the same function have a parallel structure. Choice **(B)** is correct. "To prevent" is in the infinitive form like the earlier verb in the sentence, "to reverse."

35. A

Difficulty: Hard

Category: Organization: Transitions

Getting to the Answer: Look for the choice that most concisely and correctly joins the two sentences. Choice **(A)** is the best fit. This option joins the sentences concisely and correctly.

36. C

Difficulty: Medium

Category: Organization: Conciseness

Getting to the Answer: Remember that the best answer is the most concise and effective way of stating the information while ensuring that the information is complete. Choice **(C)** works best here. It uses the fewest necessary words to convey the complete information.

37. C

Difficulty: Medium

Category: Organization: Transitions

Getting to the Answer: Eliminate any choices that use transition words inappropriately. Two complete thoughts should be separated into two different sentences. Therefore, **(C)** is the best choice.

38. B

Difficulty: Hard

Category: Graphs

Getting to the Answer: Examine the graphic for details that suggest which answer is correct. Choice **(B)** accurately reflects the information in the graphic. Beginning in the 1990s, the size of the ozone hole began to level off.

39. C

Difficulty: Medium

Category: Development: Precision

Getting to the Answer: Check each word to see how it fits with the context of the sentence. While all of the words have similar meanings, only one fits the context of the paragraph. Choice **(C)**, "measured," has a connotation that corresponds to "gauge" in the following sentence.

40. B

Difficulty: Easy

Category: Agreement: Pronouns

Getting to the Answer: Remember that the possessive form must agree with its antecedent. The correct answer will reflect the gender and number of its antecedent; in this case, the word "treaty." Therefore, **(B)** is correct.

41. A

Difficulty: Hard

Category: Development: Relevance

Getting to the Answer: To find the central idea of a paragraph, identify important details and then summarize them in a sentence or two. Then find the choice that is the closest to your summary. Choice **(A)** most clearly states the paragraph's central idea, that the ozone layer is beginning to return to normal.

42. D

Difficulty: Medium

Category: Development: Relevance

Getting to the Answer: To find the correct answer, first determine the central idea of the paragraph. Choice **(D)** is the least essential sentence in the paragraph, so it is the correct answer.

43. D

Difficulty: Medium

Category: Development: Precision

Getting to the Answer: Context clues indicate which word is appropriate in the sentence. Check to see which word fits best in the sentence. The word "reverse," **(D)**, fits with the context of the sentence and connotes a more precise action than does "change."

44. C

Difficulty: Hard

Category: Organization: Sentence Placement

Getting to the Answer: Examine the entire paragraph. Decide whether the sentence provides more information about a topic mentioned in one of the other sentences. This sentence provides more information related to sentence 1, "The Montreal Protocol is a living document"; it describes how the document is "living." Choice **(C)** is the correct answer.